THE LIBRARY
ST. MARY'S COLLEGE OF MARYLAND
ST. MARY'S CITY, MARYLAND 20686

W9-AFM-121

Against Stalin and Hitler

Translated from the German with a foreword by
DAVID FOOTMAN

AGAINST
STALIN and HITLER

Memoir of the
Russian Liberation Movement
1941-1945

WILFRIED STRIK-STRIKFELDT

THE JOHN DAY COMPANY • NEW YORK
An Intext Publisher

Library of Congress Cataloging in Publication Data

Strik-Strikfeldt, Wilfried, 1896 or 7—
   Against Stalin and Hitler.

   Translation of Gegen Stalin und Hitler.
   1. Vlasov, Andrei Andreevich, 1900-1946. 2. Russkaia osvoboditel'naia
armiia. 3. World War, 1939-1945—Campaigns—Russia. I. Title.
DK268.V56S7713 1972   940.54'21   74-162596
ISBN: 0-381-98185-1

FIRST AMERICAN EDITION 1973

Original German text copyright © 1970 by Wilfried Strik-Strikfeldt
This translation copyright © 1970 by David Footman

All rights reserved. No part of this book may be reprinted, or reproduced or
utilized in any form or by any electronic, mechanical or other means, now
known or hereafter invented, including photocopying and recording, or in
any information storage and retrieval system, without permission in writing
from the Publisher.

The John Day Company, 257 Park Avenue South, New York, N.Y. 10010

Printed in the United States of America

Contents

Illustrations   *following page 124*

Translator's Foreword

Table Showing the Structure of the German Reich

Some Equivalent Ranks for the German Army, Waffen SS
   and the United States Army

Glossary of Abbreviations

  1. Advance into Russia   19

  2. The Question of Policy   37

  3. Oberkommando des Heeres   56

  4. First Meeting with Vlasov   69

  5. The Viktoriastrasse   82

  6. Dabendorf   95

  7. The Smolensk Proclamation   103

  8. The Volunteers   112

  9. Visits to Army Group HQs   124

 10. A Set-back   137

 11. Hitler's Decision   143

 12. Tour of the Third Reich   150

 13. Dabendorf under Fire   157

 14. The Volunteers in the West   173

 15. The SS Show Interest   187

 16. 20 July   200

 17. Himmler and After   206

 18. The Prague Congress   215

 19. Last Meeting with Vlasov   222

20. The End   231

Author's Epilogue   246

APPENDIXES

  I. The Russian as Human Being   251

  II. General Vlasov's Open Letter   253

  III. Extracts from Report of Captain Peterson on His Inspection of the Dabendorf Camp   256

  IV. The Prague Manifesto   258

Index of Names   265

Translator's Foreword

I T can be argued that it was Hitler's idiotic policy towards Russia and Russians that lost him the war in the East, and, incidentally, ensured the survival of the Stalinist regime. By the summer of 1944 when Himmler (of all people) sponsored a change of course it was already too late. In the event the German armies were overwhelmed, and the Russian Liberation Movement under General Vlasov became one of the might-have-beens of history. The movement, however, has a significance of its own, apart from the moving human story of its leaders and its followers. During its brief existence it had, of course, its bitter enemies both on the Right and Left, and since the war has been the object of a smear campaign on the part of certain interested parties; but here we have an authentic account from the man best qualified to give it.

Wilfried Strik-Strikfeldt was born in 1896 of a family of German Balts. He went to school in tsarist Petersburg, becoming bilingual in German and Russian. In the First World War he served in the Imperial Russian Army. During the Revolution he was in the Baltic area where, for a time, he was associated with the British Military Mission under General Gough. In 1920 he set up in Riga as representative of German and British heavy engineering firms. His interests extended far beyond his business. He was very much a European; he wrote poetry; and he took an active part in the work of the International Red Cross for Famine Relief in Russia. In 1939, following the Ribbentrop–Molotov Pact, Soviet forces took over the Baltic States and local residents of German race were evacuated to German-occupied territory. Strik-Strikfeldt settled in Posen (Poznan) and set to work to reactivate his business. In the late spring of 1941 he was invited to join the staff of Field-Marshal von Bock, commanding the Central Group of Armies. From then till the end of the war he served in the Wehrmacht with the rank of captain. All that time he kept a full and intimate diary (names and dates omitted as a precaution against the Gestapo). It is on this diary that this memoir is closely based.

For the first few weeks of the campaign the author's duties were to tour the area behind the advancing armies and to report to the field-marshal on feeling and conditions in the occupied zone. He was impressed by the eager response to Nazi claims that the Germans were there to free the population from the Bolshevist yoke ('Hitler the Liberator'), and by the almost universal readiness to cooperate with the invader. It seemed as if a spontaneous anti-Stalin revolution had come into being throughout the occupied area. Within a few months of the start of the offensive some 800,000 ex-Red Army personnel were serving in the Wehrmacht, a very large proportion as combatants. But as the fighting troops moved on to new objectives, an ignorant and arrogant Nazi civil administration took over, and the SS were given a free hand for their brutal excesses. Conditions in the prisoner-of-war camps were appalling. What could be gathered of the Führer's war aims might be summed up as annexation, confiscation, exploitation and enslavement.

The author's deep concern was shared by a very large number of Army officers. Apart from the humanitarian aspect there were now some 60 million men and women under German occupation, and a disaffected and mutinous population could be a serious threat to military security. At one stage the author, with two senior staff officers, drew up plans for setting up a Russian Volunteer Army to serve alongside the Wehrmacht. The pre-conditions suggested included an announcement of war aims – the men must at least know what they were fighting for – an overhaul of the administration in the occupied zone and improvement of conditions in the prisoner-of-war camps. The memorandum was approved by von Bock, and submitted to the Commander-in-Chief, Field-Marshal von Brauchitsch. The latter minuted: 'Of vital importance for the issue of the war' and passed it on to Führer HQ. There it was ignored. Matters of policy, it was held, were no concern of the Army. In December 1941 both field-marshals were dismissed and Hitler himself assumed supreme command.

Early in 1942 Strik-Strikfeldt was transferred to Fremde Heere Ost, an information section of the Oberkommando des Heeres (OKH) where he came under the command of General Reinhard Gehlen. Here he found many who shared his views. Furthermore he came to realize that a number of senior officers were determined to do all in their power to bring about a reversal of current policy regarding Russia. Apart from Gehlen himself, the group included Colonel von Stauffenberg and others destined to be victims of the aftermath of 20 July 1944. In the OKH the idea of a Russian Liberation Movement was favoured, and the need felt to find a suitable personality to lead it. In the summer of 1942 the author, on instructions from his superiors, visited a prisoner-of-war camp to interview the Red Army Lieutenant-General A. A. Vlasov. Vlasov had been taken prisoner after his command (the Soviet Second Shock Army) had been wiped out in desperate fighting along the Volkhov river.

Vlasov, throughout, felt himself a Russian patriot. What moved him to act was the degradation to which the Stalinist regime had reduced the mass of his compatriots. His aim was a free, independent Russia within the frontiers of 1939. He rejected the role of quisling or mercenary. The Nazi leadership he regarded with increasing dislike and contempt. But only the Germans had declared war on Stalin, and he was prepared to cooperate with Hitler in the way (as he liked to put it) that Churchill and Roosevelt were cooperating with the Kremlin. He was sure of himself and of his fellow-countrymen. 'Let me have 200,000 Russians under my command, and I guarantee to finish the war for you, or rather for us, in a very few months.' The relationship between Vlasov and the author soon became, and remained, one of close friendship and complete mutual confidence.

In late 1942, on the initiative of the OKH, a special camp was set up at Dabendorf near Berlin with Captain Strik-Strikfeldt as commandant. Its ostensible task was to train Russian propagandists for the Propaganda Department of the Oberkommando der Wehrmacht; but hope persisted that pressure of events – the position at Stalingrad was becoming ominous – would force Hitler to change his policy. For those in charge of the camp, and for their friends and allies, the real function of Dabendorf was to be the centre of the Russian Liberation Movement. It was here that Vlasov should assemble his staff, select his cadres, prepare his military and civilian administration. It was from Dabendorf that the message of the new, free Russia should go out to the volunteer units, to the prisoner-of-war camps, to the *Ostarbeiter* settlements, to Russians on either side of the firing line.

Against Stalin and Hitler is the story of how that venture fared in face of persistent attacks by rabid party organs and in the ever-increasing shadow of impending military defeat. It is a story of achievement and set-back, of loyalties and compromises, of inter-departmental jealousy and intrigue, of risks taken and of hopes dashed. The record ends with the author's last service to his Russian friends: in April 1945 he took part in a delegation to cross the front and put the case of the Liberation Movement to the American authorities. The party arrived in the American lines, were courteously received by General Patch, and the matter referred to Washington. But before any answer was received the Armistice was signed, and the delegates became prisoners of war.

The author spent eight months as a prisoner in American hands, much of the time in solitary confinement, without news of the outside world or of the fate of Vlasov and his associates. On his release he set to work, once again, to build up his engineering business. He has now retired and lives in the Allgäu in Southern Bavaria.

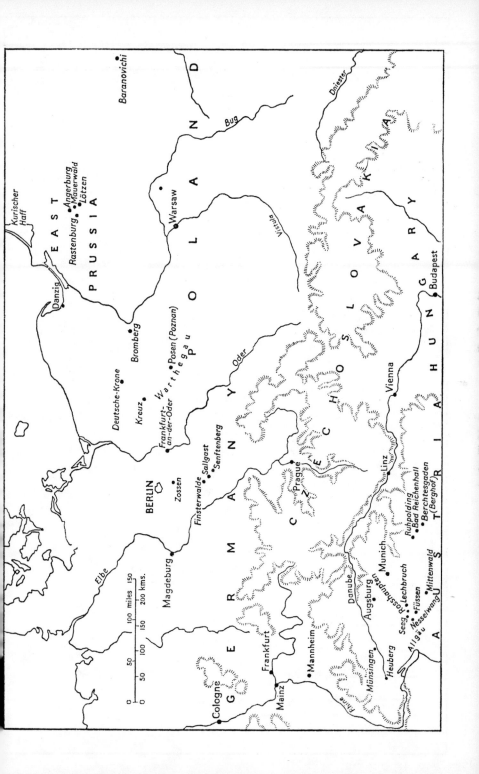

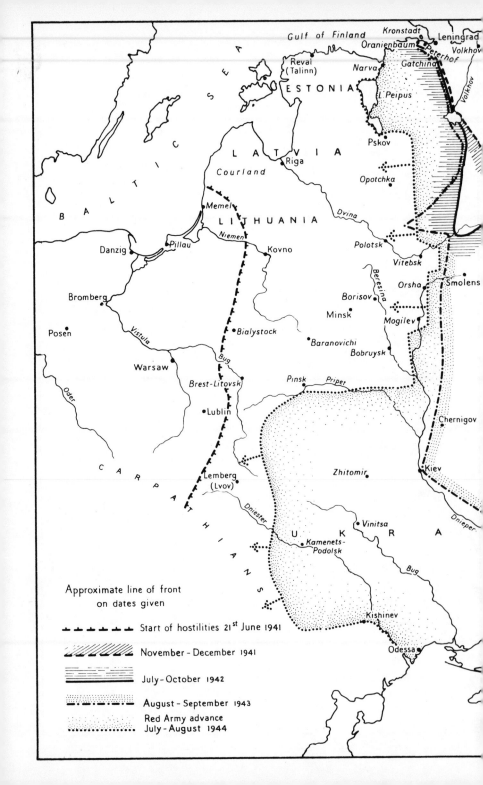

Approximate line of front
on dates given

━ ━ ━ ━ ━ ━ Start of hostilities 21st June 1941

▨▨▨▨▨▨ November-December 1941

━━━━━ July-October 1942

∙∙∙∙∙∙ August-September 1943
Red Army advance
••••••••• July-August 1944

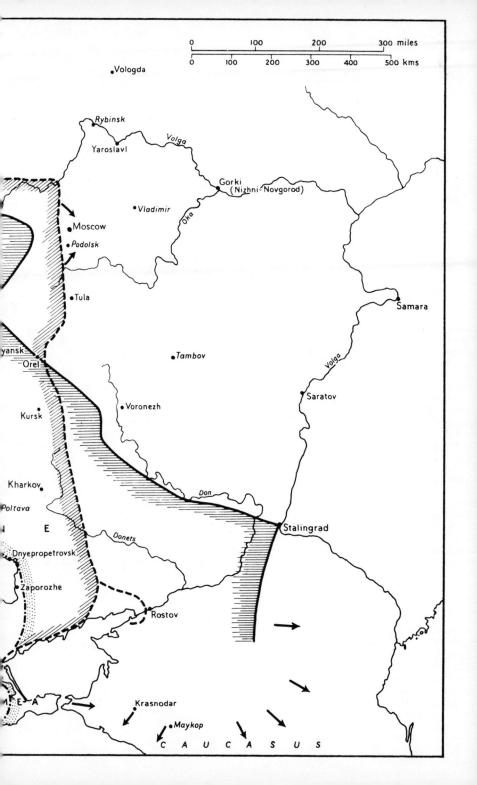

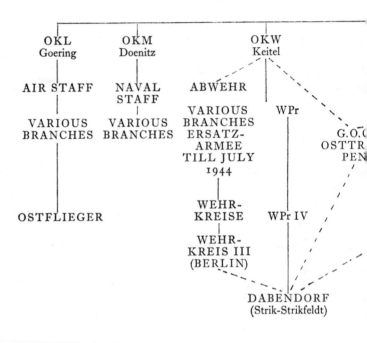

OKL Goering	OKM Doenitz		OKW Keitel	
AIR STAFF	NAVAL STAFF	ABWEHR	WPr	
VARIOUS BRANCHES	VARIOUS BRANCHES	VARIOUS BRANCHES ERSATZ- ARMEE TILL JULY 1944		G.O.(OSTTR PEN
		WEHR- KREISE	WPr IV	
OSTFLIEGER		WEHR- KREIS III (BERLIN)		
			DABENDORF (Strik-Strikfeldt)	

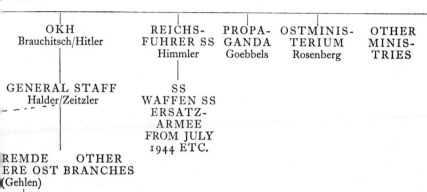

OKH	REICHS-	PROPA-	OSTMINIS-	OTHER
Brauchitsch/Hitler	FUHRER SS	GANDA	TERIUM	MINIS-
	Himmler	Goebbels	Rosenberg	TRIES

GENERAL STAFF
Halder/Zeitzler

SS
WAFFEN SS
ERSATZ-
ARMEE
FROM JULY
1944 ETC.

REMDE   OTHER
ERE OST BRANCHES
(Gehlen)

SOME EQUIVALENT RANKS

(1) *German Army*	(2) *Waffen SS*	(3) *U. S. Army*
Rittmeister (Cavalry)		
Hauptmann (other branches)	Hauptsturmführer	Captain
Oberst	Standartenführer	Colonel
–	Oberführer	Brigadier-General
Generalleutnant	Gruppenführer	Lieutenant-General

GLOSSARY OF ABBREVIATIONS

Gestapo	Nazi State Secret Police
GOC	General Officer Commanding
GPU	Soviet Secret Police up to 1934
NKVD	Soviet Secret Police, 1934–46
NTS	Narodni Trudovoi Soyuz (Russian émigré anti-Bolshevik organization)
OKH	Oberkommando des Heeres – High Command of the German Army
OKL	Oberkommando der Luftwaffe (Air Force)
OKM	Oberkommando der Marine (Navy)
OKW	Oberkommando der Wehrmacht – Organization of the Supreme Command of the German Armed Forces
OKW/Pr	Propaganda Department of the OKW
SA	Sturm-Abteilung (Nazi para-military force)
SD	Sicherheits-Dienst (Security and Secret Intelligence Service, working under the head of the SS)
SS	Schutz-Staffel (Nazi para-military organization)
Waffen SS	SS combatant troops

Against Stalin and Hitler

I

Advance into Russia

IN January 1941 a German staff officer called at my office in Posen. He told me he was aware of my experiences as an officer in the Imperial Russian Army, of my subsequent service with the British in the Baltic and of my work with the International Red Cross. He even knew that I and a number of my friends had been trying to initiate large-scale famine relief in Russia before ever the Nansen and Hoover organizations had been set up. He then, to my great surprise, announced that Field-Marshal von Bock would like to have me as officer-interpreter at his headquarters.

My first reaction was astonishment at all this detailed information regarding my past life. I then asked myself – why should the field-marshal need a Russian interpreter? As partners Hitler and Stalin had destroyed Poland and the Baltic States, and had shared the spoils. Were they not allies? My friendly visitor explained I should hear more from the field-marshal himself. Shortly afterwards I was summoned to call at his headquarters.

Fedor von Bock was in the tradition of the best type of Prussian officer – distinguished, modest, courteous, no monocle, none of the arrogance of 'shining armour' that we Russian-born Germans found so distasteful. At our interview we talked about the First World War, about the Russian Revolution, and then about the Baltic branch of the Bock family to which my mother had belonged. A Bock cousin of ours had been Imperial Russian Naval Attaché in Berlin some time before the First World War. In conclusion the field-marshal told me, 'All I can say to you at the moment is that we may soon be in need of your services.'

I gathered I was to be called up with the rank of acting major. Meanwhile I could carry on with my own civilian business. In due course I was called to Berlin to take the interpreter examination. I was asked about my education, and, on being told the school I had been to in Petersburg, the chairman of the Board remarked to his colleagues, 'Gentlemen, this examination is a waste of time. The candidate speaks better Russian than we do.' I was awarded a certificate as Interpreter Class A.

Then came a hitch, owing to a recent regulation forbidding the enrolment in the Wehrmacht of former officers of the Imperial Russian Army of German race. There seemed little sense in this regulation, the more so as it was explicitly stated that it did not apply to officers who had subsequently served in the Estonian, Latvian or Lithuanian forces. Bock's staff reacted sharply, and it was eventually conceded that I should be taken on but with the rank of captain. It was all to the good that I never became a major. But of this more later.

Field-Marshal von Bock's HQ in the Warthegau seemed like an oasis in the desert of German-occupied Poland, where conceptions of law, order and decency had come to be empty words. Polish property was confiscated, Poles of any position were expelled to the so-called Generalgovernment Ostpolen; Jewish reserves were to be established even farther east. In place of the banished Poles and Jews, Balts and other *Auslandsdeutsche* were brought in to 'German Warthegau'; and a swarm of (mostly rather shady) adventurers arrived from the Reich. The new colonizers soon found out that the area's economy would collapse unless a number of Poles were retained; but these Polish 'robots' had no rights and no future. Crime and terror marked the beginnings of the New Order under Himmler and his SS.

The older generation of the incoming settlers realized the wrong that was being done and the consequences likely to follow. But the younger ones were carried away by heady dreams of a new and glorious future. The Führer was building up a new and a better world. One cannot make an omelette without breaking eggs. Poles and Jews were enemies, and conquered enemies. (One had, of course, in those days no inkling of the horrors that were to come.) Of the darker side of things one could speak frankly only when talking to the older people or (thank God) when talking to officers on the staff of Field-Marshal von Bock's HQ.

One afternoon in June 1941 Major von Gersdorff of the Intelligence Staff of the Central Army Group passed me a leaflet. There I read that the German Wehrmacht had gone over to the offensive against the Red Army to free the peoples of Russia from Bolshevism. (The offensive had not yet been launched, but that is what it said in the leaflet.) I was astonished. This was something in which hitherto I had refused to believe. This meant war on two fronts, which Adolf Hitler had once so strongly condemned, war against the West and the Soviet Union. I wondered when. In the next few weeks? In the next few days? I had no further pointers. At that period I only occasionally came to HQ and spent most of my time on my private business.

The leaflet contained an appeal to the population and to the Red Army rank and file to offer no resistance and to welcome the Germans as liberators. At the same time soldiers and civilians alike were urged to rise against their oppressors and to kill all commissars, Communist Party and Komsomol officials and members, etc. My task was to make sure the text was linguistically correct and do a German translation for Gersdorff.

I made a few corrections and handed the papers back. Then I went home. I was to take my wife to the theatre. The piece was Lehar's *Land of Smiles*, which was far from my mood. My head was full of what I had been reading. War with Russia. And then the injunction – no resistance, but the people's appointed leaders condemned to death. What, I wondered, could have been in the author's mind? Was he mad? This affront to the dictates of God and of humanity was, at the same time, sheer idiocy. Those thus condemned to death would fight to the very last and force their countrymen to fight with them.

I had no idea as to what was happening on the stage. At the end of Act One I told my wife I must go back to HQ and would come and collect her after the performance. I found Gersdorff and explained to him what was on my mind. One should imagine it the other way round – an enemy leaflet condemning to death all Nazi Party members, the SS, the SA, the *Arbeitsdienst*, the Hitler Youth and all the other Nazi organizations. Gersdorff saw the point at once, and we sat down to draft a memorandum to be submitted to the field-marshal that same night. 'Not more than half a page,' said Gersdorff. 'Nothing about God and Humanity. Irrelevant. Keep it to the stiffening of resistance that the leaflet would be bound to provoke.'

When I arrived at HQ next morning I was summoned to the field-marshal who congratulated Gersdorff and myself on our memorandum's success. It had been passed on by teleprinter and the competent authority had decided to strike out Communist Party and Komsomol members. Commissars stayed put. So a stroke of the pen had preserved the lives of numberless Russians, and had saved thousands of German women from the loss of a husband or son. But the fact that a talk late in the evening between a Riga businessman and a junior staff officer could have so important a result raised the first doubts in my mind as to the infallibility of the German war leadership. Was it possible that no one at the top could have taken into account the political aspects?

(ii)

When the Second World War broke out in 1939 my family and I were living in neutral independent Latvia. We soon learned that the neutrality and non-aggression treaties between Stalin and the Baltic States had become null and void following the Nazi–Soviet Pact. Berlin had handed over the three Baltic States to the Soviets. The German Balts were transferred to the Warthegau, and the Red Curtain came down over Estonians, Latvians and Lithuanians – their leading and professional classes being for the most part liquidated or transported to Siberia.

Thus Hitler betrayed the West.

On 22 June 1941 German troops crossed the Soviet frontier without declaration of war. Now at last could Hitler, as he formally declared, throw off his mask and fulfil his special

Western mission. What had been done – the Berlin–Moscow Pact – would be undone. He was marching against the Kremlin ostensibly to free the peoples of the Soviet Union from the Bolshevik yoke.

Early in the campaign the Central Army Group HQ was advanced to the neighbourhood of Warsaw. General von Greiffenberg gave a talk to the headquarter's officers. 'We should be in Moscow in five to six weeks,' he said. 'I see,' he added, 'our Russian gentlemen are smiling.' Thereupon the two Russian-speaking gentlemen, Captain Schmidt and myself, were summoned to his office.

We did not know we had smiled. If we had, the smile must have welled up from the depths of past experience. Schmidt had been adjutant of the Imperial Cavalry School in Petersburg. We had both attended the centenary celebration of the Battle of Borodino. We had both served as officers in the war against the Kaiser's Germany. We knew the vast extent of Russia, and all the difficulties that these huge distances entailed.

This we explained. The general was extremely friendly. 'Perhaps I can help dispel your doubts,' he said. 'There has been enormous technical advance since Napoleon's day. Problems of long-distance transport are no longer what he had to face. I believe we have found the solution. I think you underestimate our technical resources.' Schmidt and I, of course, knew nothing about all this. 'But will Moscow mean the end of the war?' we asked. Greiffenberg smiled. 'I doubt if we should worry about that for the moment,' he said.

The first Russian prisoner brought in to our HQ was a battalion commander. Before that he had been a political commissar. This he admitted frankly. The war had been going on for only forty-eight hours, and he could not possibly have known that the Wehrmacht had orders to shoot all commissars. He was astonished at the imposing uniforms of the officers of the General Staff. 'Are they all Counts and Princes?' he asked me. There was an unbridgeable gulf between the poverty from which he came and the world of these splendid beings. This new world, he said, must assuredly be a better one. All he had seen of it was the cleanliness and tidiness, the quality of the uniforms of officers and men, their cars, their quarters. But what had impressed him most was the correct and humane treatment he had had from the Germans. He was dismissed after a short interrogation. 'Let no one know,' his case officer told him, 'that you were once a Red commissar.' The Russian thanked him. He had no idea what this advice might signify, but he felt that the Germans were well disposed towards him.

Army Group HQ moved on to Baranovichi and later to Borisov on the Beresina. Throughout the zone behind the advancing Germans one would come across parties, sometimes quite large ones, of Red Army troops who had been cut off and who (often still fully armed) were wandering aimlessly around the country. One night not far from Baranovichi I, alone with my driver – we had lost our way in the forest – ran into a group of forty. I spoke to them in Russian and they dropped their arms. It was the first lot of prisoners I had captured single-handed, and I passed them over to a guard in Baranovichi.

On one occasion Captain Schmidt, in charge of a billeting party, had to spend the night in a village. Our tanks were 50 kilometres ahead, having cut through and by-passed enemy formations up to battalion and regimental strength. The villagers knew of this and, spontaneously, posted watchmen all round the outskirts of the village to warn the German captain of any possible attack by the Reds.

In the first weeks of the campaign I, alone or with my driver, must have travelled hundreds of kilometres and passed through countless villages. My orders from the field-marshal were to report to him on general conditions and feeling, what the local population felt and what they wanted. There was in those days nothing sinister about these endless forests and isolated hamlets. One was sure, everywhere, of a friendly welcome once the initial shyness was dispelled. If one could speak their language, hearts were opened. In spite of poverty the old Russian tradition of hospitality was still alive. What they had to eat or drink was set on the table. The samovar, if they still possessed one, was brought out. And then came a flood of questions about the other world, our world, of which they knew nothing whatever. 'But surely,' I would counter, 'they have told you all about the Fascists and their crimes?' And then it would appear that Soviet horror propaganda had made little impression on the villagers. Too much propaganda is merely propaganda. Truth is something different.

I remember an old peasant, pushed forward by his fellows to act as speaker. He had, he said, been taken prisoner in the 'First Imperialist War' (1914–18), and had worked on a German farm. The Germans had been good to him. Their houses were clean and well furnished, their farm equipment magnificent. In fact, *Kultura*. So he had not believed the propaganda about the 'German beasts', and had advised his fellow-soldiers to drop their rifles and surrender. He himself had had the luck to get back to his village.

This, I was to find, was just one case of many. Whole Red units laid down their arms at the instance of soldiers who had been well treated by the Germans in the First World War as prisoners of war in a factory or on a farm. When Smolensk was taken the local NKVD archives fell into German hands. There was a list of names and particulars of all in the Smolensk area who had returned to the Soviet Union in 1919 after being prisoners in German hands. These persons the NKVD had marked as unreliable and subject to special, continuous, super-vision even though it was more than twenty years since their return. We used this document in a report to show that the Soviet authorities considered good German treatment of Russian prisoners as a threat to the Soviet regime. Here was proof.

Reports of grave deficiencies in the care and feeding of Soviet prisoners of war arrived almost daily at Group HQ from army, corps and divisional staffs. Von Gersdorff and his assistants verified their accuracy and passed them up to the competent quarters. (These quarters, alas, had at that time no Gehlen.)

The reports fell on stony ground. At some level, presumably, they were collected and filed away. We received no acknowledgement, nor did we ever find evidence of action being taken as a result of these reports.

(iii)

There were very many instances of Red Army officers wishing to place themselves and their troops under German command – one case being that of a battery commander with four of his guns still intact. They were eager to go into battle against Stalin and his gang and could not understand why they should be disarmed and marched off to a prison camp. 'But you yourselves,' they protested, 'were calling on us to rise against our common enemy. Were these empty words?' It was hard for a German officer to find an answer. Hitler had declared the Germans had come as liberators. In the little towns crude pictures of the Führer were pasted up on walls and hoardings, and, underneath, the slogan: 'Hitler the Liberator'. And yet line-crossers and prisoners, anti-Bolsheviks and unpoliticals must now alike set out on the weary road to the prison camps.

But there were certain German commanders who made use of Russians as guides through the forests and marshes, and subsequently enrolled 'their Russians' in their units to serve in various capacities. And, as will be seen later, other German commanders made far greater use of this potential source of manpower.

On the road from Minsk to Smolensk I came across an endless, tattered column moving East. I learned that these men, five to six thousand of them, peasants and workers, had been sentenced to forced labour for various infringements of the Soviet Code, and then drafted for punitive work on extensions of the Minsk aerodrome. Soviet aircraft on the airfield were destroyed on the ground by the Luftwaffe. Then German tanks and infantry arrived and the men were free to go home. But their homes were far away – round Moscow, at Yaroslavl, along the Volga. They explained they would willingly stay on and work for the Germans but as yet there were no arrangements for *Ostarbeiter*.[1] A few days later a new German officer took charge of the aerodrome and the men were thrown out; and they decided to set out on foot, in the wake of the liberators, for Moscow, Yaroslavl or the Volga.

The combatant troops, ever advancing towards new objectives, could not be expected to do anything about these people; but I wondered that no one had thought of making use of them. Russia is huge. One could never have too big a labour force, or too much mechanical transport. Wherever one went there were hundreds of tractors abandoned by the roadside. It was still warm and dry. It should not be difficult to tow them to repair shops. (The peasants had not yet had time to pilfer parts they thought might be useful.) A few German technicians and semi-skilled Russian labour could put them in order. But even the Army Group staff only smiled at the suggestion. In late autumn when German tanks and guns were bogged down in snow and mud there were no tough, primitive, Russian-built tractors to pull them out.

(iv)

Along the roads were endless columns of German infantry pressing on, gay and confident, through the heat and the dust towards the East – manhandling, when need be, their guns and trucks across the broken patches. Ever eastwards. I thought of what General von Greiffenberg had said, and felt it would be as well if Adolf Hitler for once were to give up his plane and march with his infantry. Only thus would it be possible to realize what Russian distances can mean.

In the other direction, from east to west, trailed grey columns of hungry and ragged Red Army prisoners – a couple of weary territorials at the head of a convoy of several thousands, with three or four more bringing up the rear. The prisoners were resigned and silent as they tramped on – towards what? It was still warm in July and August. They were used to hardship. They may well have hoped they would not fare worse with the Germans than they had under Stalin.

I had a number of talks with these prisoners, on the road or in

[1] Men and women drafted from the eastern areas for labour in Germany.

transit camps, and made notes of what they said to me. Here are some extracts:

'I was wounded and the Germans tied me up. I shall manage to get to a camp or a hospital. Is Germany big? Are there Russians living there?'

* * *

'Shall we soon be able to go home again? Will they let out those from Samara? And from Rostov?'

* * *

'Let us hope the war will soon come to an end. Then there will just be one big country and one government, and peace at last for everybody.'

* * *

'When peace comes and there is no more Red Army we can go back to our wives and families.' (They nearly all talked about their families.)

* * *

'How old are you?'
'Forty-nine.'
'A soldier?'
'No. They called me up for digging, and then I was taken prisoner. I have a wife and five children. When the Germans were coming nearer they drove my wife and children out of the village. I would like to go and look for them. The devil take that swine Stalin. He took away our little farm – that was years ago. Are you going to give us our land back?'

* * *

'Is it true the Germans are going to give us peasants our land back?'
'Where do you come from?'
'The Urals.'

'That is very far away.'

'But if you get there. This is something very important for us. And you certainly will get as far as the Urals.'

*　　*　　*

Then I had this experience:

In the transit prisoner-of-war camp at Orsha a group of prisoners were trying to make themselves cooking utensils out of old tins. I threw a few packets of tobacco over the wire to them. In an instant all was turmoil. The prisoners rushed like wild animals at any comrade who had got a packet. They fought with anything they could pick up; blood was flowing copiously. It was no good shouting at them. Only when the camp guard weighed in with their truncheons was some sort of order restored.

The commandant told me of his troubles. No shelter, no beds, no medical stores. The bread ration had to be divided into ten, to make sure that everyone had something. The bare essentials just were not there, and every day more and more prisoners were crowded in. He was at the end of his tether. This commandant was a decent German officer who was doing his very best; but they were not all like him.

(v)

For me these first few weeks and months in Russia were a voyage of discovery into the unknown. What did we know of these Russians, their lives and their joys and sorrows, their wishes and their hopes? I knew the old Russia, and I had to take care lest my reports to the field-marshal be in any way coloured by my memories of the distant past.

In my notes jotted down in those early weeks I can find no reference to politics. The Russians with whom I talked were completely unpolitical. They were in the grip of a new and overwhelming experience – they were free. I shared their hope of a better future, their faith in the indubitable victory of their liberators and their longing for peace – that is, a good life for the peasants, each perhaps with his own little holding.

Meanwhile my superiors were exclusively concerned with what was happening at the front. Though Gersdorff, his assistant von Schack and others realized the relevance – an important one – of what I have described to the situation on the enemy side of the firing line. On a number of occasions I was called to report personally to the field-marshal, who must have drawn his own conclusions.

One evening I accompanied von Bock and his adjutant, Count von Lehndorff, to visit a collective farm. The Soviet-appointed manager was still in charge; presumably he was a decent man and as the peasants had nothing against him the German officer concerned had left him in his post for the time being. This officer, like the rest of us, imagined that in any case collective farms were soon to be abolished.

It so happened that just before our arrival a German artillery officer had turned up to requisition horses. He produced no requisition order, and refused to give the farm manager a receipt. 'Why should I?' he said. 'There is a ruling that these *Untermenschen* should not be treated like the French or Belgians. Property means nothing to Russians.' At this moment the field-marshal arrived. He went into the case himself and ordered that no more horses be taken than the battery actually needed, and that an official receipt be given. Later he told us: 'Unfortunately there is an order that the provisions of the Geneva Convention do not apply to Soviet citizens or Soviet prisoners of war – ostensibly because the Soviet Union has not adhered to the Convention. A pity. If law and decency have been trampled on for years it is all the more desirable for us to show that we respect and uphold them. Our task as soldiers is to beat the enemy. But we must do so while observing the accepted rules of warfare.' This was the first time I heard that there were different rulings for the conduct of war in the West and the East.

There was an Orthodox church in Borisov. The Bolsheviks had used it as a store. The Wehrmacht restored it to its proper use, and this not as 'an opium for the people', but because, thank God, to act like this has always been an army tradition. The church was decked out with flowers and greenery, the approaches spread with clean white sand. The locals came out in their best clothes. The field-marshal and his officers attended the opening service. There were thousands crowded into the square in front of the church and into the streets leading off it. The service was one of Thanks and Prayer. The people could feel that the conquerors themselves bowed down to the Lord of All.

That same evening an officer wrote an account of the ceremony and of the deep impression it had made on the Russians; he sent it to the Berlin newspaper *D.A.Z.* A few days later he had an answer back that the coverage of church affairs was undesirable. His article would not be printed.

On the subject of religion I might mention that the way the Russians crowded to their churches in those early weeks was very moving. Many brought their children, aged between one and twelve, to be baptized. As most of the orthodox clergy had been evacuated, if not murdered, in many areas there was a shortage of priests. But a number of Catholic priests, from Eastern Poland and White Russia, had followed on after the Wehrmacht on foot. They spoke Russian, and thanks to them baptisms, marriages and burial services were conducted without regard to race or denomination.

After the move of our HQ to Borisov I had less opportunity to travel round. My duties now were the evaluation of reports from the front areas and the interrogation of important prisoners. My work brought home to me that it was the Russian-born Germans and the older Balts, who spoke Russian as fluently as their own mother tongue, who were able to make real contact with both civil population and prisoners. The Russians, naturally, took these intermediaries to be the representatives of Germany. They trusted them. They did not realize that all these men could do was to pass on what they saw fit. They did not know how these men suffered when 'the other Germans' ignored their warnings, and when decency and human rights were trodden underfoot in ignorance, arrogance or sheer egoism.

Quite often I saw reports from men who were known to me, school friends and business friends, now serving as interpreters in divisional corps or army staffs. Some of them wrote to me personally in the hope that I in my position at Army Group HQ could effect some improvement. I did what I could because I felt as they did. But we Army Group interpreters possessed no authority. In the Third Reich an intermediary counted for nothing since those in power had no desire for mediation.

I felt more and more convinced that the achievements of our soldiers would be in vain unless some proper solution could be found for the political, economic and human problems of the occupied zone with its 50–70 million inhabitants.

(vi)

Our convictions seemed confirmed by what we heard from important prisoners of war.

One day Stalin's son, Major Yakob Dzhugashvili, was brought in to our HQ. His face was intelligent, with strongly marked Georgian features; his bearing upright and correct. At first he refused the food and drink we offered him. Only when he saw that Schmidt and I were drinking the same wine did he raise his glass.

He told us his father had said goodbye to him on the telephone as he was leaving for the front.

On our mention of the abject poverty in which Russians were living under Communism, he replied that since the Revolution the Soviet Union had been encircled by technically developed and well-armed Imperialist States. Hence to rearm had been the urgent priority. 'You Germans attacked us too soon,' he said. 'You found us ill equipped and also poor. But a day will come when we can not only maintain our armaments but also raise the standard of living of all the peoples of Russia.' He admitted that day was far distant, and might not come until the proletariat had seized power all over the world. He did not believe in any compromise between Capitalism and Communism. Lenin had considered coexistence to be 'a pause for breath'.

He described the German attack as sheer gangsterism. He did not believe in the liberation of the Russian people by the Germans. He did not believe in a final German victory. Russia had produced world-renowned writers, composers, scientists. 'But you look down on us as if we were primitive South Sea Islanders. Well, for the short time I have been in your hands I have seen nothing to make me look up to you. True, people have been friendly, but then our NKVD can be friendly when it serves their purpose.'

'You said,' one of us asked, 'that you do not believe in a German victory?'

He hesitated.

'No,' he said. 'Do you intend to occupy the whole vast country?'

We had the feeling from the way he said it that Stalin and his gang were afraid not of a foreign occupation but of the 'internal enemy', of a revolt in their own ranks to coincide with the German advance. This seemed to Schmidt and myself to be of enormous importance and we pressed further. So Stalin and his friends were anxious about a National Russian Revolution, or Russian National Counter-Revolution?

He hesitated once more. Then he nodded.

'That would be dangerous,' he said. He went on to say he had never discussed the matter with his father, but there had been talk on these and similar lines among Red Army officers at the front.

This was what Schmidt and I had been thinking ourselves. Here was our opportunity to bring it to the notice of the highest level. What we thought was of no account. But what Stalin's son thought was surely something to be reckoned with by the OKW, by the commander-in-chief and by Führer HQ itself. Gersdorff, who knew more about such matters than we did, agreed with us.

'Stalin, according to his son Yakob Dzhugashvili Stalin, is afraid of a National Russian Movement against him. The setting up of a National Russian Government in opposition to Stalin could pave the way to a speedy victory.' Such was the keynote of our report which Field-Marshal von Bock passed on to Supreme HQ.

A former Red Army Corps commander told us there was some evidence of a new Russian national patriotic movement. This was not, as yet, official Soviet policy, but there were undertones in

speeches and even on the stage. The appeal to patriotism was
sure to meet with a warm response after the German attack,
especially in the Red Army. (This was news to us.) I saw this
officer a few months later after he had been in a number of
prisoner-of-war camps. He was disillusioned and bitter. He spoke
of German arrogance, of their inhuman treatment of prisoners.
'Are you blind?' he said. 'This is the way to lose the war and
bring suffering to mankind for generations.'

A number of captured senior officers and commissars were
brought to Army Group HQ in the course of that autumn. For
the most part the combatant troops ignored Hitler's order to kill
all commissars. One of them told us his story. Before the First
World War he had been a delivery boy in Petersburg; then clerk
in an army supply office. He had taken part whole-heartedly in
the October Revolution. Then a spell as quartermaster in a Red
Army unit. After the Civil War he had attended schools and
courses. It had not been easy for him; he had had to work
very hard to make up for his lack of early education. But in the
end he had come to be head of the Q Branch of a Soviet army.
Never had he dreamed that he would reach that height. He had no
illusions about the top Soviet leadership with their cruelty and
their ruthlessness. In the Soviet system of today there was no
longer any trace of real Communism; but he himself was still a
convinced Communist. He had done his best for his people, and
would still do his best if the Germans were willing to give a
Communist the chance to do so.

Then there was a colonel of the Red General Staff – pale,
intellectual, well-read, distinguished. He looked a born aristocrat,
but his father had been a miner in the Urals. He himself had
passed through a number of Staff College courses. He had been
involved in the Tukhachevski affair and sent to prison, but brought
back to the army when war broke out. He told us of Stalin's
pronouncement that all Red Army personnel falling alive into
enemy hands were traitors. He, like the others, hated the regime
and loved his country. He had done his duty to the end, had
been wounded, had lain hidden in the forest for several days till

the Germans had picked him up. He told us, too, of the NKVD informers secretly infiltrated into every unit to report on any unguarded remark that might be made about the leadership. He told us of the special squads behind the firing line with the task of driving the troops into battle and shooting down any laggards or fugitives.

We knew about all this from other sources. But these draconic measures had had the result of stiffening the Red resistance, and this was something our Supreme Command should take into account.

General M. F. Lukin had been captured while in command of the Soviet Nineteenth Army, wiped out in the course of the German advance. He had lost a leg; now it became necessary to amputate the other leg. He bore it all with extreme stoicism, but it was doubtful whether he would survive. Gersdorff reported the case to the field-marshal who gave orders that we should do everything possible for him. General Lukin was transferred to a German hospital with first-class doctors. At his request a badly wounded friend of his, General (or Colonel) Prokhorov, was also brought there.

Once out of danger Lukin showed a keen interest in the outside world. He did not like Germans, but he gratefully appreciated what had been done for him and his friend. He and I had a number of talks.

If this war, he told me, should prove to be not a war of conquest but a crusade to save Russia from Stalin's tyranny, then we could still be good friends. The Germans could still win the friendship of the peoples of Russia if they seriously meant to do so. Friendship was a bond between equal partners. He went on to say that cripple as he was he would lead a company, or an army, in the fight for freedom; but not against his country. He would only fight under orders of a national Russian government serving the interests of the Russian people, not, he kept repeating, a government of German puppets. The Germans need have no qualms. The inhabitants of the occupied zones could and would only elect a government that was nationalist Russian and uncompromisingly anti-Stalin.

He noticed that not all his German listeners were pleased at what he was saying. He smiled. 'Surely,' he said, 'your Hitler was talking on some such lines before he came to power.'

I suggested that if unbridled nationalism were to count above all else we would run the risk of unceasing chauvinist wars. Would not a United States of Europe be the best solution? The general reminded me that the Russian State embraced vast tracts of Asia where Russia had brought culture and civilization; but the thought of some vast Eurasian confederation seemed to fascinate him.

I saw General Lukin once again, in 1943; but of that more later.

2

The Question of Policy

THE world, not excluding Adolf Hitler, had long hoped for an upheaval in Soviet Russia. I do not know what politicians of all shades expected to ensue, or how they imagined the upheaval would take place. A mass rising in Moscow with barricades and bloodshed? And then? No one knew how many had met their death in the past decades, and especially under Stalin, in 'the most free country in the world' – gentry, middle class, workers, peasants, even leading Communists. In 1941 there was hardly a family in Russia that had not lost one or more of its members through death or banishment. The late thirties had been the era of the Great Purges – Tukhachevski and many thousands of army officers in 1937, Bukharin and the 'Anti-Soviet Bloc of Rightists and Trotskyites' in 1938.

For those in the West who knew the facts an anti-Stalin revolution was unthinkable without the shock of war. Now, in 1941, the shock had been administered, and the revolution was there. Not indeed in Moscow where the regime had too tight a grip and where the masses were tired and listless. (One becomes conditioned to living in prison: that I was to discover from my own experience.) No, the revolution took place in the field, where Red Army officers laid down their arms and were prepared to rally to their liberators – whoever they might be – in the struggle against their oppressor; in the towns and villages where townsmen and villagers alike were eager to collaborate with their new liberators, of whom, at the time, they knew next to nothing. All that they knew, or cared to know, was that now at last they were free from terror.

Only those few of us on the spot, who could see with our own eyes, could fully realize what was happening.

This revolution had first come into being in the lands along the Baltic. For Latvians, Estonians and Lithuanians memories of independence were fresh in their minds. They had lived through the Soviet invasion of 1940, the clamp-down on all freedoms, the arrests. The seamy side of Nazi rule was still unknown to them. After all, the German Führer himself had promised to respect the independence of small nations. When the Wehrmacht marched into Kovno a Lithuanian National Government was set up, soon to be done away with by the Germans. 'Partisan' groups of Latvian and Estonian patriots harried the retreating Reds and helped the Wehrmacht in their advance towards Leningrad. When German tanks first entered Riga the traffic was regulated by Latvian Territorials in uniform. So it was here, along the Baltic, that came the first revolution within the frontiers of the Soviet empire. But there were only a few who saw it and realized its significance.

I must emphasize that I do not in any way wish to belittle the sensational German military achievement, but it must be assessed against the background of the revolution that I have described.

It follows from all this that further military successes would to some extent depend upon the German leadership's policy towards the peoples of the USSR. This was much in the mind of Field-Marshal von Bock, who often quoted what my cousin, the Tsarist Naval Attaché, used to say before the First World War: 'One cannot pick up Russia with one's hands.' (*Rossiyu rukami ne vozmesh.*) We knew little of Hitler's plans, or those of the OKH, but it was believed that the industrial area Kharkov–Rostov, the Caucasus with its oil wells, the Crimea and, to the north, the area east of Leningrad should all be occupied before the onset of winter. We wondered what then.

It was not for von Bock to be concerned with political aspects. He believed, with the instinct of a good staff officer, that Moscow was the main military objective and that Moscow must be taken before winter came on. He believed that once Moscow had fallen it should be possible to insist on some reasonable solution of the political problems; Hitler could not risk losing so hardly won a prize. Von Bock had naturally to base his proposals on purely military considerations. Moscow was the core, the heart, of the enemy's whole being. All available striking force must be concentrated on the assault on Moscow. This was equally clear to Stalin: all available forces must be concentrated for Moscow's defence. Time and again the field-marshal pressed his views, but it appeared that the tug of war of rival strategists at Führer HQ was not yet ended. And time went by.

(ii)

One day Central Army Group in Borisov had a visit from a special representative of the Minister for Eastern Affairs (Alfred Rosenberg) and another high party official. The field-marshal invited them to a meal. Von Bock, as he told us later, derived the impression that there were marked differences in the respective attitudes of Rosenberg, Himmler and indeed other ministers regarding Russian problems. The gentlemen seemed only to agree on one point. Territory conquered should be subjected and colonized. It is true that before ever the campaign was launched Hitler had harangued the field-marshals on the intended subjection of Russia and on the special role designed for the SS on Russian soil. But at the time no one had taken this very seriously. No details had been given. One might therefore assume that in view of the vastness of the tasks to be fulfilled sound common sense would ensure an appropriate policy. (On the posters the slogan was 'Hitler, the Liberator'.)

But what these two emissaries went on to tell the field-marshal was, as he admitted to us afterwards, so alarming that he began to wonder whether or not his guests, or perhaps their superiors, were in their right minds. He told us so frankly; but of course he might have misunderstood them, for what he had imagined them to say could not possibly be the policy and aims of reasonable men. The two emissaries had set out the aims of the Government of the Reich more or less as follows:

White Russia (called 'White Ruthenia') to be incorporated in East Prussia; huge Russian areas as far east as Smolensk perhaps Moscow, perhaps even farther east and including the

Ukraine and the Caucasus, to be occupied and colonized; a
German top layer, Russian and Ukrainian slave labour, and
for these last no education, no opportunity to better their lot.
It was the sort of fantasy with which (albeit on a much smaller
scale) irresponsible political thinkers had been playing in the
First World War. Finally, most shattering of all, there were
40 million too many Russians who must disappear. And how
was this to be brought about? Famine; there was every
indication of a drastic shortage of food. And supposing this
particular problem could be solved? There would still be 40
million too many Russians. Meanwhile, on the other side of the
new Eastern frontier what was left of Russians, Jews and other
Untermenschen could lead some sort of existence in the Steppe.
The Steppe would never again be a danger to Germany and to
Europe.

This was the programme of the liberator. The field-marshal
could not and would not believe it.

A few days later I was ordered by von Gersdorff to take a plane
to Berlin and call on Alfred Rosenberg, Minister of the Occupied
Territories, to check the authenticity of what we had heard.
Thanks to a friend of mine, Herbert Dumpf, I was assured of a
private meeting with the minister. A few hours later I was in
Berlin. Distances seem very different when travelling by air. It
turned out that Rosenberg, unexpectedly, had to be absent from
Berlin, and I was received by two senior officials of the Ministry.
Dumpf was with me.

Famine? There was, of course, no magic remedy for famine;
but deliberate murder had never entered anyone's mind. Colonization? Certainly; but there were differences of opinion as to how
far this would be practicable. Collective farms? For the time
being collective agriculture must stay, as in wartime one could
not risk experiments for the return of private holdings. It was a
question of supplies for the Wehrmacht and the German population. Also, land in the east would have to be made available for
German peasants. In any case there were still conflicting views
in the various ministries. Accordingly what was here and now

being said should be taken as off the record and only for the personal information of the field-marshal. The political objectives had still to be finalized. They could still be discussed with the Führer. That, in short, was the minister's special message to the field-marshal.

Finally I was assured by one of the officials that the Ministry was concerned with evolving a policy that took full account of the facts. Fantasies emanating from the SS and other quarters would inevitably dissolve like evil dreams in the light of realities and of the needs of the army in the field. The minister intended to make a stand for the proper treatment of the civilian population and of prisoners of war.

On their part the two officials took the opportunity to question me closely on my impressions of the occupied areas. I gave details of the crying needs of the population, and in particular of the prisoners, and emphasized that only the adoption of a policy that the population could accept would bring about the changes desired.

It was with profound relief that I returned to HQ at Borisov. My superiors were shocked at what I had to report, but took comfort in the thought that Berlin would be forcibly brought to its senses. 'At the start of a victorious campaign,' remarked Major von Schack, 'no one can conceive the possibility of a set-back through his own fault. But, when there are no longer victories, they come creeping back to the Cross.'

(iii)

The Central Army Group staff tried to make use of every contact they had with policy-making quarters so as to bring about a change in the political line. An excellent opportunity was thought to lie in Hitler's visit to our HQ in early August, seven weeks after the start of the campaign.

Field-Marshal von Bock had definite operational views; either capture Moscow before the onset of winter, or else halt in fortified positions and await the spring. The onslaught on Moscow demanded the concentration of every available striking force, which entailed a temporary postponement of moves against other operational objectives on the wide front from the Baltic to the Black Sea. This conception demanded if not a final solution to the political problems, at least a secure and contented rear, i.e. a reversal of the current deceitful and inhuman treatment of civilians, line-crossers and prisoners of war.

Captain Schmidt and I were ordered to work out a draft memorandum, to be finalized by von Gersdorff and von Tresckow, GSO I of the Central Army Group. The field-marshal himself wished to arrange that Schmidt and I should have an audience with Hitler. We had, owing to the nature of our duties, a first-hand knowledge of conditions and problems; it seemed desirable that we should have the chance to report direct. This is perhaps an unimportant episode, but it illustrates the atmosphere at our HQ.

Accordingly during the Hitler visit Schmidt and I sat in the waiting-room: we might be called in at any moment. It was nearly 2 a.m. when von Gersdorff told us to go to bed. There was no desire to hear what we had to say.

When Hitler left the HQ next day, the officers were to take leave of him in the park. When we were assembled a lieutenant-colonel appeared and ordered all present to remove all cameras and arms. An odd directive from the Supreme War Lord to his officers at the front. A number of officers returned to their quarters and did not come back. I had no revolver, and decided to wait for Hitler and hand him our memorandum as his car went past; but a heavily armed bodyguard screened the car against any approach, and I stood as if turned to stone as the Führer with ashen grey face drove slowly by.

A few weeks after our HQ moved from Borisov to Krasny Bor (near Smolensk) we were notified of an early visit on the part of Propaganda Minister Goebbels. This seemed to offer a chance to explain our views to a prominent member of the government. The field-marshal, Greiffenberg, Tresckow and Gersdorff intended to speak very frankly to the minister. He was believed to have an open mind on Russian affairs and to make no secret of his disagreement with Rosenberg. We had gathered from an official of the Propaganda Ministry that Goebbels had drawn up a far-reaching programme for 'a new Russia', with the aim of winning over the peoples of Russia for the idea of a New Europe based on Freedom and Equality of Rights. Our directive for the discussions was: No politics, merely the measures necessary from the strictly military angle. The main point that the field-marshal and his senior officers wished to emphasize was the impossibility of keeping down 70 million men and women by force alone, and that the front could be in danger should these 70 million mutiny.

I was instructed to write a short memorandum (which I later was to expand into my lecture 'Russians as Human Beings'). My main point was that we had now the choice of two alternatives: (a) to win the Russians over to our side (as desired by the military leadership), or (b) not to win them over (by continuing our present policy and practice). Course (b) entailed holding them down by force. Course (a) entailed recognizing their rights as equal partners in the European Community of Nations.

I was further assigned the task of taking the minister on a tour of Smolensk, showing him the citadel, the museum, etc., and arranging for him to meet leading representatives of the local intelligentsia so as to let him see something of Russian culture and form his own impression of the country and its people.

But the day before he was due we were informed that the minister must unfortunately postpone his visit. He never came. We later learned that Hitler had told him not to get involved in what was not his business.

(iv)

'Cannibalism in the prisoner-of-war camps. . . . Only Russians could be capable of that. . . . Our theory of the *Untermensch* is shown to be correct.'

An SS colonel was sent from Berlin to our HQ at Krasny Bor to confirm this theory of Himmler's by observation on the spot. I was detailed to look after him. I was delighted to have this chance to enlighten him, the more so as he told me that Himmler himself had sent him on his mission. This SS officer was open-minded, honest and intelligent. He soon realized that it was ill-treatment and starvation that had brought about the prisoners' dehumanization. He realized, too, that the root of all this evil lay in the ruling of the leadership that Russians were to be enslaved.

'The scales have dropped from my eyes,' he told me. 'I would be grateful if you would write me a memorandum to be attached as appendix to my report. SS Gruppenführer Müller is chiefly concerned with these matters, and a copy of my report will go to him. When next in Berlin you must call on Müller and explain things to him. I imagine he has no idea of what is going on.'

I knew little about the SS at that time, and had no idea that this Müller was the formidable Gestapo boss. I set to work with gusto on my memorandum. Soon after the SS colonel was back in Berlin he sent me a note that Müller would like to thank me for my 'interesting observations'. So, apparently, even in the SS there were men who were not only sensible but human. I was glad to think my memorandum had fallen on fruitful soil.

Or had it?

Another visitor to our HQ was a young Nazi Party member who had to decide whether to take on the post of mayor at Kharkov or at Reval (Talinn). He knew no Russian and no Estonian, but apparently both posts were vacant and Berlin had earmarked him for one of them. He had no experience and no knowledge of the tasks and problems involved, which was why he had come to spend a couple of days with us and intended to pay a similar visit to Northern Group HQ.

'If you have a family,' I said, 'and if, as you tell me, Russia is a closed book to you, I would suggest Reval. Estonia has a western cultural tradition. There would be a German school for your children, you would feel more at home in Reval, and you would be in a better position to make a success of your job.'

The young man did not seem to be very interested. 'The point is,' he said, 'that if I went to Reval all that I could hope to be would be mayor. But in Kharkov I would be Lord Mayor [Oberbürgermeister] from the start. That would be promotion. I have been a mayor since 1938, and after all I want to get on.'

The young man had in fact been mayor of some tiny commune in the Harz, which I was unable to find on the map.

This was how Berlin selected candidates for key communal posts in the occupied zone.

(v)

In Smolensk there was lively contact between certain officers from HQ and a number of leading local families. Russian hospitality, in spite of the apparent poverty, was unbounded. Talk was on a high level, whether we were discussing education, art, philosophy or politics; but we soon came back to the main issue:

'You Germans have rescued us from Stalin's tyranny, which, if you please, had no longer anything to do with Communism. We thank you for the liberation. Our Communists and Socialists will also be grateful. But what comes next? The longer we enjoy the blessings of the freedom you have brought us, the more our doubts begin to grow. On your present showing you will never get to Moscow, never win the war – let alone win over the Russian people.'

A German lieutenant-colonel – formerly in the Imperial Austrian Army – tried to dissipate our hosts' misgivings, suggesting that 'the Prussians have never shown much skill in their treatment of other nations. The Nazis certainly have not, as one can see from their behaviour in Austria, Poland and the Balkans. They should, of course, have put Austrians in charge.'

Unfortunately I have forgotten the name of this excellent officer, who got together a number of Jewish craftsmen from Smolensk and neighbourhood. His workshops were thus able to provide the Wehrmacht with much of what was needed, and, incidentally, secure a decent livelihood for the Jewish craftsmen. Our Russian friends remarked that under Stalin such initiative from an individual officer would be unthinkable. 'So with you there is still freedom and independence.'

This Smolensk group was ready to take the initiative in promoting the active cooperation of the population of the occupied zones in the war against Stalin. We gave them our advice. There was a great gulf between the closed world in which they had lived and the world outside as known to us: and it was only by close collaboration that realistic proposals could be evolved. (But of course here lies the essential task of the intermediary.) And so together we composed an address from the city fathers of Smolensk to the Führer of the German Reich. The group, who assumed the title of 'Russian Liberation Committee', expressed its readiness to summon the Russian people to arms against Stalin and to raise a Russian Liberation Army of a million men. Conditions were the recognition of the 1939 frontier, equality of rights for the Russian people and the formation of an independent Russian National Government on a democratic basis.

The address was illuminated by a Russian artist and bound in ecclesiastical brocade. One of Napoleon's cannons from the Smolensk citadel was presented to Field-Marshal von Bock, in thanks for the city's liberation. Von Bock inquired of Führer HQ if he might pass on the address, of which he gave a summary. Approval was given for it to be submitted, and we were delighted to feel there was still hope of a change in policy towards Russia.

Weeks went by and no reply came back from Führer HQ. After repeated inquiries word came that the address would remain unanswered as questions of policy were not the concern of the Army Group. Bock gave orders to his Chief of Staff, General Greiffenberg, to convey to the city fathers his personal thanks for the Napoleonic cannon and to inform them of the negative attitude of Field-Marshal von Keitel. I accompanied Greiffenberg to Smolensk. *En route* we discussed how best to break news of the fate of our brain-child without causing further distress. As ointment on the wound two truck-loads of medical stores were, at the instance of the field-marshal, handed over to the Smolensk Russian Hospital.

When Greiffenberg, with much hesitation, came to the subject of the Address, a Russian interrupted my translation by saying:

'Please tell the general not to bother with an explanation. If, in a decisive moment like this, it takes so long to reply to our offer, the answer must certainly be negative. Obviously your government has still not grasped what the position is.'

Greiffenberg thanked him. He had no need to sully the honour of a German officer with a lie. The Russians showed extreme tact and asked no further questions. The general bowed and left the room in silence.

(vi)

In the first few months of the campaign a very large number of Red Army officers and men, and indeed civilians (townsmen as well as villagers), had joined up with, or rather had been taken on by various units of the Wehrmacht. They served in a variety of capacities as combatants, for reconnaissance, construction and road work, transport. German casualties, both for officers and men, had been heavy – in the Central Army Group some 18–20 per cent up to November 1941 – and officers in command of units welcomed the opportunity to complete their establishments with these 'Russian drafts'. Subordinate commanders took advantage of the initiative allowed them by German military practice to build up their effective strengths.

Professionals at the front – as opposed to politicians in Berlin – knew perfectly well that if a man is to work he has to eat, and, if a Russian, to smoke as well. Unit commanders found a way to fix matters with the supply services; and by some means or other these men were all given their rations. If one stopped a German army lorry on the road to ask the driver a question, one would often get as an answer '*nix ponemai*' (don't understand). Russian drivers carried Wehrmacht supplies, safely and surely, over hundreds of kilometres of road.

The troops at first used to call these men 'our Ivans'. Then the designation 'Auxiliaries' (Hilfswillige) was approved. They included many with the sincere desire to fight for freedom, but, very naturally there were also others who wished to avoid the hardships of prison camps or who foresaw some advantage to themselves in offering their services to the Germans.

At first the higher military authorities had no confidence in ex-Red Army officers, so an appeal was made to émigré ex-officers to volunteer – in particular to émigrés in France. A number of them passed through our Army Group HQ; others proceeded to corps, divisions and regiments. According to Y. S. Zherebkov, head of the Émigré Centre in France, he and General Golovin (President of the Russian Officers' Association) had registered over 1,500 officers ready to enrol unconditionally in the struggle against Bolshevism.

The first batch to arrive numbered some two hundred, who were decked out in fancy uniforms. Their showing in the firing line was satisfactory, and a number were decorated for acts of bravery. Some were killed in action, some severely wounded. I was in touch with many of them, and could share their initial enthusiasm and their subsequent disillusionment and bitterness. After a few months the OKW brought back all émigré officers to the Reich, forbade them to wear their decorations and left the wounded and disabled to fend for themselves. A resourceful paymaster in the Berlin Wehrkreis, who had to deal with these émigrés, succeeded, on his own responsibility, in entering some hundreds of Russian officers on his own establishment under a special schedule, and maintaining them there for several months.

(vii)

'We cannot alter policy,' Tresckow and Gersdorff used to say. 'But, with the aim of assuring better security for our combatant troops, we can bring into being a new factor. And this new factor in itself may perhaps induce our leadership to reconsider the policy so far pursued.'

The new factor they had in mind was the setting up of Russian Volunteer Formations on a large scale. I was allotted the task of working out detailed proposals for the immediate enrolment of 200,000 men, who were to be trained and ready for active service by late April 1942.

The idea of mercenaries is foreign to Russians. There would be no point in trying to recruit Russians on behalf of German interests, particularly in view of the anti-Russian policy in the occupied zone; but experience had shown that Russians, and other races in the USSR, were willing to fight to liberate their homes from Stalin's yoke. Accordingly I proposed a 'Russian Liberation Army' led by Russians. An essential condition for the success of this project would be an improvement in the treatment of prisoners and in the administration of occupied territory. This was my basic thesis, and I went on to work out detailed proposals for the setting up of a 200,000-strong army.

Tresckow and Gersdorff showed a lively interest in my draft, and took care that the arguments should be so worded as to be based on purely military considerations. Soldiers must not interfere in politics. The memorandum, as finalized, was in line with Field-Marshal Bock's own views, and he passed it on, with his warm recommendation, to the commander-in-chief, Field-Marshal von Brauchitsch. It has since been suggested in various quarters that I was the sole author of this memorandum; but I would like to emphasize that my proposals were merely a résumé of what many of my countrymen and a number of German officers were already hoping, and perhaps had already expressed. All the same I was extremely proud when von Brauchitsch sent back my memorandum with the comment: 'I consider this of decisive importance for the issue of the war.' (The German commander-in-chief to a Riga businessman!)

Von Bock, Tresckow and Gersdorff congratulated me. Only old von Schack shook his head. 'One doesn't put a bridle on a horse's tail,' he said. 'Nothing will come of it.'

As things were the position at the front ruled out any immediate steps for the implementation of the project. And on 19 December 1941 von Brauchitsch was dismissed, and Hitler himself assumed supreme command. In due course the Wehrmacht was to enrol in its ranks nearly a million Russians, Ukrainians, Turkic racials, Caucasians, Latvians and Estonians; and Hitler continued to forbid discussion of the considerations put forward in the memorandum. But of that we were then unaware.

(viii)

The abject misery in the prisoner-of-war camps had now passed all bounds. In the countryside one could come across ghost-like figures, ashen grey, starving, half naked, living perhaps for days on end on corpses and the bark of trees. Gersdorff and I visited a prison camp near Smolensk where the daily death rate reached hundreds. It was the same in transit camps, in villages, along the roads. Only some quite unprecedented effort could check the appalling death roll.

In the twenties Herbert Hoover – subsequently President of the USA – had headed a vast organization (the ARA) to fight famine in Russia. Would it not now be possible to appeal to Hoover for help? Or perhaps to the American president? The idea occurred to me because I and a few friends had launched an appeal for famine relief in Russia before ever the Hoover or the Nansen committees had come into being. Later I had worked for some years with the Nansen Relief Organization, and I had thus been in contact with members of the Hoover Administration.

In the autumn of 1941 it was not only possible to express such ideas in the Central Army Group HQ; one could also take steps. Three officers, who had been connected with both the German and the International Red Cross, signed a memorandum *Inter Arma Caritas*. It was doubtful whether effective action would be possible while the fighting was still going on, but once the fighting was over, or after the capture of Moscow and Leningrad, there would be enormous need and scope for relief work in the battle against famine and epidemics.

There seemed no serious difficulties over a private approach to our American contacts. Field-Marshal von Bock, after cautious consideration, expressed his approval. He was aware that the Führer had given orders to the German Navy to do nothing that might endanger the state of neutrality between the USA and the Reich. Though President Roosevelt was supporting the British, Hitler was determined to avoid an open break. This gave the field-marshal some hope of our chances of success. Later it transpired that the memorandum must be passed through official channels, so that our idea of a private approach had to be abandoned. 'Official' channels meant Nazi Party channels and that meant there was little hope of success, although the Soviet authorities had not refused the offer of help from Hoover and Nansen. (Our memorandum had cited the Hoover and Nansen relief work as precedent.) Von Bock, when he heard the appeal was to be routed through the party, regretfully gave instructions for the memorandum to be withdrawn.

A few weeks later, on 7 December, the Japanese attacked the American fleet in Pearl Harbor; and on 12 December Hitler declared war on the USA.

(ix)

Those long autumn and winter nights I sat up very late, busily writing. To explain, persuade, enlighten, was the task I had set myself – to act as intermediary between two worlds, to mitigate the appalling misery around me. Papers on military matters must be passed through the official service channels. But no one could stop me, in my private capacity, from writing stories, plays and sketches (unfamiliar as I was with that kind of composition) and ensuring they were widely circulated. Thus I wrote my play *God, Hammer and Sickle*, which I sent off in instalments, by the military postal service, to my wife who had it multigraphed. In January 1942 two hundred copies were dispatched. The first recipients were senior Wehrmacht officers. But it was important that leading politicians should also read it. Having no contacts myself I wrote to suitably placed friends of mine and asked them to pass it on; in this way copies reached Emmy Göring, Alfred Rosenberg, Alfred Ingemar Berndt (of the Propaganda Ministry), Gauleiter Greiser, Minister Frank and others. I had, of course, my own business contacts, and so was able to post it direct to prominent industrialists in the Rhineland and elsewhere.

Another piece, started in 1941 and completed later, was what the reader could not fail to recognize as a criticism of current Nazi policy, albeit camouflaged as an assessment of the errors of Kaiser Wilhelm II and his advisers. I quoted a number of wild statements made between 1915 and 1918 which, in fact, were just what rabid Nazis were saying in 1941. 'If,' I wrote, 'we wish to build up a new Europe, we must clear our minds of the illusions of Wilhelm's imperialists. . . . Shadows of the past must not be allowed to cloud the relationship between the rest of Europe and the German Führer who, on 7 March 1936, declared: "The nations of Europe are now one family."' My concluding words were: 'If a new Europe were to be founded on the old imperialist methods of oppression, robbery and exploitation, then even a dismembered or subjected Russia would still present a danger. Woe to the victor who has cause to fear the vanquished!'

These essays were finished and distributed in the course of 1942. It brought me a number of letters expressing agreement. From the Ostministerium came two separate, and contradictory comments. One expressed appreciation, the other (from von der Milve, deputy head of the Department of Culture) to the effect that the dissemination of such views should be forbidden. I had a friendly letter from Field-Marshal von Bock. Of those prominent in political circles there were favourable comments from Ingemar Berndt, SS Gruppenführer Otto Wächter and from Frauenfeld, commissar in the Crimea. These three last were quite unknown to me, but I had the satisfaction of feeling that some of the seed had fallen on fruitful soil.

(x)

In Krasny Bor it was often my privilege to accompany the field-marshal on his walks in the woods and thus become acquainted with some of his innermost thoughts. The attack on Moscow had already been initiated, and this was his constant preoccupation. Would we find it possible to consolidate, once the town had been taken? Even more ominous were the possibilities should Moscow not be captured but, like Leningrad, merely be encircled.

Von Bock was no Nazi. By background and upbringing he was the antithesis of Hitler; but it was this same background and upbringing that precluded any act of insubordination against the constitutionally appointed Head of State. Von Bock, like so many others, had welcomed, as a German patriot, the rise of Hitler without accepting the tenets of the Nazi ideology. The successful reoccupation of the Rhineland without any counter move from the West convinced many Germans (and not only Germans) of the soundness of Hitler's judgement. The campaign in the West in 1940 offered further evidence. It was Hitler, and not his generals, who had correctly assessed French military weakness, and this was something the generals were unable to forget. Would Hitler prove to be right once more over Russia? So far he was behind in his timetable. Von Bock, doubting whether the objectives would ever be attained and envisaging the possibility of disaster, was filled with grim misgivings; but he saw no other course than to continue to do his duty as a soldier in the face of the enemy.

From time to time I wrote occasional verse, with the object of making my ideas better known. Count von Hardenberg, the field-marshal's ADC, was one of the recipients of my efforts. One day I took him a new poem, *Achtung vor dem Menschenleben*. Hardenberg glanced at it.

'You must show this to the field-marshal at once.' Then he asked: 'Have you heard of yesterday's horror in Borisov?'

I had not. Army Group HQ had once been in Borisov. The area was now in the rear lines of communication. Perhaps the civil administration had already taken over. An SS commando had evacuated the Jewish quarter in Borisov, and driven out the whole community, men and women, old people and children. Many hundreds of them had been massacred with machine-pistols.

'A small consolation for us,' said the count, 'is that we, the Wehrmacht, wear a different uniform from the SS, and so are not responsible for their crimes. But the Führer is head of the German State. We are Germans and the field-marshal must not let this pass in silence.'

Hardenberg took me into the field-marshal's room. Von Bock stood by the window, nervously tapping the panes with his fingers. Outside snow was falling in thick flakes. Hardenberg handed over my poem, which the field-marshal read through more than once.

'I know,' he said in an expressionless voice, 'but what am I to do? . . . Hardenberg tells me I should resign. But what then? Look outside. Ice and snow. The fighting for Moscow goes on and on. The demands on our men are for their utmost. I initiated this operation. I carry the responsibility. If I resign I am deserting my officers and soldiers in their hour of need.'

'You would not be leaving them for long,' said Hardenberg. 'Things cannot go on as they are. It is your duty to God and to history to protest against this crime.'

'Even when committed outside the zone of my command?'

'The security of the front depends upon the security of the lines of communication, which makes it possible for you to make an official *démarche*.'

'That should have happened long ago. Think of Poland. That was on our lines of communication. It still is. Think further, think of Germany.'

'Quite true.' Hardenberg's tone betrayed his feeling. 'But this case makes it essential for you to act.'

'It was so before the campaign in Russia ever started. I am, as you say, responsible to God and to history, responsible too to the German nation for the lives of those men who today and tomorrow are facing death in the Russian winter. Who can weigh the scales of my responsibility? I know, Hardenberg, what you mean. But I do not know what is my duty. If I leave, another will take my place. I do not know what he will do. I am certain only of this, that a change of command will cost many lives. And I know that it is here, in front of Moscow, that we will either win or irreparably lose the war.'

The field-marshal looked at me as if he was hoping for my silent approval. I was conscious of von Bock the man, the good old-school officer deeply and bitterly aware of his responsibility to his superiors, and to the men in the icy fox-holes, in the marshes and woods, on the roads and in hospitals, to the men and women far away at home. He felt his powerlessness and he did not attempt to hide it.

Hardenberg told him of the indignation of those officers of the Army Group who had heard the news. The field-marshal stood motionless. Then suddenly stiffened and said: 'I will not pass it over in silence. But I know it will be useless.'

Hardenberg and others worked out a draft for the field-marshal's note to the Führer and von Brauchitsch. It seems there was embarrassed silence at Führer HQ when this note arrived from the commander of the sorely tried Central Army Group front. Bock's protest resulted in there being for a time no further atrocities of this kind in the Central Army Group zone; but it also had the consequence that von Bock had foreseen. On 18 December he was retired 'at his own desire and on grounds of health'; and Field-Marshal von Kluge was appointed to succeed him.

3

Oberkommando des Heeres

(i)

I HAD only one interview with Field-Marshal von Kluge who succeeded von Bock in command of the Central Army Group. He had every sympathy with the increasing demand for the proper treatment of prisoners of war; he was very much a soldier, and this was something near his heart. He was highly critical of the way the occupied zone was being administered, but he was unwilling to accept the idea of the setting up of a Russian Liberation Army. I told him of the comment of von Brauchitsch – 'of decisive importance for the issue of the war' – and his short answer was, 'We can talk about that later on.' He agreed to the employment of Russians on various tasks as required by the Wehrmacht, but he looked on things from a narrowly military angle. The wider problems that had so preoccupied von Bock – the question of peace, the fate of the Russian people, the German task on Russian soil – were, for him, of no interest.

This talk with von Kluge took place in early January 1942, when his whole attention was absorbed by what was happening at the front. Bock had been right. Not only had the fighting in front of Moscow brought heavier casualties than ever before but an irreparable blow had been struck at the structure of the higher command. Hitler had declared himself Supreme Commander on 19 December, and proceeded to destroy the instrument to which he owed his rise to power.

(ii)

The soldiers' word for rumours was 'latrine gossip'. Although we at Group HQ were better informed than those in the firing line, as far as high policy was concerned we had to depend on rumours. They were apt to be contradictory. Some were thoroughly depressing, others gave us new hopes. Here are some samples from my diary:

The Abwehr under Admiral Canaris have started a campaign against the ill-treatment of prisoners of war and against Himmler's and Rosenberg's policy in the occupied zone.

A number of German officers have, on their own initiative, released prisoners of war whose homes are in occupied territory.

Russian prisoners of war are being transferred to the Reich as a labour force and are being ill-treated.

Minister Rosenberg intends to appeal to the Supreme Command for prisoners to be treated according to the dictates of humanity.

Russian schools reopened by the Wehrmacht are being closed again by the civilian authorities on the grounds that Russians do not need education.

Prominent Nazis believe that medical care is not required for non-Germans in occupied territory.

Although the USA has adhered to the London–Moscow alliance, it has been officially declared in Washington that Communism is as intolerable as National Socialism.

Germany's immediate economic aim is to ensure raw materials for the Reich. The Eastern territories must therefore deliver raw materials as against subsequent deliveries from Germany of manufactured goods to a population whose standard of living must be kept as low as possible.

The former German Ambassador in Moscow, von Schulenburg, has proposed the formation of Russian and other National Governments in the occupied zone, these governments to be recognized as allies.

Reichsmarschall Göring, in his capacity as head of the Four-Year Plan, is in favour of a radical change in our policy towards the Eastern territories.

(iii)

The balance sheet of the past six months and prospects for the future were the main topics at Smolensk in the early weeks of

1942 at little gatherings with my own particular fellow-country-men. By these last I mean those Russian-born Germans and Balts who had not only understanding of but also sympathy for the peoples of Russia. There were of course other Balts who followed Rosenberg in his theory of the Nordic German master race.

I shall always remember Andrik von Sivers, whose modest job was to go round the villages to seek out butter and eggs, or some-times *valenki* (Russian felt boots) for the officers. At these gatherings of ours he would quote Napoleon's dictum that one can win a battle against a superior enemy but not a war. He would go on to warn against underestimating the Russian soldier when fighting on and for his own soil. Andrik's father, General von Sivers, had commanded a Russian army against the Germans in the First World War. For this reason it was hard for Andrik to get a hearing. As so many others of his like he was labelled pro-Russian.

We were all agreed that the Soviet system under Stalin had proved to be brittle. We had seen the break, once it had been subjected to a shock from outside. The Russians, and the other racials, had awoken from their lethargy once the cord that bound them to their rulers had been cut. Past efforts to make a stand against their oppressors had all been in vain. Now at last they were given an opportunity that held a real chance of success.

This unrecognized 'Russian Revolution' came into being from the impulse of the individual – of many million individuals. There was within the Soviet Empire no organized movement; every attempt at organized resistance had been bloodily suppressed. And outside the Soviet frontiers there was still no organized movement to which these liberated Russians could turn.

Here we had a compulsive urge for freedom, felt by millions. To talk of 'collaboration with Hitler' or of 'treachery' is irrele-vant. How could these Russians know of Hitler's war aims when we Germans ourselves did not know of them? They did not turn to Hitler, but to those Germans whose genuine aim was to free the Russian people from Stalin's tyranny.

We, in our little gatherings at Smolensk, were convinced that this war could not be won on the field of battle; but it could be brought to an end through sincere collaboration with the liberated population. We were encouraged to find that more and more Wehrmacht officers were coming to share this view. After all it was the Germans alone who could bring about the essential pre-conditions of a genuine collaboration. The Russians could do nothing.

But here, after six months of fighting, the outlook was bleak. In the party the old ideological fantasies still held sway – Nordic superiority, *Untermenschen*, annexation, confiscation, slave labour. We tried to comfort ourselves with the thought that the failure in front of Moscow must have opened the leadership's eyes. We endeavoured to hope that Brauchitsch, Bock and the others, so arbitrarily dismissed by Hitler, might find means to make their views prevail. For the strategist a set-back does mean ultimate defeat: it is an occasion to reconsider, to correct past errors, to formulate new and better plans. This, we felt, should hold good also for one who controlled both strategy and policy. But suppose, in spite of Moscow, ideological fantasy prevails over common sense? All one could say was that that would be lunacy. There are cases, of course, where mental illnesses are cured. In other cases, if the trouble proves incurable, the only course is for the patient to be put out of harm's way in a mental hospital. ('Do you mean the Führer?' asked a young Balt who was present. 'I never mentioned Hitler,' said Sivers. 'I was talking about lunatics.')

The spring saw the beginnings of Partisan activity throughout the occupied zone, causing grave concern to the front-line commanders and to the civilian administration in the rear. This was not, as some thought at the time, a mere matter of security control. It was one of the fruits of a masterpiece of political innovation by Stalin, who, unlike certain others, was prepared for the time being to put ideology into cold storage. He appealed to Russian love of country and announced the Great Patriotic War. Warrior heroes of the old Russia, Suvorov, Kutuzov, were recalled in honour. In the newly reopened churches prayers were offered for the victory of Russian arms.

(iv)

Early in 1942 I was granted sick leave, to recover from the after-math of frostbite in my right foot. I made use of this interlude to continue my crusade on behalf of a new approach to Russian problems. I called on the Ostministerium where I saw Dr Braütigam and Dr von Knüpffer. My impression was that neither of these two gentlemen nor Minister Rosenberg were in a position to take action in the sense I desired. But Ingemar Berndt, who (as I have mentioned) had read my essay, asked me to go and see him and kept me talking for hours. I left him feeling he had been won over for our cause. He promised to put the case for a change of policy to his minister (Goebbels) and to other highly placed contacts. He even gave me to understand he might have a chance to speak to Hitler himself. I, of course, had no knowledge of the workings of the top hierarchy, but the interview filled me with hope. My travels took me as far as the Rhineland, where I went to see the heads of important firms for whom I had been agent in the Baltic. All showed a lively interest, coupled with a frightening degree of ignorance (and, indeed, illusion) as to what the facts really were. I left with them copies of memoranda, essays and other pieces. It was, incidentally, thanks to this that I was able to recover some of my material after the war.

A few days after my return from this excursion I received my orders. I was not to return to Army Group HQ but was trans-ferred to the Oberkommando des Heeres.

(v)

I proceeded to Angerburg (East Prussia) and reported to Lieu-tenant-Colonel Dietz, head of the 'War Booty Collection Centre' of the General Staff. I thought of the tanks and tractors abandoned by the Russians during the German advance and left to rust. At last, after ten months, had it been decided to put them in order? But it turned out that 'booty' meant soldiers' letters, reports, books, papers, prisoners' interrogations and Red Army orders, which were here to be assessed by Fremde Heere Ost[1] of the

[1] Department of Foreign Armies East.

General Staff so as to provide information on enemy order of battle, armament and morale.

Dietz was a good-natured cavalry officer and obviously intelligent, but he knew no Russian and frankly admitted he was a square peg in a round hole. He told me much of the material coming in was out-of-date, and, at best, of only historical value. This came as a shock to me. While at Army Group HQ I was concerned with action, here apparently I was to be buried in a mass of paper.

Our section was soon renamed 'Group III of the Department of Foreign Armies East at the General Staff of the Army'. My colleagues were Balts and Germans from Russia – engineers, pastors, lawyers, businessmen, professors: a mixed lot but with a high level of capacity and a sense of responsibility. 'It grieves me,' Dietz remarked, 'to have all these clever gentlemen sharpening their wits for the wastepaper basket.' I was to remain in the Department of Foreign Armies East (under the command of Major-General Reinhard Gehlen) up to the end of the war, and I learned to value the spirit and the comradely feeling of what before long we came to call 'the club'.

We were soon put under one of Gehlen's officers, Colonel Alexis von Roenne, born in Courland and with a good knowledge of Russian. Sharp, clear-headed and purposeful, von Roenne was to steer our little ship out of the realm of paper and into the world of action. A few days after his arrival, after supper in the mess, Roenne referred to an article of mine in the *Deutsche Offiziersblatt* and asked me why it was that I was always taking the Russian side in my reports and memoranda. I replied: 'In the first place because I feel it my duty to God. Second, because in this way I am serving the German people. Third, because I am fond . . .' Roenne interrupted me. 'Don't say you are fond of Russians. Your point one: God has been abolished. Your point two: how best to serve the German people is for the Führer alone to decide. Finally, point three, if you are fond of Russians you have no business to be here.'

For the moment I was tongue-tied. But I had no need to speak. My colleagues – Schabert, Kerkovius and Eckert – fell upon the colonel like a pack of hungry wolves. Captain Eckert had been a pastor in Courland, and von Roenne may well have been in his or in a neighbouring parish, and Eckert, after the practice in Courland, called him 'Baron Roenne' and not 'Herr Oberst'. The duel went on for a whole hour, on one side the cool, incisive staff colonel and on the other the vehement 'club members'. As we said good night under a clear moon in the old market-place of Angerburg, von Roenne suddenly remarked: 'Thank you, gentlemen, for our talk. I entirely agree with Strikfeldt and the rest of you. But I enjoy an argument.'

This was the seal of our alliance with von Roenne, which was to last right up to his death.

(vi)

Colonel von Roenne would regularly call his officers together to keep them informed on the situation at the front. The Northern and Central Army Groups had stabilized their positions. In the south the Southern Army Group had regained the initiative. In spite of what had happened in the winter Hitler appeared to have no intention of bringing hostilities to an end; in fact he was widening the scale of the operations. The objectives of the Southern Group offensive were first the Caucasian oil fields and the mountain passes, and, second, Stalingrad so as to cut communications between the heart of Russia and the south.

It appeared that Field-Marshal von List and other senior generals had expressed grave misgivings regarding this operation, as the striking force available did not seem adequate in view of the enormous areas to be covered, i.e. a front line some 3,500–4,000 kilometres in length. (Field-Marshal von List was dismissed in September 1942. At the end of the war, when he and I were fellow-prisoners, he told me about his arguments with Hitler and with Keitel.) 'I fear,' said von Roenne at one of his talks, 'we are going to miss the million or so Russian volunteer levies. To fight against Stalin on their own soil would make sense, and they would fight. But to be sent off into the blue across the Caucasus with a lot of Italians, Hungarians and Romanians must seem to them to have no point.' 'No more than it does to us Germans,' said Pastor Eckert. Von Roenne made no comment.

Führer HQ was moved forward to Vinitsa and the OKH with its various departments moved with it. My section was housed in a former hospital. I myself never visited Führer HQ.

This was the first time I had been in the Ukraine. My colleagues and I were of course eager to learn what we could of local conditions and local feeling. It would be hard for me accurately to assess Ukrainian political aspirations. I was there for too short a time, and I spoke only Russian, not Ukrainian. I was not in a position to check the reactions of either Ukrainians or locally domiciled Russians to the views of Ukrainian émigré nationalists arriving from the West. I could only compare the general atmosphere of the summer of 1942 with that of the previous year.

In 1941 the Ukrainians, like the Russians, had welcomed their 'liberators' without reservation. Today Ukrainians and Russians doubted whether the Germans would ever give up the territory they had occupied. They fully recognized the achievements of the German Army and they appreciated the army's correct behaviour. Certain difficulties and incidents are inevitable in the stress of war, and that was generally understood. The soldiers completed their task and then moved on, but they were followed by SS contingents, police, Ostministerium officials and commissars. They were for the most part arrogant and out for their own advantage. Their methods were very similar to those of the Red commissars, but at least these last spoke the same language and one could talk to them. In the towns the best living quarters were taken over by the Germans. But, as has been said, this was wartime. In general, requisitioning by the Wehrmacht had been less drastic than by the Red Army.

This was what we heard from the various people to whom we spoke.

Production was at a low level. There was praise for the German effort to get industry going again, but no heed seemed to be paid to the needs of the population. Up till now all of them, workers, peasants, technicians, artists, Russians or Ukrainians, had all been citizens. True they hated the State machine, but still they were citizens. The State did not do much for them, but it did do something. Everyone had his place and his job. But what was going to happen now? Why should engineers be sacked from their posts even though they had never been members of the Communist Party? Why were workers treated like slaves?

It was quite natural that the Germans should want young Ukrainians for work in their armament industries in the Reich. There was a war on. And after all, why not? According to the Germans labour and living conditions in Germany were very good. A spell there would be a valuable experience for these young people. They would learn something. But why should they be rounded up, like criminals, by SS and police and packed into cattle trucks without even the chance to take leave of their families? It was all too reminiscent of the way that Stalin's gangs had behaved at the time of forced collectivization.

And what was going to happen about the land? German pundits were now proclaiming that collective farms were more productive than private holdings; but German peasants still retained their holdings. Who was to benefit by increased production? The invaders? What was to happen once the war was over?

Secondary schools were still closed. In many localities the Wehrmacht had allowed them to start up again; but then came the civil administration, and the only instruction permitted was in reading, writing and arithmetic. Why were Ukrainians and Russians forbidden to learn the German language? Many hospitals had to hand over their accommodation to the occupation authorities. Even under the Bolsheviks some provisions had been made for the sick. What about freedom of movement, of trading, of speech? And municipal and rural district councils? And the right to form associations?

The behaviour of the new 'liberators' or conquerors was so arbitrary and often so inconsistent that it was impossible to tell if the Germans had made their minds up as to whether or not they should stay in the area permanently. In the minds of the population there lurked the dread that they had merely exchanged one tyranny for another.

(vii)

In the OKH we no longer wrote memoranda to be passed on to a higher level. After all, militarily, the highest level was the OKH itself. And what had all the numerous reports and memoranda pleading for a fresh approach been able to effect? My joint paper with Gersdorff and Tresckow had at least had the result of causing von Brauchitsch to modify his views. But then he had been dismissed.

General von Schenkendorff, in command of the Central Army Group's lines of communication, had subsequently submitted detailed proposals on similar lines. The proposals were ignored.

Both papers envisaged a speedy termination of hostilities to be brought about by the adoption of a realistic, and humane, policy. Implicit in both was the abandonment of any idea of territorial aggrandizement.

Following the setbacks at the front, a number of prominent generals had sent in proposals of a not dissimilar tenor but based on purely military considerations. They called for a change of policy in the occupied zone, and for the intensive recruitment of Russians and Ukrainians in view of the army's pressing need for manpower. Nothing came of these proposals, even when backed by men of the calibre of Field-Marshal von Reichenau (believed to be pro-Nazi) and later Field-Marshal von Kleist. It must have been Hitler himself who was refusing to consider any change of attitude. Indeed this was more or less an open secret in the OKH, though of course the Führer's name was not directly mentioned, and criticism ostensibly directed at his various advisers.

It was in those few weeks in the spring and early summer of 1942 that I was privileged to be associated with a group of officers in OKH who disapproved of the official Eastern policy and who, in the light of their experience, were now prepared to take action on their own responsibility. The group included General Wagner, head of Q Branch, General Reinhard Gehlen, head of Fremde Heere Ost, Colonel Schmidt von Altenstadt, General Stieff,

Colonels Claus von Stauffenberg, Roenne and Herre, Lieutenant-Colonels Klammroth and Schrader and others. My impression was and is that the main initiative came from Gehlen, Roenne and Stauffenberg.

Colonel von Roenne, who was my closest contact, took me into his confidence. He drew a clear line between 'war aims', which were no business of ours, and 'political warfare directed to the attainment of military objectives' which he regarded as our own special and immediate task. He was in full agreement with the 'war aims' as proposed and elaborated in my memorandum; but he saw that the only chance of getting these adopted was by first persuading the Führer, 'or whoever it may be', to accept our proposals for political warfare. We must act, von Roenne emphasized, with extreme circumspection, and take advantage of any outside support, from whatever quarter it might come. 'Political warfare on the lines we envisage must inevitably lead to a new conception of war aims, and this alone can bring about a successful conclusion of the war in the East.'

The first problems to be tackled were those concerning the locally raised auxiliaries and the security of the combatant troops, which last involved, particularly in view of the Partisan danger, the whole question of policy and administration in the occupied zone. As a satisfactory solution of these problems was irreconcilable with what we know of the Führer's own war aims, it was essential to proceed with caution, resource, flexibility and indeed camouflage, making use, when occasion demanded, of some of the earlier Nazi slogans. All arguments must be put forward as based on 'absolute military necessity'.

At that time I had no reason to suspect that the officers with whom I was in touch were involved in a plot against Adolf Hitler. Their aim was to 'get round' (*umkrempeln*) not overthrow the leadership. This last would have meant too great a responsibility at a time when our enemies aimed at the destruction of Germany.

(viii)

I have already noted that, in the early months of the campaign, a very large number of officers commanding units had, on their own initiative, made good their casualties by taking on Russian, Ukrainian or other local volunteers and auxiliaries. The Abwehr under Admiral Canaris had gone further, and had systematically established for their own purposes a number of small locally recruited commando and other units. Finally it was known that Hitler, as early as the autumn of 1941, had approved a 'Turkic Legion'; and some Caucasian units were subsequently raised.

In the Central Army Group, General von Tresckow (on the authority of the former ruling of Field-Marshal von Brauchitsch) had started to set up a number of Russian units. Cossack troops were being enrolled in the Southern Army Group sector. Since Hitler had approved the Turkic and Caucasian formations the hope seemed justified that he would agree to further developments on these lines, if only in view of urgent military needs. At least that is what we thought.

The OKH accordingly was faced with the task to take in hand the many hundred thousand 'Volunteers' or 'Auxiliaries' who had now become indispensable, to arrange for their rations, pay, uniforms, etc., and, above all, to regulate their position in the Wehrmacht, and their relationship to German officers and other ranks. It is typical of the way things were then being done that before any of these basic questions were tackled an order was issued providing for the award of decorations to Eastern racials locally recruited. Medals might be all very well, but what was more likely to be of concern to these people was the ill-treatment of their fellow-countrymen in the prisoner-of-war camps, the whole conception of *Untermenschen*, the appalling conditions in the occupied zone. My friends in the OKH were well aware of the dangerous situation that would arise from these preoccupations in the minds of the local levies. Something must be done, and that quickly.

23 July was my birthday. Thanks to the resource and enterprise of Lieutenant Blossfeldt, ex-manager of the Hotel de Rome in Riga, it was celebrated in some style. At dinner I sat between Gehlen and von Roenne. There followed some amusing speeches and sketches, one of which took an unexpected and hilarious

turn. Gehlen left us at 11.45 p.m. as he had to make his situation report to the chief of staff. Pastor Eckert then took the stage, and proceeded to give us his version of that interview, impersonating in turn both Gehlen and Halder. After a few minutes Gehlen, unseen by the good pastor, came back by the rear door – General Halder having postponed the meeting – and the delighted audience were treated to the spectacle of Eckert–Gehlen lecturing the chief of staff on the mental limitations of the Big Hats, with the real Gehlen standing a few feet behind him.

In late July, at the instance of General Gehlen, I gave a lecture to a large audience of OKH officers on the subject of 'The Russian as a Human Being'.[1] This was based on my paper of the previous autumn and amplified with the help of my Berlin friends, Professor Scherke and Theodor Krause. Gehlen had my lecture multigraphed and distributed to all intelligence officers on the Eastern front. Later, in 1943–4, the lecture was printed (in several impressions) by the Propaganda Department of the OKW, and issued, not only to officers at the front but also to commandants of prisoner-of-war camps and to the various ministries and government offices who had to deal with prisoners and with *Ostarbeiter*. The title page merely said 'by Captain Strik-Strikfeldt', but the fact that it was issued by the OKW gave it an official character, and thus for many of its readers raised the hopes of a change of heart at the top: for the OKW there was, it seemed, no longer any such thing as an *Untermensch*.

On Gehlen's instructions I gave this lecture (and also a second one on 'The Treatment of Prisoners of War') to officers' courses on a number of occasions right up to July 1944.

[1] The concluding passage of his lecture is given in Appendix I, see page 251.

4

First Meeting with Vlasov

IN the summer of 1942 Gehlen and von Roenne gave me a new assignment, which was to call for my exclusive dedication with every fibre of my being up to the end of the war.

The idea of liberation from the Stalinist yoke came spontaneously to the Russian people as soon as the German advance made this liberation seem possible. The thought of setting up a Russian general as an ally against Stalin came from the OKH. As it became apparent, after the first winter campaign, that the Reich government was incapable of working out a plan of political warfare, it occurred to responsible officers of the OKH that it was for the military leadership to initiate and exploit all possible political measures to ensure a speedy and satisfactory termination of the fighting.

General von Wedel, chief of Wehrmacht Propaganda, showed interest in the idea. In the military chain of command, between von Wedel and the Führer there was only Field-Marshal Keitel. Between the OKH and the Führer there was only Colonel-General Halder. By making use of those two channels of approach it should not be too difficult to induce Hitler to modify his so mistaken conceptions of anything to do with Russia. At least that is what the officers thought. Our first task was to provide a convincing, factual brief for the two senior officers with access to the Führer.

General A. A. Vlasov, one of the successful defenders of Moscow, was taken prisoner in the summer of 1942. He had fought to the end and shared the hardships of his troops.

There was nothing he could have done to prevent the destruction of his command – the Soviet Second Shock Army on the Volkhov. For Vlasov (as for every Soviet commander) that defeat sealed his own doom. He was well aware that a court martial and sentence of death awaited him in Moscow. When the position round Volkhov became obviously hopeless, Soviet planes landed at Vlasov's headquarters. They had come to 'rescue' the command. The general preferred to lead his soldiers to the very last and perish with them in face of the enemy. The idea of suicide did not appeal to him.

Fate decided otherwise. He survived. Where the situation was such that it was no longer possible to direct operations, Vlasov withdrew to the woods with a small group. Before long only very few were left. For weeks they trekked hither and thither, from one hiding-place to another, living off what food they had with them or bread begged from peasants late at night in some lonely village. The villagers were not forthcoming – at times even they were hostile. True, these were their fellow-countrymen in dire need: but they wished to have nothing more to do with their former oppressors – especially when and if there were German units in the vicinity.

It could not last. On the evening of 13 July Vlasov laid down to sleep in a barn. Probably someone notified a German patrol. In any case he was tracked down and thus became a prisoner. He was not entirely uninfluenced by Soviet propaganda. He did not believe all he had heard about German atrocities, but still (like, alas, every Red Army soldier) he had good reason to fear for his life.

In late July Vlasov was brought to the prisoner-of-war camp at Vinitsa. The commandant was an elderly German American – an intelligent man, but he knew no Russian. Odd, yet typical, that he should be put in charge of a Russian camp whereas in a camp for Americans or British he could have done good service. Vlasov was marched through the streets of Vinitsa where once he had held high Soviet command. He was 6 feet 5 inches tall, marching at the head of the column, and must have been recognized by many. This arrangement seems to have been deliberate; small minds wished to humiliate him. Once in the camp Vlasov initiated his first resistance movement: he refused to parade with the other prisoners for the roll-call, insisting that the roll of officers be called separately. 'If,' he protested to the 'American' commandant, 'you feel you can conquer and refashion the world by this sort of behaviour you are mistaken.' The commandant smiled and reported the matter to Captain E. Peterson who, in the OKH, was responsible for senior officer prisoners. Peterson growled, as he was apt to do, but he appreciated the point: the roll-call procedure was altered. Vlasov told me of this incident when first, at von Roenne's instance, I called to see him at the camp.

Vlasov's original mistrust had been dissipated by his correct and tactful treatment, at the time of and after his capture, by German officers and by the chivalrous attitude of General Lindemann (his opponent in the battle of Volkhov). This had confirmed to him what he had wished to believe – namely that Germans were not animals but human beings: that, as soldiers, they respected an honourable enemy; and that in a comparison between Bolshevism and National Socialism the Germans were likely to come off the better. The man himself impressed me with his modesty, his intelligence, his reserve, and with a bigness, hard to define, about his personality. On this first visit we talked about almost everything except military matters. It seemed to bring us together when we talked of the hard lot of ordinary Russians, on both sides of the front line.

He told me about his life. His father was a poor peasant in the Nizhni-Novgorod province. His mother, to whom he was devoted, wished him to become a priest, though perhaps the real reason was that fees for a seminary were less than for any other school. A German cheese dealer in the neighbourhood lent, or gave, his father enough money for his education. So Vlasov felt that Germans could not be so bad as Soviet propaganda made out.

Then came the First World War and Vlasov was called up. But it turned out his year of birth was wrongly entered on his baptismal certificate and he was sent home again. The November Revolution filled him with enthusiasm. 'Bread, Peace and Land for the Peasants' were the Bolshevik slogans. The war-weary troops were sent home, and promises made to split up the big estates among the peasants. Young Andrei could never forget that his father was a poor peasant.

He left the seminary and joined a group of revolutionary students. He volunteered for the Red Guard, to defend the new freedoms and the peasants' land. He became a company commander. The White reactionaries and the foreign imperialists were defeated and driven out, and Andrei decided on a military career. Under the tsars he could hardly have hoped to become an officer. This was one of the achievements of the Revolution.

He had in him the qualities of organization and leadership. Promotion came rapidly. He commanded a regiment, then a division. Then came appointment to the Soviet Military Mission to the Chinese Generalissimo, Chiang Kai-shek. And so for the first time this poor peasant's son travelled abroad, but travelled as someone of high position and importance. In China for the first time he met representatives of the West. He was a keen observer. He came to know and to appreciate China's ancient culture. He studied Sino-Japanese relations, and formed the opinion that the Japanese were bound to fail: they might conquer China, but they could never win over the Chinese people. (An interesting deduction, I thought, and one that we ourselves might take to heart.) His stay in China afforded him insight into Moscow's schemes for Asia. It opened his eyes, and broadened his view. He spoke of Chiang Kai-shek with great respect, but had doubts as to his ultimate success.

Back in Moscow he was forbidden to wear the Chinese decorations that the Generalissimo had awarded him. 'Not for internal Soviet use,' he remarked. He was then given a division. It was in very poor shape when he took over, but not long afterwards, at an army competition, Stalin himself singled it out as a pattern of what a division should be.

What he told me was of absorbing interest. I was impressed by his clarity, his shrewdness, his keen observation, his sense of humour.

Throughout all his experience in China he had kept an eye on conditions in his homeland, and had never lost touch with the feelings of his fellow-countrymen. He knew their little joys and their grim needs. He remained, I felt, the champion of the ideals that the November Revolution had proclaimed. After all, he had the Revolution to thank for all that he had become. But in the course of time he had become acquainted with the seamy side of the regime. He knew well how the villagers lived and felt. His father, like millions of Russian peasants, had been dispossessed and robbed of all he had ever managed to acquire. When he, Vlasov, went to the village the collectivized peasants would not talk to him. They were frightened of the Kremlin's favourites in their imposing uniforms. Not even vodka would loosen their tongues. Their silence itself helped Vlasov to understand the peasants' needs, their disappointed hopes, their sacrifices, their innermost fears. He knew, too, the party bosses, their lack of scruple, their cruelty in pursuing their own ends. He knew the leading figures on the Kremlin stage, and also what they were like behind the scene. He knew the intrigues and manoeuvres of the higher and lower functionaries serving the regime but not their fellow-men.

But of all this we talked later.

(ii)

On my next visit I had to tell the general about Germany. He was interested in everything, but in particular he wanted to know more about German war aims. It was surprising how much he already knew. In spite of guards and barbed wire the prisoner-of-war bush telegraph worked quickly and accurately. German treatment of prisoners, together with efficient Soviet whispering propaganda, had left the prisoners in no doubt of their lot. Russians on this side of the line were second-class human beings, *Untermenschen*. They had no need of political education to draw their conclusions.

Vlasov spoke openly, and I did too in so far as my oath of service allowed me. He accepted this and continued to do so throughout the whole of our collaboration.

Frankness and honesty brought us together. I asked him whether the war against Bolshevism was purely a German concern, or whether Russians and other races of the USSR should not themselves be interested in the outcome of this struggle. He considered. Then he spoke of the struggle for freedom that for years had been carried on by peasants, workers, officers, students, men and women. The outside world had watched in silence. Commercial and other motives had led to alliances and treaties with the men in the Kremlin whose hands were stained with blood. Would this encourage the Russian people to take their fate into their own hands?

His expression was as inscrutable as the proverbial Chinaman. I wondered what this all was leading up to. He made a further point. In the USSR not only the masses but many officers and responsible officials were, not indeed against the system, but against Stalin. In view of the terror in Russia an organized resistance movement was unthinkable; but here in prison, he, Vlasov, had had the chance to talk with a number of senior Red Army officers. Only a few of them took the attitude of wait and see. Most of them felt it was the patriotic duty of Russians to take up the struggle against Stalin. But along with whom? 'The English in the past have left us in the lurch. The Germans apparently do not need our help. The Americans have made a pact with Stalin. Although neither English nor Americans are interested in annexations.' He watched what effect these last words would have on me. I asked: 'How do you envisage practical participation on the part of the Russians in the struggle against Stalin?'

He asked me what I would suggest. I told him I and my friends, when the campaign started, believed it to be a war of liberation to free the Russian peoples from the Bolshevik yoke; but I also told him of the wretched conditions of the prisoners, about which we could do nothing. I told him that the Nazi leaders were obsessed with arrogance and thereby blind. The result was the catastrophic position of the 50–70 million in occupied zones; but I explained that the army's attitude was very different. Vlasov seemed to have found that out for himself. He mentioned General Lindemann and his staff. He seemed also to be well informed on the position in the occupied areas.

'But what can we do?' he asked once more. 'And what does your Führer think?'

'The Führer is still surrounded by men who are blind. But the field-marshals and the senior officers here in the General Staff are doing what they can to modify the war aims, and thus put our relationship with the Russian people on a new footing. Are you willing to collaborate with those who are prepared to fight against Stalin?'

'Against Stalin, yes. But for whom and what? And how?'

'Hundreds of thousands of Russians are helping the Germans in this war against Stalin, very many as combatants. But they have no rallying point.'

'Would the German officers of whom you spoke allow us to raise an army against Stalin? Not an army of mercenaries. It must take its orders from a National Russian Government. It is only an ideal that can justify the taking up of arms against one's own regime. The ideal here is that of freedom and human rights. I am thinking of the great American champions of freedom, of George Washington and Benjamin Franklin. In my case, only if I put human values before nationalist values would I be justified in accepting your aid in a fight against the Kremlin. In any case the Kremlin is now only of pseudo-nationalist and not of patriotic import.'

He here was expressing only what other senior Red Army officers had already said, i.e. their willingness to fight against Stalin on behalf of a free, independent, national Russia. No annexations, no government of quislings by the grace of Hitler. But Vlasov had gone one step farther than the others. He had put freedom and human rights before national interests. That was the decisive point.

I asked the general to put his views in writing. The moment was opportune, as Halder, Chief of the General Staff, had ordered Gehlen to produce a detailed report on Red Army reactions to Stalin's recent abolition of military commissars. Here was a chance to put Vlasov's appreciation into the hands of the chief of staff with minimum delay.

Colonel Boyarski, formerly in command of a Soviet Guards Division, had been present at some of our talks – Vlasov would call him in to help clear up certain points – and his contribution had been valuable. The man himself made an excellent impression. He was anti-Stalin, but, as he frankly emphasized, no friend of the Germans. The draft appreciation covered the various points we had discussed, and included Vlasov's explicit declaration that he was willing to offer his services *to his nation* in the struggle for freedom. It was an admirable document, but, as drafted, far too Russian. I had learned myself that Prussians like things to be put briefly and without frills. Von Roenne made the further point that when dealing with Nazis one should make some appeal to their vanity and their special interests. So I and the two Russians set to work on a shortened and revised version. Vlasov was rather amused at this phase of our effort, but he understood the reasons for it.

(iii)

Vlasov, I found, was always to take this line. Adamant as far as the essentials were concerned, he was willing to make small concessions so long as the essentials remained unimpaired.

Boyarski, later on, was apt to lose patience; but for the moment he showed great flexibility and for this reason his cooperation was extremely valuable. Colonel von Roenne was extremely pleased with the result. He had a number of talks with Vlasov, and told me that if and when we had to select a collaborator his choice would certainly be Vlasov. There were, at the time, a number of other senior Soviet officers in Vinitsa, including a Colonel Shapovalov. Shapovalov was a first-class officer and a convinced anti-Stalinist. He found favour because in appearance and bearing he was of the type of good German officer; but he had not Vlasov's personality, and a yes-man would in the end have been no good either for us or for the Russian people. I mention Shapovalov because I considered it most important to have a strong and independent personality at the head of the Russian Liberation Movement. The essential precondition for an ultimate alliance was the will to cooperate in all sincerity with the Wehrmacht, but not to give way to German whims. I do not wish to accuse Shapovalov of this tendency; but to my mind Vlasov alone possessed the qualities that would successfully serve both German and Russian interests.

It was, we felt, a personal triumph for Gehlen (whose proposals were largely based on the paper we had drawn up with Vlasov) when Hitler authorized the OKH to draw up and to implement regulations for the remuneration of the Auxiliaries and for their position *vis-à-vis* the Wehrmacht. This meant that the OKH could now take in hand the establishment and the legalization of Volunteers and Auxiliaries. This was a big step forward. 'We have now got going,' von Roenne said to me, 'and you can tell Vlasov.' I suggested that in due course these volunteers would all have to be placed under Vlasov's command. 'That you must not tell him, as yet,' said von Roenne. (This was an order, though he smiled as he said it.)

I, of course, told Vlasov only what I was authorized to tell him, but he at once came out with the logical conclusion. 'Once you have organized all these volunteers – you tell me there are eight-hundred thousand to a million of them – you have only to pass some two to three hundred thousand of them over to me, and I guarantee that I and Boyarski will have finished the war for you (or I should say for us) in a very few months.'

Vlasov did not think like Halder did, or even like his German friends. He thought in Russian. For him it was not a war against an external enemy. The issue was internal – between Russians. Nothing could have been done up till now. All the armed force had been in Stalin's hands, and his position could not be threatened. 'Now it will be threatened. And the threat comes not from you, but from us. You, Wilfried Karlovich, see the point. So does Colonel von Roenne. And I imagine you will make sure your superiors see it too.'

When we parted we understood one another even better.

One senior officer who correctly assessed the position was General Halder, Chief of the General Staff. Halder had realized, at the time of the advance towards Moscow, that political as well as military action was needed to bring about an early and satisfactory end to the campaign; and he had repeatedly tried to convince Hitler. I was told later that Halder, quite early on, had

remarked that 'we are bound to lose the war unless Hitler takes
into account these views of the military leadership'. This I heard
from Gehlen.

(iv)

A further success for the OKH was that from now on all divisions
of the Eastern armies, at the front or on lines of communication,
were authorized to enrol a certain percentage of Russians and
Ukrainians in order to make up their strengths. The figures
suggested were some three to four thousand men per division, and
Hitler himself was believed to have approved. Could this be the
beginning of a new policy? I myself never saw the written order,
but I was present when officers of the OKH A Branch were
telephoning their instructions to subordinate commands.

Meanwhile von Roenne had taken steps to mobilize the
Ministry of Foreign Affairs; and one day Gustav Hilger, a
former German Counsellor of the German Embassy in Moscow,
arrived in Vinitsa. I had known Hilger since 1920 when he had
been in charge of the repatriation of German and Austrian
prisoners with which I was also concerned on behalf of the
International Red Cross. I was glad to see him, and took him to
call on Vlasov with whom he had a long and satisfactory talk.

Hilger's views coincided with what we in the OKH were
thinking and with what Vlasov felt himself; and we all believed
that the prospects were very favourable. No western expert could
rival Hilger's profound knowledge of the Soviet Union and its
rulers. We did not realize that his views on Russian affairs were,
alas, completely ignored by the Nazi leadership.

Another visitor was First Lieutenant Dürksen, assistant to von
Grote in the Propaganda Department of the Oberkommando der
Wehrmacht (OKW) in Berlin. He had been born in Russia, and,
though he was German to the core, I was delighted to find his
heart was in Russia. His mission to Vinitsa was the result of von
Grote's wish to find a prominent Red Army general to issue an
appeal to Red Army soldiers, and his (Dürksen's) immediate task
was to get Vlasov to sign a leaflet to be dropped over the enemy

lines. Should this leaflet result in an increasing number of desertions and line-crossers coming over to the Germans it would be evidence that both OKH and OKW/Pr (Propaganda Department) were thinking on the right lines.

Furthermore, Dürksen expressed his willingness to arrange for Vlasov to join the little group of Soviet prisoners of war attached to the OKW in Berlin. Von Roenne thought the idea excellent. It would give Vlasov an opportunity to learn something about Germany, while the OKH were getting on with their plans and fixing things up with the appropriate authorities involved. Then, when all was ready, they could come back to Vlasov. Von Roenne told me that the next step – to be based on the new arrangements for 'Volunteers' that were now being worked out – was to have the Berlin group released from prison, and given the status of 'semi-Allies'. He would at once take up the matter with General Stieff and Colonel von Stauffenberg. I was authorized to inform Vlasov of what was intended. We seemed to be making progress.

Some time before Dürksen's visit, von Roenne had asked Vlasov if he would issue an appeal to the Red Army troops to lay down their arms and come over to the Germans. Vlasov categorically refused: he was a professional soldier and could not call on troops to infringe their duty. Von Roenne saw his point. What Vlasov desired was formal establishment of the Liberation Movement, and nothing less. All the same von Roenne continued to plead. Unless, he urged, one could point to some tangible achievement the higher authorities could not be persuaded to agree to further steps. This tangible achievement, in the eyes of the German High Command, would be an influx of Red deserters following Vlasov's appeal. 'They will come over,' Vlasov replied, 'without any appeal from me to act against their duty.' But all the same he understood that the 'decent officers', as he called them, in OKH were for the time being unable to force their superiors to take the radical decision they hoped for. We must either abandon our plans altogether, or adopt a policy of little by little, of small deeds. 'Here,' Vlasov said, 'it is very different from Moscow. Here you find people ready to act, on their own responsibility, for what their conscience tells them is right. Over there such

opposition would be unthinkable. The slightest hint of the
dictator's whim and they all fall flat on their faces.'

I had a number of talks with Vlasov.

'We want,' I told him, 'an appeal from you in order to prove to
our political leaders that Red Army officers and soldiers listen to
what you, a fellow-Russian, say to them. We want to raise your
standing, to make our politicians realize your importance. Once
they are sensible enough to realize that we are much closer to our
goal. Meanwhile, Andrei Andreyevich, all we can do is to tread
the thorny path of opposition, against Stalin, and against —'

'And against those blind idiots round Hitler.'

There it was. He had said it.

'Won't you help us?' I asked him. 'Not only with this first
appeal on a leaflet, but with all the other moves that are bound to
follow?'

He asked for twenty-four hours to think it over.

I now felt that Vlasov and I understood each other.

At that time I, like the other officers, believed that Hitler must
ultimately see reason, alternatively that the generals would enforce a sensible solution. I told Vlasov this, and, at the same time,
asked him never to reproach me if it should turn out that I had
been mistaken. He gave me his promise, and kept it throughout
the time we were together. I hope, too, that I kept the promises I
made him. We made a pact always to be completely frank, one
with the other, to hide nothing, except when my oath of service
commanded silence.

Our talks ranged wide. The Berlin proposal opened up all
sorts of possibilities. . . . And yet he still hesitated. Was he the
proper man to head a liberation movement? Would this policy of
'small deeds' ever lead to the goal we aimed at? To win a struggle
against tyranny makes one a hero; to lose it, a traitor. Some
Higher Power led me at that moment to bring out a thought that
had lain deep in my mind since the First World War and my
work with the Red Cross.

'I cannot tell,' I said, 'whether we shall live to see our political
aims achieved. But are our political aspirations all that count? If

the OKH does only half of what we wish, we will certainly see a vast improvement in conditions for the Russian prisoners now starving in the camps. That achievement at least we can surely count on. We shall be serving our fellow-human beings, according to the divine commandment.'

'You are right,' said Vlasov. 'That alone would make it all worth while.'

If he had been moved merely by ambition, by the will to come to power, he would not have understood me. For Andrei Andreyevich Vlasov what mattered was to serve. This was the proof, and it was to be proved again and again.

So we started off on the policy of small deeds. Vlasov agreed to make an appeal to the Red Army, on his own terms. The text of the leaflet was drafted by Boyarski and amplified and finalized by Vlasov. It consisted, entirely and exclusively, of an indictment of Stalin and his clique. There was no appeal to come over to the Germans.

The die had been cast. The result was tens of thousands of line-crossers on every sector of the front. There had been nothing like such numbers for months. Russians had been addressed by a Russian general, and one who had fought bravely and well for the defence of Moscow. It was of course true that Vlasov's name was unknown to quite a number of Red Army units, and a demand soon came in from several German divisions that, to ensure greater effectiveness, the appeal to Russians should come from a Russian national leadership or government, and to Ukrainians from an Ukrainian one. What we few had been suggesting for over a year was now recognized by many to be an urgent necessity. But those who more than all others should have realized what was happening – since they were responsible for policy – still seemed unable to grasp the point.

5

The Viktoriastrasse

IN September I had to leave our 'club' and my good friends at the OKH and proceed to Berlin and the unknown Oberkommando der Wehrmacht. General Gehlen informed me that as *Betreuer*, i.e. the man responsible for Vlasov, I was to be seconded to the Propaganda Department of the OKW. Personally I was to remain under his command. Official regulations were such that it was only the OKW who could authorize a Russian, i.e. Vlasov, to appeal to Russians.

I had told Gehlen of my agreement with Vlasov. The question was how long he would continue to cooperate if we failed to make any progress along the lines we desired.

Meanwhile Colonel von Roenne had been sounding Tresckow and von Gersdorff as to the possibility of resuscitating the 1941 project of the Smolensk Liberation Committee with General Vlasov as its central figure: it appeared that the former Smolensk participants were no longer available. Tresckow and von Gersdorff approved von Roenne's proposal.

My immediate task was to secure the approval and support of the OKW. Once this was achieved, I was assured that the A branch of the OKH would agree to an establishment for an all Russian propaganda unit.

Before leaving I was warned by Colonel von Stauffenberg that the SS was already setting up Estonian and Latvian units. That meant we must hurry on our plans for an overall Russian authority. In spite of their theories of the *Untermensch* the SS would go ahead ruthlessly; and if Himmler conceived the idea of setting up his own Russian Liberation Committee, he would win over hundreds of thousands of Russians for the SS, some of them believing his promises and others with an eye to the main chance. This would be a disaster for everyone. I was delighted to find that von Stauffenberg and his friends in the OKH realized so clearly the problems that would still have to be faced when the fighting was over. I did not then realize how great was the trust he must have placed in me in talking to me as he did.

I explained that we had no need to be anxious about Vlasov himself. He would never agree to be taken in tow by the SS or to help substitute a brown dictatorship for a Red one.

Von Roenne warned me to say nothing about the idea, so often put forward in the club, of a Russian government as a member of a European Union. 'We must confine ourselves to political *warfare*, and our tactics are little by little. If you have no success in Berlin we must bring you back here.'

(ii)

In late August 1942 I arrived in Berlin. The so-called Russian Collaboration Staff of the OKW/Pr was located in the Viktoriastrasse under lock and key. Barred windows, wooden bunks. Straw mattresses. No permission to leave the building. All doors locked at night. I was shocked. The meagre meals were brought in daily from a tavern in the Potsdamer Platz. The worthy Territorials who acted as guards often added something from their own rations. They felt that any one who was working for us should have enough to eat.

Lieutenant Dürksen of the OKW/Pr expressed his satisfaction at seeing me again. My immediate superior was Captain von Grote. He had been, for a short time, at the same school as myself. Later he had served in the Grand Duke Michael's division, and later still in the Baltic Landeswehr where he had been highly regarded. Head of the Aktiv Propaganda section was Colonel Martin. Von Roenne had been right in warning me to keep within the limits of political warfare in dealing with Martin. Only Dürksen declared straight away that we could only succeed if the wider issues were successfully handled. But before very long all three of them became active supporters of the thesis that the

German mission in the East involved full recognition of the rights and interests of all the nations of the USSR.

Soon after my arrival in Berlin Vlasov asked me what had come of his talk with Gustav Hilger of the Ministry of Foreign Affairs. I had to admit prospects were dim. Either the Ministry had made no impression on Hitler, or else Ribbentrop had taken no notice of Hilger's report.

'So the Germans will do nothing,' said Vlasov. He went on to criticize the 'privileged' treatment accorded to Russian freedom fighters at the OKW HQ. 'But if we could even secure similar conditions for all the other Russian prisoners we should have done a wonderful service to our people.' He meant what he said, but his tone implied a slightly bitter reflection on our agreement at Vinitsa – i.e. that his collaboration was the price to be paid for helping the prisoners. 'I have thought a great deal,' he said, 'about what we agreed then and what we have to do. My countrymen can be roused from the lethargy, be made to work and to help, only if offered a new and better future. They have no interest in your German Reich. They want to see their own problems solved.'

Our talks would go on for hours.

(iii)

The Russian collaborators, in their shabby but very noticeable prisoners' uniforms – with SU[1] on the backs in big letters – were allowed on the streets only in column of fours and under military escort. Vlasov refused to take part in these excursions to be a show for passers-by in the Tiergarten. He stayed in his room. From time to time these collaborators were summoned to one or other of the ministries and government offices as experts in some special field, such as agriculture. This made it essential for the rules to be made more flexible. We decided we must acquire civilian clothing for these occasions, and also improve general working conditions.

Alas it turned out that this was more than the OKW could do

[1] Sovietische Union.

for us. First, it was against existing regulations; second, no funds were available for such extravagance. Vlasov and his Russians would smile at our efforts: 'This is the élan by which you expect to conquer the world?'

Of course it would have been possible to get what we wanted from the Abwehr, but this we rufused to do. Those of us who were plotting to bring to life a national and independent Russian movement could not afford to join with the Abwehr, and thus make the movement the Abwehr's tool. (Even though, as I found out later, there were many Abwehr officers of good faith who supported the Russian, and the German, struggle for freedom.)

So we made private appeals to our friends for overcoats, suits, underclothing, etc. Bit by bit the clothing came in and was altered so as more or less to fit them. But there was nothing to fit General Vlasov, 6 feet 5 inches tall, until one day a junior employee of a Berlin clothing depot came in with a passable blue suit and overcoat. The employee (whose name I forget) said: 'If the general wants to help us we ought to help him.' There was general rejoicing, and Colonel Martin, who officially had not to know what we were doing, was much amused.

(iv)

Vlasov was now in a position to start building up 'his staff'; and I accompanied him on visits to prisoner-of-war camps in the immediate neighbourhood of Berlin.

Of the Russians in the Viktoriastrasse, Mileti Aleksandrovich Zykov was the outstanding personality. Zykov had been a prisoner for some time. We, of course, could not check his claims to have worked for leading Soviet newspapers and to have been on close terms with Bukharin and other prominent Bolsheviks proscribed by Stalin. He was a man of quick intelligence and wide knowledge. He maintained he had never been in the West, which no doubt was true, but he was well informed on Western Europe. He had no illusions about Germany – the ambitions of the Nazi Party and the various party organizations, the complete lack of coordination (in spite of the Gleichschaltung) between ministries and party offices, the vacillations of Rosenberg, the almost impossible

position of the senior officers of the OKW/Pr who, Zykov
suggested, 'have to serve up sober truth untouched by any
ideology and sometimes even contrary to Hitler's pet theories'.
Typical of Zykov was a remark he made to Vlasov in my presence:
'The Nazis have lost their war, but that means all sorts of possibilities for an anti-Stalin Europe. It is up to you, Andrei
Andreyevich, to exploit them . . .' And then: 'If the Germans are
too small-minded for large-scale policies, then we must exploit to
the utmost their policy of small deeds.' This was the line he took,
right up to the autumn of 1944. Zykov was un-Russian in that he
never expected to have everything all at once. He would think
out the first modest steps, and then the next.

Vlasov asked me if we could keep on Zykov permanently, in
view of the fact that he was a Jew. I told him that Captain von
Grote, in charge of the Viktoriastrasse group, had guaranteed
Zykov's safety. As soon as we had our own Russian unit it would
be for Vlasov and myself to look after him. Vlasov told me he
attached great importance to having Zykov with him. He had
need of outstanding personalities. 'Zykov is the only one I have
found here so far, and we would be hard put to find a second
Zykov. There are very few of that calibre in the USSR. Stalin
has liquidated them.'

Zykov, who had spent four years in exile in Siberia, was
passionately opposed to Stalin, but not to the system as such. In
this his views differed somewhat from those of Vlasov and of the
other generals who were to join him. But none had any quarrel
with the state of society that had allowed them to become what
they had become in Russia. This was the bond that united them.

(v)

The Russians were continually suffering from petty restrictions
on the part of their new German friends, and from the rigidity,
not to say stupidity, in their conduct of political warfare. The
ex-Soviet officers had to help the Germans interpret Soviet
announcements, assess what was happening in Russia and at the
front, and compose leaflets for Red Army soldiers; but, in the
OKH/Pr it was only a few of the German officers who were

allowed to listen to Soviet broadcasts. How then could our Russian associates do their job? The answer was only by illegally procuring clandestine receiving sets.

When one day our Russians told us that Stalin intended to bring back the old imperial uniforms for Red Army officers, the OKW were sceptical. They had no concept of the political and military implications – what interested them was 'How did these prisoners get this news?' Von Grote and I were told to intensify our supervision. A few days later Fremde Heere Ost at OKH confirmed the information, and within a month it was an established fact.

(vi)

The OKW had no cars available for small fry like ourselves, so Vlasov (in his civilian suit) and I had to make use of public transport. Besides our visits to prisoner-of-war camps, I took him to the Berlin parks and cafés. He made his observations.

One day he remarked: 'You Germans are hard-working, diligent and capable. You are modest and economical. You do your utmost for your families and homes. I really believe that all Germans like to work. But throughout your history you are haunted by some evil fate. As soon as you had achieved something there came on the scene some king or Kaiser or Führer, and with one stroke all was lost. Is that not so? And so the German had to start all over again, by hard work and privation, to get back to his former level. It made him small-minded and envious, and narrow. He can never acquire the mentality of a nobleman, of a gentleman in the real sense, even though he now likes to call himself a *Herrenmensch*. I am really sorry about this decent German. But that is how I see him and that explains a great deal.'

(vii)

I accompanied Vlasov on his visits to prisoner-of-war camps within easy distance of Berlin. The atmosphere in the camps was everywhere heavy and depressed. The Red Army generals were mostly pro-Soviet, or rather pro-Russian. They were definitely anti-German. Even those officers who, at the time of their capture a year before, had been willing to fight on the German side against the Red dictatorship were now disillusioned and embittered. There is no need to mention those opportunists who had worked their way up under the Soviet regime and were ready to serve any master, or those who offered their services to the Germans as camp informers. They were called spies and stool pigeons to their face, by all ranks.

There were a number of good men among the younger staff and regimental officers – scientists, engineers, teachers, agricultural experts. The mass of soldiers who had escaped death many times on their way to Berlin were dazed and indifferent. Only when one talked to them in their own language, about wife and children, about the hope of going back to their homes, did their eyes light up, and something human came back to their worn features. God's image, I felt, can never be entirely destroyed.

Vlasov went from camp to camp and asked questions. Only a few of the generals recognized him. To the others he introduced himself in his accustomed modest manner.

'Have you ever considered, gentlemen, that we, former commanders, have the duty, here in prison, to serve our nation, that is, to serve our people? Not because we are forced to do so. In fact because we are not forced to do so. It gives the Germans no satisfaction to see us help and serve our people, to act as an example to them, on our own free initiative. Serve – here in the prison camp – by aid and example. Serve, perhaps go on serving when we are free again.'

Vlasov invariably opened his talks on this note. These were simple yet unexpected words, and he made us think of the Sower in the parable.

General Vasili Feodorovich Malyshkin told me Vlasov had made him ashamed. What had he, or the other Red Army officers, done for their men in prison camps? And, after all, the struggle against Stalin was primarily a matter for Russians. 'Why did this never occur to us?'

Malyshkin had once been Chief of Staff in an Army or Military

District in the Far East. He had been arrested in connection with the Tukhachevski Affair, but in spite of torture during his interrogation none of the charges against him had been established. On the outbreak of war in 1941 he had been released from prison and sent to the front. At this period – late 1942 – he had been a prisoner for some nine months. He had been hungry, had contracted dysentery and typhus, had met with ill-treatment from his captors (though at least he had not been tortured). He was gentle, with artistic sensibilities. He would exercise his memory by reciting poetry – the Russian classics and the poems of his contemporary Yesenin.

Malyshkin and another general, Blagoveshchenski, offered to cooperate with Vlasov when they learned he was not in German pay. Vlasov had approached them just as he had approached all the others: 'I am a Russian, one of the many taken prisoner by the Germans. I am not a traitor, whatever Stalin may say about Red Army prisoners. I love my people and wish to serve them. I can do so only by working for the freedom and well-being of the individual. Otherwise I can do nothing. I can play my part in the struggle to improve the wretched conditions of my countrymen in the prison camps, but only if I take a stand for the freedom and human rights of Russians generally. I am not in German pay. There are German officers who sincerely desire the good of the Russian people. They have offered me their support and I am working with them. Only the future can show what comes next.'

It was much on the lines of what I had myself said to Vlasov back in Vinitsa a few weeks previously, when he was about to make his big decision. I must make clear that, as was then the case with many Germans, my whole being was consumed with the hope that right and reason must inevitably triumph in the end. Vlasov derived his strength from this same hope. It was the bond between us. I found it astonishing that without ever departing in any way from the truth he could always find words that would touch the hearts of his fellow-countrymen. The path we had to tread was a hard one, and we were sustained only by the faith that we were fighting the good fight.

(viii)

I was involved in an incident with General Malyshkin.

The day I was due to collect him from Wulheide a Führer's Order was issued to the effect that any German officer responsible for the custody of an enemy general was liable to the death penalty should that general escape. (A French general had succeeded in escaping a few days earlier.) Colonel Martin informed me of the order and offered me an armed escort for Malyshkin. In my eyes Malyshkin was already our ally, though according to the letter of the regulations this view would not be acceptable. I asked myself whether Malyshkin would still feel himself an ally if I arrived for him with an escort.

'No, Colonel,' I said. 'That will not do.'

'I have warned you, and you carry the responsibility.'

Colonel Martin, as ever, understood what I felt, and at the same time had to carry out his orders. He let me have my way, even though by doing so he ran a risk himself.

We took the train from Wulheide to the Friedrichstrasse. Coming out of the station I suddenly realized I had lost him in the crowd. In a panic I rushed back down the stairs and tore round the labyrinth of corridors, barriers and exits of the, to me, unfamiliar Friedrichstrasse Station. No trace of Malyshkin. He was in civilian clothes which made it even more difficult. Finally I went back to the platform where I had last seen him, and there he stood, as if rooted to the ground. He had remembered the old rule – always go back to where you last saw the other party.

'We have that rule,' he said, 'in common with thieves and gangsters.'

'Did you know where we were going?' I asked him. He did not. Vlasov had only told him he was in the prisoner-of-war quarters of the OKW; he had no idea of the street or what the place was called.

'I would have asked for the Ministry of War in the Alexanderplatz.'

'Why Alexanderplatz?'

'We learnt at school that there is an Alexanderplatz in Berlin. Tsar Alexander freed the Germans from Napoleon.'

Police headquarters and the interrogation cells were in the Alexanderplatz. A sad outlook for us should Malyshkin have landed there following the Führer's latest order.

(ix)

Mention should be made of another recent adherent to the little conspiratorial group in the Viktoriastrasse, one who was to play a big part in the Liberation Movement – Major-General Georgi Nikolaievich Zhilenkov.

Zhilenkov had been army commissar, and on the death of the army commander he took over. The army was wiped out in front of Moscow, and Zhilenkov disappeared into the grey mass of prisoners of war. Later he volunteered to drive a lorry: otherwise he had only the choice of starving or being shot as an ex-commissar. For some months he drove German munition lorries between Minsk and Smolensk.

His opportunity came in the summer of 1942 when Colonels von Tresckow and von Gersdorff set up the so-called Russian Probation Unit. Zhilenkov risked his life by admitting his past as commissar, but the German officer concerned (von Tresckow) was a man prepared to accept a dangerous responsibility. Zhilenkov's rank had been equivalent to that of major-general. He was accordingly dressed up in a fancy uniform with the insignia of a major-general and made joint commander of the unit. His colleague was the Colonel Boyarski who had helped draft Vlasov's first appeal to the Red Army.

The 'unit' was of brigade strength, officered exclusively by Russians. Von Tresckow's idea was that a number of similar Russian units should be formed, provided this one proved its worth in action. Hence the provisional title 'Probation Unit'. It was a modest first step to implement those proposals which, in the autumn of 1941, Field-Marshal von Brauchitsch had described as 'decisive for the issue of the war'.

Field-Marshal von Kluge appeared at first to be in agreement, but later ordered the brigade to be disbanded, and the various battalions or companies to be incorporated into German regiments. Zhilenkov and Boyarski refused to follow these instructions on the grounds that they were contrary to their agreement with von Tresckow. They were not and would not be mercenaries. They were willing to fight alongside the Germans so long as German and Russian interests ran parallel – i.e. to free the Russian people from Stalin, but that was all.

Field-Marshal von Kluge regarded this as mutiny and gave orders that the two Russians be arrested and court-martialled. They were saved by von Tresckow and von Gersdorff who passed them over to the OKH where Gehlen and von Roenne could look after them. Captain Peterson, whose duties included supervision of the OKH prison camp in Lötzen, had the difficult task of ensuring that the two were treated as 'allies', and that the 'mutineers' did not escape. Luckily nothing more was heard from von Kluge, and in due course von Roenne phoned me to take over Zhilenkov and see that he disappeared once more into the mass. 'It is unlikely,' said von Roenne, 'that they will be after him, but if they do find some excuse to send him back to Peterson at OKH, and we will do what we can.'

Zhilenkov told us he had been one of the *bezprizornie*, that host of waifs and strays that once used to haunt the streets of Moscow. He seemed to have made a rapid career in the Moscow Soviet and even to have come to the favourable notice of Stalin. That had not blinded him to all that was wrong in the regime, and he had a very sharp eye. Eager and intelligent, he was sometimes suspected of being lacking in principle, because no consideration ever seemed to deter him; but he never made a pact with Hitler or with the devil. I was to be with him, after the capitulation, in an American prisoner-of-war camp where his helpfulness and comradely loyalty made him an example to everyone. He had the self-respect and bearing of a born gentleman, without fear and without reproach, right up to the day when the Americans handed him back to Stalin's butchers.

(x)

But there were Russian officers who, in the circumstances, were not prepared to cooperate with Vlasov. One was General Lukin. It was he whose life we had done our best to save in the autumn of 1941, and in whom Field-Marshal von Bock had taken a keen interest. Lukin had then declared himself ready, in spite of the loss of his leg, to command a company or an army in the struggle against Stalin. But the bitterness of prison life and the brutality of German policy had completely disillusioned him.

'You, Vlasov,' he asked, 'have you been formally recognized by Hitler? Have you guarantees that Hitler will restore the former Russian frontier?'

Vlasov had to say no.

'There you are,' Lukin continued. 'Without such guarantees I am not prepared to join you. After my experience as a prisoner in German hands I do not believe that the Germans have any intention of freeing the Russian people. I do not believe that they will change their policy. Accordingly, Vlasov, all you can do is to serve German interests, not those of our homeland.'

Vlasov maintained he had no intention of serving Hitler and the Germans, only his own people and perhaps others who were being oppressed. Many millions were suffering under both Stalin and Hitler, but the arch-enemy of the Russian people was Stalin. Hitler alone had declared war on Stalin. The issue would be a clear one but for Hitler's treatment of the Russian people. However, were the people's leaders to stand by with folded arms and look on at the wretched plight of the millions under Soviet rule, the millions under Nazi occupation? He, Vlasov, could not stand idly by: he had to do what he could within the narrow limits fate allowed. Stalin had branded as traitors all those taken prisoner by the Germans. His, Vlasov's view, was that the only traitors were those who refused to act. He himself, in this unparalleled situation, was determined to fight, on two fronts, against Stalin and against the other oppressor.

One could see Vlasov doing his utmost to secure the cooperation of this splendid man and Lukin's refusal was a severe blow.

But this was no longer the hesitating Vlasov of the days in Vinitsa; he was master of his soul.

'I am just a cripple,' said Lukin. 'You Vlasov are still unbroken. If you think you must fight on two fronts, which in fact is a fight for freedom on one front, then you must carry on. I wish you success, though I do not believe success will come your way. As I have said, the Germans will never change their policy.'

'But if these German officers now helping us can one day bring about a change?' I saw how Vlasov clung to this last hope, which was also mine.

'In that case, Andrei Andreyevich, we can have another talk.'

Vlasov was depressed as we left. Lukin, in a way, was right. He wanted a treaty with Hitler against Stalin. Vlasov was against them both.

'I find it inexplicable,' Vlasov said to me, 'that the German leaders – Hitler, Göring, Goebbels – do not understand that their present policy is tantamount to signing their own death warrant. Or have they in fact formed a suicide club as Zhilenkov suggests?'

One was often to hear the term 'suicide club' in Vlasov's entourage.

(xi)

Von Grote's staff included a young Russian journalist, Aleksander Stepanovich Kazantsev, who was a member of the émigré organization NTS and who had never been a prisoner. I had been officially warned against the NTS, and no doubt so had von Grote. But von Grote was a Balt and a gentleman: what mattered to him was personality, and Kazantsev was a personality, sensitive and intelligent. He loved Russia and his fellow-Russians, though he himself had been an émigré nearly all his life. He was thus in a position to explain the West and Western ways to those coming fresh from the Soviet Union.

6

Dabendorf

THREE months had gone by since the matter of a Russian centre for General Vlasov had been discussed and approved by the OKH. But for the time, there was no possibility for setting it up except under the umbrella of Wehrmacht Propaganda, and this was headed by General von Wedel, in charge of OKW/Pr. At last, early in November 1942, Gehlen and von Stauffenberg, with von Wedel's approval, were able to authorize the establishment of a 'training camp' for Russian volunteers, to be known as Ost-propagandaabteilung z.b.V. That meant I could begin to take on to my establishment Russian officers and other ranks released from camps. The proposed camp, with huts, at Dabendorf, was not far from Berlin. In due course the Ostpropagandaabteilung was known simply as Dabendorf. It was the German root from which it was intended that the Russian Liberation Movement should spread its shoots and blossoms into the world; but un-fortunately this root hung in mid air, so that it had no native soil.

Although it was in no way to be compared with our venture, a start had been made with the training of Russian propagandists in the spring of 1942 in the prisoner-of-war camp at Wulheide, where Soviet prisoners of war were trained for the press and broadcast purposes of the Ministry of Propaganda, and also for work among prisoners of war.

One could offer no programme, no prospect of a better future to these men in the barbed-wire cages. Prisoners and outlaws as they were, they were supposed to appeal to the population of the occupied zone. What could they tell them? They could not give them more to eat. They could not stop them being kicked around by the jackboots of their conquerors. There was not the slightest gleam of hope to offer. They were impotent in face of the

ever-increasing Red propaganda in the camps – fanned by the
Nazis' own behaviour. A number of German camp commandants had, in their ignorance, appointed the dregs of the prison
inmates as camp police. These creatures soon earned the hatred
of the prisoners of war (and *Ostarbeiter*). Moscow could not wish
for more effective allies. It turned out in due course that many of
them were working for the NKVD.

Conditions in the Wulheide camp were quite appalling although
the commandant, a former Imperial Austrian officer, was doing
his best. It was proposed that I should take over Wulheide for our
new assignment. Having seen what it was like I refused, and
Martin and von Grote backed me up. From Wulheide I took on
the training officer, Lieutenant von der Ropp, who had had a
year's experience with Russian prisoners. I was struck by what he
told me of the terrifying grip of Marxist theory on the younger
Soviet generation.

Nazi propaganda was too crude to have any effect. An example
is one of the many anti-semitic Nazi propaganda films, *The Bone
Mill*, designed to expose the horrors of the Stakhanovite system.
The film was too incredible to be taken seriously by Russians, and
was sharply criticized by the prisoners. There were inaccuracies
due to the ignorance of the German producers, a totally false
presentation of conditions of life in Russia; and the Nazi gospel
of anti-semitism left most Russians quite cold.

The OKH had been in touch with the commandant of the
Berlin Wehrkreis, and there was a possibility that we might take
over one of the Wehrmacht's camps, formerly used for French
prisoners of war. I was instructed to report to the general in
person and convince him of the urgency of our claims.

'Put on all your decorations,' von Roenne advised me, 'and
tell him what von Brauchitsch wrote – the matter is decisive for
the outcome of the war.'

I followed this good advice. The friendly general, who knew
nothing whatever of Russia and Russians, listened attentively
to what I had to say and kept looking, with extreme interest, at a
white cross hanging from my neck (it was the Latvian Order
'*Pour les honnêtes hommes*').

'From what you tell me,' the general concluded, 'it seems your General Vlasov might bring about a change in the tide of war. That is also what the OKH officers have been telling me. Well, your request is an urgent one. I could, as I said, make available for you a perfectly good camp in Dabendorf. And I will do so because I can see the matter is important. The Russians, as you tell me, are going to help us beat Stalin. We should have made them our allies a long time ago.'

And so we were promised Dabendorf. Our capable paymaster looked after all the details.

(ii)

In the eyes of Vlasov and his staff (and, subsequently, of all Russian Freedom Fighters) Dabendorf was an outstanding success, especially when one considers the circumstances. The Propagandaabteilung Dabendorf was given the status of an independent battalion. The officer commanding was Captain Strik-Strikfeldt. As regimental commander there was Colonel Martin for so long as Dabendorf remained under the OKW. For general directives – censorship of newspapers and leaflets – we came under OKW/Pr IV (Captain von Grote); for rations and equipment under the commandant of Wehrkreis III (Berlin). Later, when the post of General der Osttruppen was created we came under him as well. I personally continued to be under the command of the Department Fremde Heere Ost in the OKH, which after all was primarily responsible for Dabendorf's existence.

So I had four masters. I could therefore always apply to whichever of them I thought most likely to help me over any particular issue. If one of them let me down I could always go to the others; but my surest support throughout the years came from General Gehlen and his Department Fremde Heere Ost, and that still held good after the events of July 1944.

Colonel Martin had originally envisaged a small unit of some forty to fifty Russian collaborators. When I brought him a form giving an establishment strength of twelve hundred he signed it without blinking an eyelid. Then he looked at me quizzically.

'If you had brought me a form for a hundred and twenty men I would have turned it down. That you have put twelve hundred means one of two things. Either you have this strength already approved at a higher level, or else . . .' (he tapped his forehead). 'But in the latter case there is nothing whatever I could do for you.'

The Dabendorf establishment had been carefully worked out in the OKH. While argument was going on in the Viktoriastrasse about the wording of the Smolensk proclamation, I paid several visits to Mauerwald (OKH). First, basic questions must be cleared with von Roenne. It was not always easy; von Roenne, as a Balt, was more German than the Germans.[1] Gehlen was to prove more flexible and big-minded. Then I had to deal with Stieff, Stauffenberg, Klammroth and Altenstadt. Stauffenberg swept aside many of von Roenne's meticulous objections. He tripled our figure of four hundred to twelve hundred. The Dabendorf establishment must be one that could serve as the core of all possible future developments. Our establishment strength provided slots for eight generals, some sixty staff officers and several hundred officers. An agreement with the Fremde Heere Ost foresaw subsequent attachments to one hundred divisions on the Eastern front, as well as to certain specialist German units. Future provision was made for liaison officers and 'propagandists' (education officers) in all prisoner-of-war camps coming under the OKW – including camps in the west. Altogether I could later count on 3,600 slots for officers.

So the little ship Dabendorf, flying the flag of the Russian Propaganda Department – for officially it was only propaganda that had been approved – sailed out into the stormy sea. I had to find twenty-one German officers to serve under me. They had to be chosen with great care to avoid having a cuckoo in our nest. That held good, to an even greater degree, for the selection of the Russian leadership and the Russian training staff.

I decided from the start to deal myself only with the top Russians, and to leave it to them to build up the organization within

[1] Before 1914 there had been Balts who were more Russian than the Russians.

the framework of our establishment. German intervention seemed to me desirable only when the Russians found themselves stuck fast in some bog. Experience was to show that this attitude was not only the best but the only one practically possible.

(iii)

In that critical winter of 1942–3, the period of the disaster at Stalingrad and the defeat at Alamein, we were desperately working to build up our base in all the chaos involved in an unprecedented project. First we had to get the living quarters ready, then be concerned with selection and appointment of heads and teams for our various departments and sections.

Vlasov and his collaborators, and the whole of the editorial staff, were released from Viktoriastrasse and transferred to the Dabendorf establishment. At last they were free men, as far as one could be free under a Nazi regime.

Our effort and achievement must not be assessed by normal criteria. What we did must be judged, and perhaps understood, in the light of the extraordinary conditions then prevailing. Everything had to be built up and made ready to function in those few, crowded, winter weeks. There was no precedent and no pattern. As so often in my life I had to improvise. Planning was improvised. Choice of personnel was improvised. And yet the whole took shape.

(iv)

My official task, with that of my German and Russian staff, was to recruit and train 'propagandists', i.e. *Betreuer*,[1] for the Russian Volunteers and Auxiliaries and the same for all permanent and transit prison camps throughout the whole of German-dominated Europe. These last were to work in close touch with the German commandants to do all that was possible to improve the prisoners' lot. All this entailed the work of enlightenment by means of a

[1] There is no exact equivalent in English for the German word *Betreuer* (? man of trust) as used here. It was intended that these *Betreuer* should do all in their power to look after the physical and moral welfare of their fellow-countrymen in the volunteer units, in the prisoner-of-war camps and in the Ostarbeiter settlements, and should propagate the ideals of the Liberation Movement.

Russian language press of our own. Millions of Russians were to be given new hope and a sense of purpose, to be aroused from their lethargy and rallied to a cause they could feel worth while. Captain von Grote of the OKW/Pr was responsible for the moral and intellectual appeal to the prisoners of war. He was also in charge not merely of press censorship but also of all leaflet propaganda directed at the enemy. (None of his seniors understood Russian.) It was for us at Dabendorf to make proposals and submit texts. There must thus be close liaison between Dabendorf and OKW/Pr.

Such was the programme officially approved by the OKH and the OKW.

To my mind my second, and more difficult, task was, for the time being, to provide cover for a Russian centre under Vlasov's leadership. Under the wing of Dabendorf the Russians would have to think out their ideas and their programme, select and train their cadres, widen their contacts. When the hour struck all would have to be ready – the General Staff, the corps of officers, the administration, press, etc. All this must be worked out, in secret, by the Russians themselves.

Grote, Dürksen and I had to think and think again. In the Russia of Stalin twenty-four years of Bolshevik domination had soldered power and ideology into a single whole. The much younger National Socialism was striving towards a similar unity, but in this was still far behind the Bolsheviks. In the Third Reich there was still private initiative and private property. It was possible to work and live independently of the State. Germans could still express their views, even though these did not tally with official dogma, could still, to some extent, act as they thought best. True there was the ever-growing (and to us intolerable) pressure of the party. But to ex-Soviet citizens this 'unfreedom' in Germany appeared as freedom itself. That was the big difference. And it was the appeal of this 'freedom' that still brought Russians over to our side in spite of all the disappointments of 1941. I am speaking here of the élite, not of those who joined from hope of personal advantage or from fear of Stalin's threatened reprisals.

The fall of Stalingrad had dimmed the hopes of Germany's ultimate victory, and the faith in the technical and moral superiority of the Wehrmacht. But it was just this that raised Vlasov's hopes of being accepted as ally and equal partner. He no longer believed that Nazi Germany would win the war. He did believe in the collapse of Bolshevism when the fighting was over.

In late 1942 all was not yet lost. The German armies stood deep in Soviet territory. Stalin had, it is true, successfully appealed to Russian patriotism as against the imperialism of the Nazis. But there was no sign that Moscow desired to better the lot of the common people of the USSR. Sentence of death against prisoners in German hands was still in force.

I was firmly convinced that we, with Stalin on the one side and Hitler on the other, were working on the right lines. What was I to demand from myself, from the German officers with me, in our cooperation with our Russians? No interference in Russian concerns, no ideological argument, no hint of German superiority. Instead of this, integrity, comradeship, example, understanding and tact. That at least, rightly or wrongly, was the result of my long deliberations.

(iv)

I am both grateful and proud to bear witness to the sterling contribution of the German officers, NCOs and men to our work at Dabendorf; and this holds good of our women helpers under Verena von Düsterlohe ('our Verena' to the Russians) who stood by her post right up to the bitter end. To each and all of them my heartfelt thanks. A full roll-call would be too long for inclusion here, and I can but mention a few of my closest collaborators: Captain von Dellingshausen, my friend and deputy; Major Elben, our first camp commandant; Georg von der Ropp, our training officer; Hellmuth von Kleist, our Abwehr security officer; Captains von Bremen and Kaehlbrandt; Arnold Schabert; Lieutenants Semder and Brieger; *Sonderführers* Schulz and Rogoshin; Paymaster Pehla (who managed to find rations for 20 per cent more men than our allotted strength, provided clothing, underclothing and equipment, made improvements to the camp and, last but not least, managed to provide the drinks for our festive occasions); Werner Bormann, a journalist from Riga; Captain Strauch, our adjutant. And, finally, a couple whose connection was quite unofficial. My old school friend Theodor Krause, a civilian working in the OKW, was bombed out of his Berlin home and came with his wife to stay in Dabendorf, where by force of personality they won their way to our Russians' hearts. Krause, steeped in both Russian and Western culture, proved the ideal interpreter and intermediary between the two different worlds.

7

The Smolensk Proclamation

(i)

DR BRAÜTIGAM, the Ostministerium's liaison officer with the OKH, favoured a change in German Eastern policy. It may well be that his representations persuaded Rosenberg to envisage a change of policy following a conference on 18 December 1942 when senior OKH officers of the front and rear zones spoke forcibly on the military aspects. General von Schenckendorff, Colonels von Altenstadt and von Tresckow and other officers emphasized the deplorable consequences of the current political war aims and treatment of the Russian population. They demanded that Eastern volunteers be put on the same footing as German troops. General von Schenckendorff expressed the views of many when he told Rosenberg that the Führer had, apparently, been consistently misinformed about such matters.

We were told that Rosenberg had been deeply impressed, and had given the officers to understand that he would take the matter up with Hitler with a view to an early change of policy.

'The club' were delighted at this news, which I had von Roenne's permission to pass to Vlasov. We were making progress. The officers had won their battle with the party's chief ideological pundit, a victory that might well outweigh the threatening catastrophe of Stalingrad.

It was some time before we heard anything about the Rosenberg–Hitler meeting, which took place around Christmas. We learned later that Rosenberg had been uncertain and muddled, and was sharply rebuffed by Hitler. Shortly afterwards Field-Marshal Keitel issued a strict directive that the army must keep off politics; but the idea of the necessity of help from the Russians found new protagonists among the army officers. The new spirit could no longer be suppressed. Following the December conference came a flood of reports and memoranda, calling, *inter alia*, for the proper treatment of the Russian population and proper terms of service for the 'local formations'. There was even talk of 'our new allies'.

Our Russians remarked that this sort of thing would be unthinkable under Stalin.

It was significant that these signs of a change of atmosphere seemed to come spontaneously and were not due to our representations. There was an order from Field-Marshal von Manstein inspired by the new spirit. There was a new directive for the treatment of the local population in Field-Marshal von Kleist's Army Group area. General Stapf, head of the Eastern Economic Staff, called on Vlasov and gave express orders to his subordinates for the proper treatment of the *Ostarbeiter*.

I was summoned by General Gehlen and spent most of the night reading his important report on the partisan problem and on the employment of locally raised formations. I was proud to see much of it was on the lines of my lecture 'Russians as Human Beings'. Gehlen went further. He instructed me to ask General Vlasov 'as an ally' to write him a paper on the partisan question and on the Soviet military position generally. In the eyes of Vlasov and his entourage this move by Gehlen was the first step towards real collaboration. They eagerly set to work. Their 'factual General Staff appreciation', as could be expected, might be summarized as 'set the Russian people free and there will be no more partisans'. This of course was too much for Gehlen. It was impossible for him to go so far. As I explained to Vlasov, he must confine himself to purely military issues. If he embarked on politics, all we had achieved in the last few months might well be lost. Vlasov understood, but the Russians naturally felt that our progress was all too slow.

For the idea of the Smolensk Proclamation one must go back to August 1942. It was then that von Roenne had proposed to reactivate the projected 'Smolensk Russian Liberation Committee'. The Central Army Group had approved. There had been discussions between the OKH/Fremde Heere Ost and the

OKW/Pr on the subject of an appeal by this committee, setting out clearly its political aims, and of which a million copies should be printed and dropped over the enemy lines in the Stalingrad sector. It would point the way to a new future for the (at that time) hard-pressed Red Army leaders. To the Red rank and file it would emphasize the futility of further resistance. The German armies were still sweeping forward, so that the timing was well chosen.

Months went by, and, as far as we could see, no progress whatever was made regarding the political aspect. By November I doubt whether anybody still believed in the possibility of early recognition of the 'Russian Liberation Committee'. But Grote refused to accept defeat. He had conceived a scheme which, in case of recognition, would put him in a position to exploit it, and which, if recognition were delayed, should have sufficient propaganda success to bring about a fait accompli. Some time before, he had obtained approval for a leaflet containing thirteen points which in fact amounted to a political programme without in any way committing the German government. Grote had no need to apply again for approval of these thirteen points. If Vlasov and the Smolensk group would sign the leaflet it seemed assured of a resounding success.

Von Roenne kept phoning from the OKH to inquire about the appeal. It was now urgently needed in the Stalingrad section where the military position was rapidly deteriorating.

But it transpired that it was not permissible for the Smolensk residents to sign the appeal: were they to do so, the formation of a 'Russian Liberation Committee' would become a political act. And Vlasov and his collaborators flatly refused to agree to Grote's proposal. There was, however, one of them who saw in it the possibility of bringing the whole idea of Russian liberation right out into the open. It was Zykov. He supported Grote's scheme of confronting the German leadership with a fait accompli. 'Let the devil out of the bottle,' he said, 'and he will do his work himself.'

In the end Vlasov also agreed. 'You people,' he said, 'are like a man in a bitterly cold winter who cannot make up his mind to buy a fur coat for fear it may have lice. You shiver and freeze. I will buy it and wear it and take it off again.'

Zykov redrafted the thirteen points to give them greater appeal to their Russian readers. It was still the policy of small steps, but the only step that we, at the time, could take; but even this modest venture ran up against fresh obstacles. General von Wedel, as chief of OKW/Pr, felt that he could not issue the leaflet without the approval of Minister Rosenberg. Soldiers must keep out of politics. It is possible he may have heard of Rosenberg's abject failure to make any impression on the Führer.

So that the leaflet, so urgently required by the OKH on behalf of the troops at the front, lay waiting in the pending tray of the Ostminister. It is true that the action planned back in August was no longer relevant to the actual military position in front of Stalingrad and in the Caucasus; but Hitler's pet assumption that the Soviet war potential was now exhausted had been shown to be completely false, and one might suppose that he would at long last agree to the employment of political measures as urged by his General Staff. The enemy's numerical superiority was crushing, and the drafts available from Germany were insufficient to make good the Wehrmacht's huge losses. Would not General Vlasov and a Liberation Army provide, perhaps, a chance to turn the scales?

Suddenly, and quite unexpectedly, we found it possible to go ahead with our appeal.

A friend of mine had introduced me to a Dr R, a member of the Waffen SS but none the less a sharp critic of the party's Eastern policy. My friend told me that R had access to both Himmler and Rosenberg and was a considerable personality himself. Early in January Vlasov and I were invited to R's private flat. He spoke excellent Russian and proceeded to attack the party line with even greater vehemence than I had heard from the army officers. I mentioned the matter of our proclamation, still held up in Rosenberg's pending tray. Our host said he would take action.

In the night of 11/12 January I was suddenly called to R's flat, where he told me of his plan for our leaflet. It was a moonlight night with the sirens sounding and enemy bombers overhead. All the Third Reich's successes, Dr R explained to me, have come from 'pulling a fast one'. 'Tomorrow is Rosenberg's birthday, and I intend to pull a fast one over the Smolensk Appeal.' It seemed to me most unlikely that his plan would work.

The following day I was in my office in the OKW/Pr when the telephone rang. I picked up the receiver.

'The Devil's grandmother [*chortova babushka*] speaking.'

It was Dr R.

'The minister has just signed permission for the proclamation to be printed and distributed. Send someone at once to collect the document before he changes his mind. That is quite possible. It is urgent.'

Grote, our liaison officer with the Ostministerium, left at once and came back with the permission in his pocket.

What had happened was this. That morning R had called on Rosenberg to offer his birthday wishes. The two were alone together, and in the course of conversation R mentioned that the Reichsführer SS (i.e. Himmler) was showing interest in the Smolensk Liberation Committee. He hinted that Himmler was possibly thinking of himself setting up a Russian Committee. Meanwhile he (R) would be grateful for a copy of the proclamation, as just now he was going on to Himmler's HQ. (Rosenberg knew of and perhaps overestimated R's relationship with Himmler.) Now Rosenberg could not agree to allowing Himmler to acquire a greater say in matters concerning the occupied territories in the East. So he signed the permit for the proclamation in R's presence.[1]

I must pay tribute to Grote's work of organization. The rotary presses were all ready, and within a few hours millions of our Smolensk Proclamation leaflets had been rolled off. Dispatch and distribution were smooth and speedy. The Army and the Air Force played their part. We soon had reports that German

[1] The text of the Proclamation is to be found in Thorwald, *Wen sie verderben wollen* (Stuttgart, 1952), pp. 171–5.

planes 'had lost their bearings' and that the proclamation – contrary to Rosenberg's express orders – was being dropped not only on the Soviet side but on our side of the front line. The text was set up and put out by a local printing works in Smolensk. A number of locals copied it out and passed it from hand to hand.

News of the 'new spirit' spread like wild-fire. Grote and I knew well we would not earn any credit for the planes having lost their way and dropped the leaflets on our side. We were counting on the breakthrough creating a *fait accompli*, so that the idea of Russian freedom could never be suppressed. It looked at one time as if this was going to be the case.

The Army and Air Force had been waiting impatiently for months for a decision in this sense. Now they wished to exploit it to the full in spite of the short-sightedness of Berlin. The military (without any action on our part) did all they could to secure the widest possible distribution – including units along the lines of communication, who hoped thereby to counter partisan activities. Millions of Russian men and women had found new hope. That was what was important.

But in spite of the Stalingrad defeat and in spite of the proclamation's success stringent and urgent orders were issued that distribution must be confined to the enemy side of the front line; distribution on our side was expressly forbidden, any breach of this order to entail drastic punishment. The Ostministerium and the OKW (i.e. Keitel) were at one on this ruling. All the OKH could do was to bombard the chief of staff with a flood of reports on the proclamation's excellent results; but General Zeitzler, who had by now succeeded Halder, was unable to have the order rescinded.

Officers at the front failed to understand how Berlin could bring itself to play this double game, how it could perpetrate so transparent and idiotic a deception.

Vlasov was disappointed. But he was surprised that in Nazi Germany it was still possible to kick against the pricks, and that 'men like Dr R, Martin, Grote and Strikfeldt were not put up against a wall and shot'. His personal confidence in these men was increased, in spite of the setback to his hopes of ultimate success. Zhilenkov's comment was, 'There is no helping the Suicide Club. But it would be a pity if it turns out that we have to go down with them.'

(ii)

We had, for a moment, hopes of a change of wind in the Propaganda Ministry. According to Colonel Martin officials there were taking the line: why not a Russian Liberation Committee if it is going to be helpful? After all there would be no need later on to take any promises made too literally.

Zykov and Zhilenkov saw the point. This was just how Stalin would act. 'Start by making promises; later on one can see how far one has to keep them.'

'The crux of the matter,' said Zhilenkov, 'is who is going to be the stronger when the time comes.' Zykov did not speak as openly as this. He was apt to keep his thoughts to himself. Both of them considered the Ministry was showing great foresight. Let the cat out of the bag now that it seems useful; later on one can drown it. 'Always provided,' Zhilenkov remarked, 'that the cat lets itself be caught.'

One gathered from Martin's words, though he did not say so outright, that Goebbels himself was in favour of the Smolensk Proclamation.

It was about this time that I had a visit from a young German Balt in the Propaganda Ministry, formerly a fervent adherent of the Nazi Party line, but by now disillusioned. He told me Goebbels was determined to press Hitler for a radical change in Germany's Eastern policy. His idea was to urge Hitler to issue a Führer Proclamation to the peoples of Eastern Europe that should form the basis of a new relationship between these peoples and the Reich (much on the lines of what we ourselves had been hoping). Goebbels, my visitor informed me, had declared that this declaration of principle must come first and should pave the way to the solution of such problems as national committees, self-administration, economic cooperation, status and tasks of Volunteers and Auxiliaries, anti-partisan measures and so on.

'It is a step forward,' my friend remarked, 'that one of the Führer's most intimate collaborators should make so determined a stand for a change of course.'

It was indeed a step forward – was what senior officers of the General Staff, what Vlasov himself was hoping for. If only it had not come too late.

Some weeks later we heard that Goebbels had been rebuffed, either by his colleague Rosenberg or by Hitler himself. We were given no details. A proposed meeting – arranged by Martin – between Goebbels and Vlasov was cancelled or indefinitely postponed.

I might here mention that in early 1945, after the official recognition of the Committee for the Liberation of the Peoples of Russia, Vlasov and Zhilenkov had an interview with Goebbels. Months later, when we were fellow-inmates of an American prisoner-of-war camp, Zhilenkov gave me an account of it. Goebbels, who was very friendly throughout, explained that right from the start he had favoured a Russian Liberation Movement: it could always be dissolved should its members take it into their heads to turn against the German Reich. Zhilenkov then seemed abruptly to change the subject, and asked the minister if he knew who had discovered America; and persisted till Goebbels answered Columbus. 'Yes,' said Zhilenkov, 'Columbus discovered America. And America is now there. Could you, Excellency, cover America up again? This applies equally to the Russian Liberation Movement.' Goebbels smiled. Times had changed.

(iii)

The German defeat at Stalingrad made a shattering impact on our Russians. For weeks they had been following, and correctly assessing, the contradictory Soviet and German communiqués. Now they were faced with an accomplished fact. I remember how they crowded round the map, I remember the expression on their faces, I can still feel the weight of gloom. Zykov was the first to speak. 'As Russians we should rejoice at a Russian victory. As Russian freedom fighters we cannot. Every Red Army victory reinforces and prolongs Stalin's grip on the enslaved Russian people. The cruel blow that has struck the Sixth Army has fallen too on us.' Vlasov, hitherto silent, then brought out the phrase that soon became the movement's slogan. '*Rossiya nasha* [Russia is ours]. By this,' he said, 'I mean free Russia, the Russia our people long for – not over there under Stalin's yoke, but here, on our side, with the freedom fighters.'

Meanwhile we were still in the realm of little by little and small deeds. Our immediate concern was to develop what we had started in Dabendorf.

8

The Volunteers

ON the German side the immediate problem was what to call the Russian troops serving with the Wehrmacht. The designation might be 'volunteers' or it might be 'allies', but the current official title *'Hilfswillige'* should no longer be used, as in any case it sounded ridiculous when translated into Russian. (It should be noted here that use of the words Russia and Russian was officially forbidden. The ban went so far as to include the wording of traditional songs – e.g. in *Volga, Volga, Russian* river had to be amended to *great* river. The authorities were inane enough to imagine that Russians would sing their traditional songs in the new amended text.)

However, the task was to devise an official designation for the Russian troops. I vividly remember a conference at OKW/Pr where this problem was to be finally settled. Count von Stauffenberg, *en route* for his new command in Africa, had come to Berlin to attend it. I represented the Department Fremde Heere Ost. Present were representatives of the OKW, of the Propaganda Ministry and of the Ostministerium. Stauffenberg demanded a clear ruling in favour of the term 'volunteer' (in Russian, *Dobrovolets*). The Propaganda and Ostministerium delegates protested, and the argument seemed likely to go on for ever. Finally Colonel Martin intervened. 'Good,' he said. 'We will have an OKW order issued to all units and also to the Russian civilian population to the effect that these troops be invariably and exclusively referred to, whether in writing or by word of mouth, as our "Ivans".' The ministerial representatives gave up the struggle. We had got the designation 'volunteer' officially approved, both for the troops themselves and for the newspaper that we in Dabendorf were going to bring out for them.

(ii)

In passing the news to Vlasov I was ashamed to go into the details of this ridiculous conference. I merely told him the name *Dobrovolets* had been approved for the newspaper we were proposing for the troops.

We soon got together the editorial staffs, and the two newspapers – *Dobrovolets* for the troops and *Zariya* (Dawn) for the prisoners of war – started to appear. M. A. Zykov was editor-in-chief, with a Ukrainian, Kovalchuk, as his deputy.

At last, for the first time since June 1941, Russians were able to address their fellow-countrymen on the subject not only of their needs but of their hopes. There was still in force the ban on publication of the Appeal of the Smolensk committee; but Zykov found a way round. Reference could be made to the contents as 'commonly known', and also to 'the general lines of the Liberation Committee'. These two newspapers told their readers they were fighting not for Germany but for the freedom of their compatriots. They made no attempt to gloss over the hard lot of the prisoners of war, but pointed to the possibilities of a better future and of return to a homeland freed from terror. They gave no incentive to hate but rather to reconciliation, in spite of all that Russians had suffered.

Future generations will find it hard to understand how it was that Germans, engaged in a ruthless war against Stalin, should have been at such pains to hamper and suppress a liberation movement that this same Stalin so feared. The OKW's censorship directives, thanks to the influence of Grote, allowed the papers to take a patriotic line, but they were forbidden to make specific promises in the political field. The spectre of 'Great Russian ambitions *vis-à-vis* the minority races' had at all costs to be excluded. Grote did his best, within the limits of the possible. Werner Bormann, German representative on the editorial board, was forced, almost every day, to strike out long passages as 'too nationalistic', and to do so without too much discouraging his Russian colleagues. Bormann was between two fires. His German superiors were always coming up with complaints – 'pro-Russia', 'far too chauvinistic' and sometimes even 'colourless and unintelligible'. But, by and large, the papers fulfilled the task we had intended for them. The Russian editors were quick to grasp the situation. In spite of the censorship cuts they managed to include a great deal of what they felt essential. New hope came to millions in the prison camps. A new sense of purpose came to those fighting at the front: they were not mercenaries, but volunteers and soldiers. The idea of the Russian Liberation Movement took root and spread.

The papers came out twice a week, and thanks to Bormann's efforts they never, right up to November 1944, missed a single issue in spite of the air attacks.

The papers acquired a valuable secondary function. It was Grote's excellent idea to include a German language supplement, giving short summaries of the issue's contents. These supplements went to officers of all those units to which volunteers were attached and to the commandants and staffs of the prisoner-of-war camps. They served to teach them, should it be necessary, that they had to do not with *Untermenschen* but with fellow-human beings; and those already well disposed could feel that their good intentions were officially backed by the Oberkommando der Wehrmacht. There is no doubt that these supplements helped to alleviate the lot of very many thousands of Russians.

While on the subject of our press, I should mention frequent complaints from highly placed Nazis (in the Ostministerium, the Propaganda Ministry and even the SD) to the effect that our papers contained no anti-Semitic propaganda, or rather (as they put it) 'neglected the task of anti-Semitical education'. Bormann was hard put to it to resist this pressure. It was Zykov who found a solution. 'Good,' he said. 'We will include anti-Semitic items in both papers. We will take them from the German press, for instance "*Völkischer Beobachter* reports", and then quote. Our readers will well understand we insert such items only under compulsion. They have learned in Russia how to read between the lines.'

(iii)

Vlasov's original choice for Chief Training Officer was the elderly and rather impulsive General Blagoveshchenski, later replaced by the intelligent, cautious and extremely energetic General F. Y. Trukhin. Trukhin was a Russian and at the same time a European; a first-class staff officer with an imposing presence. It was Vlasov, Malyshkin and Trukhin who selected the training staff; and also the future divisional and regimental commanders. At the same time those with good administrative or economic qualifications were noted and listed. The idea was to build up a reserve of men qualified to fill the leading posts as and when the time came. However the most urgent and immediate task was the training of *Betreuer* for the prison camps and for the volunteers at the front.

All this, of course, should have been a purely Russian concern, in which, as agreed with Vlasov and Malyshkin, we had no wish to interfere. But the whole had to function within a German framework, and here came the difficulties. Von Dellingshausen had a hard time with our German superiors as it was his task to smooth out day-to-day issues between our Russian leadership and the various German authorities. I myself was constantly on the move between Berlin and the OKH in Mauerwald on questions of policy and to ensure coordination between the OKW and the OKH. Gehlen, Roenne and Stauffenberg, and the latter's successor Klammroth, did all they could to help us. The creation of a new post, that of general commanding the Osttruppen in the OKH, meant that there was yet another authority with whom we had to deal.

We worked out our Russian training programme and the texts for the various lectures and instructional courses and then found ourselves in serious difficulty. We had gone too fast. There was general agreement on the subjects on which instruction should be given, but the content and tone of what we proposed to teach showed up the enormous gulf between our Russians' conceptions and those of, for instance, Rosenberg's ministry or of the GOC Osttruppen. Von der Ropp had come across the same problem in Wulheide. My own feeling was that we must make every effort to avoid, for the time being, a head-on clash with the Ostministerium or the Propaganda Ministry – the more so as General von Wedel (OKW) refused to take the responsibility himself. He merely 'recommended' (not ordered) that the programme be submitted to the two ministries for their approval.

I hurried off to the OKH in Mauerwald. Von Roenne handed over the programme for vetting to 'the club', i.e. the Department Fremde Heere Ost. Ten days later the whole, as originally drafted by the Russians, was passed and approved. We could go ahead, without any need to refer to the two ministries.

What, as time went on, the Russian instructors actually said to the classes is another matter. But the Russians had to tackle their problems in their own way.

Under Trukhin, A. N. Zaitsev, former university lecturer, was responsible for political education. In due course he was joined by members of the émigré NTS, who came to exercise an important influence on the intellectual struggle against Stalinism. I have already mentioned that Kazantsev, an NTS member, was working for Grote; also that both Grote and I had been warned against this organization. But in view of the quality of our new recruits, of whom Vlasov also approved, we decided to ignore the warning, and we never regretted having done so. The NTS, originally founded by younger members of the first wave of emigration, had been rejuvenated by the adherence of young men fresh from the USSR. The organization accordingly had a clear grasp of the realities of life in Soviet Russia and was ready to cooperate with those who had spent their whole lives there. To Ropp, to Grote and to myself this seemed of particular importance. Another factor was that the NTS, on its own initiative, had already become active in the occupied zone, in the camps for *Ostarbeiter*, and in the other spheres where we ourselves had not yet been able to penetrate.

M. A. Zykov, while unswervingly anti-Stalin, was prepared to accept, by and large, the Soviet Communist programme. On the other hand the NTS, under the influence of their solidarist ideology, were inclined to seek new social and economic forms and patterns for the Free Russia of the future. It is proof of the wisdom and tolerance of all concerned that they were able to work together so smoothly and harmoniously at the great task they had undertaken. In all some five thousand men completed our Dabendorf courses. And the Prague Manifesto bears the unmistakable mark of their collaboration.

It was the Russian generals responsible for policy and administration who attracted the limelight. But it was men like the university teacher Zaitser who won the hearts of their hearers. Zaitser, a first-class lecturer, would frequently announce that he was 'anything but pro-German'. And soon, blameless as he was, he became the victim of all manner of unpleasant aspersions. 'Listen,' he said to me, 'these men have been starved, have been beaten, have suffered all kinds of ill-treatment at German hands. Do you seriously believe I can win them over if I now suddenly tell them that the Germans are angels? No, I must be perfectly frank about all that they have suffered. Then later, perhaps, I may succeed in creating a different atmosphere, in bringing about the sort of relationship that exists, my dear Captain, between you and me. If and when that happens I will really have won them over.'

But this seemed much too complicated to those Germans who did not understand the men's mentality. These Germans preferred Russians to be yes-men.

(iv)

Our classes in Dabendorf comprised both volunteers back from the front and volunteers just released from prisoner-of-war camps. There was a long list of practical problems calling for urgent solution: pay and rations; uniforms and insignia; national flag; pay-books; form of oath, etc. There was no general, co-ordinated procedure. Each German unit treated its Russians or Ukrainians just as it felt inclined. Russian prisoners often made themselves out to be Ukrainians because they had come to believe that it might be to their advantage. And so it came about that instead of selecting the best it was the most adaptable that were selected. In Dabendorf we had a 'Russian Leadership', and the core of what should become the headquarters of 'The Russian Liberation Movement'. Meanwhile a new authority was being set up in Lötzen (East Prussia), that of General Officer Commanding the Osttruppen under the OKH, whose immediate task it was to solve all these problems 'within a German framework'. This new authority was (and continued to be for some time) preoccupied with organizing its own staff and office. It had had no contact with the Russians such as we had had in Dabendorf and before Dabendorf came into being. Our own prime concern now was to effect a reconciliation between the Russians' needs and wishes and the new general's administrative duties. I had, in consequence, to spend even more of my time in Mauerwald and Lötzen.

Originally recommended by von Roenne (who had served in his division) Major-General Hellmich was appointed 'GOC Osttruppen' (i.e. Eastern Troops). The designation of his post was unfortunate. Once more Russians, Ukrainians, Balts, Caucasians and Turkic racials were to be lumped together under the collective title of *Ost*. The Russians, especially, were sensitive to this slight on their national pride. Furthermore the word *Ost*, applied by the Nazis to Russian and Ukrainian workers, had acquired a pejorative sense. It was, as it were, a synonym for *Untermensch*.

General Hellmich, like most of his officers, spoke no Russian. They were men of good-will and integrity, but had otherwise no qualifications for the delicate and complicated task assigned to them. They had no experience of dealing with Russians. We in Dabendorf had arranged that selection of staff, indeed all questions of personnel, be left to our Russians to settle. I did not envy the German officer in charge of Hellmich's Personnel Department, all the more so in view of the dubious character of some of the Russians he had to help him. They included opportunists who sought personal advantage in exploiting any differences between Dabendorf and the GOC Osttruppen.

Hellmich began his new assignment with energy and enthusiasm. He knew nothing about Russians, but he realized full well one can hardly make good soldiers out of men who cannot be told for what they are fighting and who see their compatriots starving and ill-treated in prisoner-of-war camps and workers' settlements. He made every effort to bring this home not only to his military superiors but also to the Ostministerium and Propaganda Ministry. The sole result was that he acquired, in certain quarters, the reputation of being 'a political general'.

I was present at his first meeting with Vlasov. Vlasov started off with a bitter indictment of the designation *Ost*: he did not understand how otherwise intelligent Germans could be so blind. 'I suppose the reason,' he said, 'is that egomania kills the brain as well as the heart.' He went on to press that the Russian units should be withdrawn from German formations, and, at the earliest possible moment, made up into national Russian divisions; that was what Stalin was most afraid of. 'We have very little time,' he told Hellmich. 'It may be already too late, but you and I must do what we can.'

Hellmich agreed with him. He explained he had done what he could to have the name 'Osttruppen' changed to 'volunteers'; but the question of putting these Russians under Russian command was a matter of policy. Only the politicians could decide. He, Hellmich, could do nothing. His task was to take charge of these volunteers, see that they had their rations, their pay and their uniforms, make sure that in every way they were put on the same footing as German troops. That, if they were expected to fight, was only their due.

Vlasov and Hellmich were at cross purposes. But Vlasov understood it was not possible to go into the question of command until Hellmich had completed what he had described as his immediate task. He asked Hellmich how long the process of taking over would take; but that was a question the German general was unable to answer. In spite, he said, of all his efforts he was quite unable to obtain reliable figures of Russian troops from the various German commanders. At present they were getting next to no drafts from Germany, and they feared that if they lost their Russians they would be seriously under strength.

Vlasov realized this was an important, possibly decisive, factor. He assumed a pathetic tone (as he often did when he wished to hide his displeasure). In his view hirelings in German pay would prove to be useless. He should be allowed to build up his Liberation Army from the newcomers, the line-crossers still coming over daily to the German lines. But this too, Hellmich explained, was outside the sphere of competence of the GOC Osttruppen.

With that the interview came to an end.

Hellmich of course reported this conversation to his superiors, and was given to understand that, for the time being, Vlasov's role was confined to propaganda aimed at the Red Army: as far as the volunteers were concerned he should be kept in the background. It became clear to Hellmich that any further attempts on his part in the realm of policy were doomed to failure. There was nothing left to him but to obey his orders as a soldier.

Grote, Dürksen and I had to keep reminding Vlasov that to remove Russian and other German combat units was an almost impossible task, even for General Hellmich. Vlasov knew nothing of the battles which Hellmich had to fight, but his good sense told him it was being very difficult for Hellmich. For a time he wondered, circumstances being what they were, whether he should not abandon the struggle. Only after long talks with his intimates did he finally decide to remain at his post.

(v)

Now that the volunteers were officially recognized there arose the question of their oath of service. They should not, and would not, swear allegiance to the Third Reich. It was agreed that the oath should be to their Free Nation and Fatherland. However, Rosenberg, head of the Ostministerium, demanded they should also swear allegiance to Adolf Hitler. The Russians asked why no such demand had been made to the Romanians, Italians, Hungarians and other free allies. Vlasov and his officers refused to take this oath, a refusal which German patriots – including a number of officers – described as 'unheard-of impertinence'. I myself had sharp exchanges in the office of the GOC Osttruppen. But in the end some of the more flexible Russians, with Grote's help, worked out what they called a 'provisional formula': the Russians should swear allegiance to their nation – the minority races to theirs – and at the same time swear obedience to Adolf Hitler as 'Supreme Commander of all anti-Bolshevik Forces'. Naturally this formula did not satisfy everybody, and some of the officers in Dabendorf preferred to go back to their prison camps.

This new formula was surprisingly and speedily approved by the Minister for Eastern Affairs. Dr Knüpffer later told me that Rosenberg had quickly come to the conclusion that it was reasonable and entirely acceptable. But later GOC Osttruppen (on instructions from above?) disallowed the formula, and all the pay-books so far issued (which contained the text, including the phrase 'Free Fatherland') were called in again. It is unlikely that the Führer had ever seen one of these pay-books, but he was believed to have inveighed against the idea of a Free Fatherland for Russians and Ukrainians, and no one wished to risk their necks. Rosenberg stayed silent.

The episode served to intensify Russian mistrust of the Germans, but this aspect the OKW chose to ignore.

National colours had by this time been approved for the contingents of nearly all the minority races. It was now high time to do the same for the Russians, but the actual composition of the flag presented difficulties. The old imperial White Blue Red was ruled out. Both Dabendorf and the office of the GOC Osttruppen worked out various suggestions, and Rosenberg himself took a personal interest. The design that took his fancy was a small St Andrew's cross, blue on white, on a red field. But on second thoughts he felt there was too much red, and himself proposed a large St Andrew's cross on a white field with a thin red border. Von Grote was delighted and on arrival in Dabendorf warmly congratulated Malyshkin: the Russians now had their national colours combined with the St Andrew's cross. General Hellmich arrived in Berlin with the designs worked out by his staff only to find the decision had been taken. He was pleased and relieved that it was so. He admitted that none of his own staff's designs would have been thought by the Russians to have been acceptable.

As to the uniforms, the time factor and the general shortage of raw materials rendered impossible the production of a special cloth. The Russians were disappointed to find they had to wear the German field grey: they had only the broad epaulettes to distinguish them from members of the Wehrmacht. But it turned out that this arrangement had practical advantages; the Russian in field grey was accepted by the German as a brother-in-arms, and was recognized as a soldier by the civilian population. Later on senior Russians were permitted to wear German epaulettes, and this served to accentuate their equal status with their German opposite numbers.

It was a great day for Dabendorf when all, or nearly all, our volunteers paraded in their new uniforms with their national badges and General Vlasov took the salute. In his speech he dwelt on the hard lot of the still enslaved Russian people. He urged his listeners to forget their harsh treatment by the Germans; without forgiveness there could be no peace and no future, either for individuals or for nations. He spoke simply and frankly. He hid nothing, made no attempt to depict in rosy colours. His listeners hung on his words. Over the camp, alongside the German flag, there floated for the first time the blue St Andrew's cross on a white field with a thin red border.

General Hellmich also gave an address, in German, to welcome the Russian volunteers as comrades in arms. 'Honourable comrades,' he said in conclusion, 'in the fight for Germany's future.' Our Dabendorf German officer who acted as interpreter rendered these last words 'in the fight for the future of the Russian people'. When, later, the general was told of this amendment he thanked the interpreter warmly. He, of course, had been thinking in German. 'When two different worlds come together,' he said, 'one has to make a lot of readjustments. I have not yet got that far.'

General Wedel, head of OKW/Pr, other generals and senior staff officers, used to come and visit us in Dabendorf, whether or not we had laid on some special occasion. This helped us to make a number of personal contacts that were to be of value to us in our role of intermediaries between two different worlds.

(vi)

There was still not a word in the German press about any of these developments. But the writer Erich Edwin Dwinger set himself up as advocate of the Russian Liberation Movement. He produced a whole series of papers which were read in quarters to which we had no access. Another champion of our cause was Günter Kaufmann, publisher of a widely circulated Nazi youth periodical. Both men ran into trouble, and Dwinger may have been brought before a court. He was forbidden to publish further articles, but this merely increased his assiduity in lobbying leading Nazi Party members, many of whom paid serious attention to what he had to say. It was believed that 'Dwinger must know'.

The Paris émigré paper, *Parizhki Vyestnik*, gave considerable coverage to the Freedom Movement. Its publisher, Y. S. Zhereb-kov, and its editor, Colonel N. Pyatnitsky, soon made contact with Zykov in Dabendorf, and reached an agreement on general policy and on educational instruction for volunteer formations. The Russian press in France was not under the jurisdiction of the OKW, and the regulations in force in France gave far more scope for free reporting and comment.

And then a Swiss newspaper published an important article on the Vlasov movement. It assumed that the movement had Nazi support, and pointed out that the Germans had the habit of doing things thoroughly. Readers were advised to look out for significant developments in the Eastern theatre of war. Zykov, of course, was quick to exploit the opportunity, and both *Dobro-volets* and *Zarya* emphasized the attention being paid to the Freedom Movement abroad. It was something that could not be hushed up, in spite of being ignored by the German press. The *Baseler Nationalzeitung* of 7 June 1943 raised the question of whether events were not moving too fast for Vlasov's plans to be implemented.

9

Visits to Army Group HQs

THE impact of the Smolensk Proclamation was remarkably successful, especially in the Central and Northern Sectors. In the south everything was of course overshadowed by the Stalingrad disaster, though even from this sector reports came in of a good reception. Divisions in the Northern and Central Groups reported increasing numbers of line-crossers coming over from the Reds. Of prime importance was the fact that the civilian population now, in spite of Stalingrad, harboured new hopes. There was a perceptible heightening of morale in the ranks of the volunteers and auxiliaries.

Gehlen, Roenne and their OKH colleagues were considering their next move. They came to an agreement with Tresckow and Gersdorff of the Central Army Group that Vlasov should be invited to visit the Army Group. The population were calling for the Smolensk Committee. Where was it? No one seemed to know about it in Smolensk. The volunteers were anxious to see Vlasov. Line-crossers were coming over with copies of the leaflet and demanding to be enrolled in the Russian Liberation Army. Field-Marshal von Kluge at last realized that something had to be done, and he authorized Vlasov's visit.

I would only too gladly have accompanied the general and, incidentally, seen my old friends at Central Group HQ, but in those crowded early weeks of 1943, Dabendorf and the tug-of-war in Berlin over the National Committee question made this impossible. Unexpectedly, and in spite of Rosenberg's negative attitude, the setting up of National Committees was now once more on the agenda. Grote, at the moment, was carrying on an all-out struggle. A decision, one way or another, was at hand.

I do not know who were the initiators of this latest move in the

General Vlasov

FRONT ROW, LEFT TO RIGHT:
*Malyshkin, Vlasov,
Strik-Strikfeldt,
von Kleist, Zhilenkov*

Field-marshal von Bock

Hitler leaving von Bock's headquarters (cameras were forbidden, but somebody cheated)

LEFT TO RIGHT:
General Herre,
von der Ropp,
Colonel Pozdniakov

LEFT TO RIGHT:
Colonel Nauck,
General Gehlen,
Colonel Wessel

General Trukhin

Colonel von Roenne

Captain von Grote

Colonel Freytag von Loringhoven

Vlasov and Malyshkin

Von Dellingshausen and Vlasov visiting Northern Army Group

LEFT TO RIGHT: *Strik-Strikfeldt, unidentified SS officer, d'Alquen, von Dellingshausen, Zykov, Zhilenkov*

FRONT ROW: *Gehlen, Strik-Strikfeldt, Malyshkin*

Vlasov talking to volunteers

Boyarski, Zherebkov and Malyshkin arriving in Paris

LEFT TO RIGHT: *Vlasov, Zhilenkov, Kroeger, Goebbels*

Father Alexander, Trukhin, Aschenbrenner, Vlasov

Ostministerium. The names of Leibbrandt, Knüpffer, Zimmermann, Kleist and Mende can hardly be mentioned in the same breath, as each one of them represented a different tendency. It all started with the already mentioned conference in December 1942 attended by Rosenberg, General Wagner and other officers. As has been seen, their recommendations had been rejected by Führer HQ. However, since then there had been the successful leaflet operation with the Smolensk Proclamation, and in view of the Stalingrad defeat, problems of security at the front and in the rear had become very urgent. Rosenberg had long been aware that something must be done. He still opposed the Great Russian conception of a 'One and Undivided Russia', but seemed inclined to favour the recognition of a number of national committees, including a Russian National Committee. This last should have no overall authority for the whole of Russia but should take its place alongside the national committees of the minority races. I will deal later with our discussions with Vlasov on this particular issue.

(ii)

I myself was unable to leave Dabendorf, but von Roenne arranged that Lieutenant-Colonel Schubuth (who had served under General Köstring, Military Attaché in Moscow) and Captain Peterson (my former chief in Fremde Heere Ost) should accompany Vlasov on his tour. Here are some extracts from Peterson's report:

Before we started I gave the general my revolver. One could not let him go to the front completely unarmed . . .

Our first stage was Bialystock–Minsk–Smolensk. The arrangements were made by the Army Group's propaganda section, and worked out admirably . . .

Great enthusiasm everywhere on the part of the population. Visits to Smolensk Cathedral, the Russian theatre, receptions, mass meetings, speeches . . .

Vlasov was especially impressed at his reception by General von Schenckendorff, an avowed champion of the common interests of the German and Russian peoples. 'A magnificent man,' said Vlasov after the interview.

There were of course some awkward questions from volunteers and from Russian civilians. For instance:

Question: Why is it that since the Smolensk Proclamation we have heard nothing more of the Smolensk Committee or of yourself, General?

Answer: Russia is big. You must not take the little word Smolensk on the leaflet too literally. You know how things were under Stalin. You will soon be hearing more and more often from me. We are just beginning.

Question: Why have we still got to have collective farms?

Answer: These things cannot be settled in twenty-four hours. First, win the war. Then, land for the peasants.

The Army Group had arranged for Vlasov to broadcast a speech on the Bobruysk transmitter. But someone in authority – probably in OKW – must have heard of the impact of the visit, and the broadcast was banned. But it is significant that, in spite of this ban, Bobruysk announced there was present in the studio an important guest, 'General Vlasov, now on a tour of inspection of the liberated areas, who sends his greetings to all sincere Russian patriots' . . .

Our visits to the various Russian units took us through forests and isolated tracts. We had to travel in armoured cars or with an escort of volunteers. This in an area where months ago partisans had not even been heard of . . .

Everywhere, reception enthusiastic and discipline good . . .

We visited a Cossack regiment, the men mostly ex-Red Army soldiers, the officers ex-Tsarist émigrés. Vlasov was surprised at the excellent comradely spirit prevailing among these very different elements. The commanding officer (himself an émigré) asked Vlasov what was his attitude to the émigrés. Vlasov answered: 'We are engaged in a life or death struggle. Anyone prepared to risk his life against Stalin is – whatever his background – our welcome ally and comrade. But there is no place in our ranks for anyone joining us from selfish motives, from wanting to get his property back or (like certain Red Army men) from hoping to curry favour with the Germans.' Vlasov's answer was greeted with a roar of applause.

Peterson concluded his report with the words: 'We are now on the right path which can lead us to further political and military successes.'

Vlasov came back to Berlin in exalted mood. For the first time he had been able, as a free man, to make contact with his compatriots in the occupied zone. He was convinced that he was on the right path with his Russian Liberation Movement. 'If only,' as he kept repeating, 'it is not too late.'

Together with his senior Russian collaborators he set to work on a memorandum containing a number of 'demands', including abandonment of the colonization policy, recognition of the Liberation Committee, and the establishment of a Russian Liberation Army under Russian command. The memorandum was passed to Captain Grote of the OKW/Pr. Grote, of course, had sad experience of the likely fate of such representations. Nevertheless, after tactfully altering 'demands' to 'proposals,' he passed on the memorandum to General Wedel and to the Ostministerium. There it remained in somebody's pending tray.

(iii)

It would be quite impossible to give an account of all the points and problems which our Russian friends were continually bringing up to us, and which all had to be discussed at considerable length. But the nationalities question, with which we had to deal at the beginning of 1943, was of special importance.

Rosenberg was willing to agree that the Ukrainians and certain other races should have their own State (under German tutelage) and a certain measure of autonomy. But, apparently, not the Russians. Could this be the last word? Vlasov and his staff in the above-mentioned memorandum had taken the line that there should be no splitting up of Russia for so long as the war lasted: all effort should be devoted to the struggle against Stalin. Later, he declared, the nationalities question should be settled by the freely-arrived-at decisions of the peoples concerned. He was in favour of cultural autonomy and for the other national minority rights as laid down in the Constitution of the USSR. But he went further. He was entirely sincere when he spoke of national self-determination. The tragedy was that the Germans had no wish to see genuine self-determination, and they did not believe that Vlasov meant what he said. For Rosenberg he remained a Great Russian, a champion of the idea of a 'One and undivided Russia'.

My own view was that nationality problems and differences could be settled in the framework of a European Community. But it was not for a Riga businessman to pontificate on such matters, and I accordingly sought expert advice. In the early days of National Socialism, Ambassador Werner Daitz, at one time a fervent supporter of Hitler, had formulated a concept of a German foreign policy that should respect the inviolability and sovereignty of other nations. It was from Daitz that I first heard of the idea of the '*Lebensraum* of the European Family of Nations'. I quote some of the points made by Daitz:

> The good of Europe as a whole takes priority over nationalist (chauvinist) advantage . . .
>
> It is important that each nation should possess a territory. Next comes the question of the legal obligations arising from such possession of territory . . .
>
> Force must be replaced by the laws governing the community of nations . . .
>
> All nations of Europe, including the Russians, must adapt their economic, legal and territorial concepts so as to fit in with the new European order . . .
>
> In the new Order account must be taken of the varying productivity potentials of the respective nations . . .

These are only a few, and perhaps not the most significant of Daitz's pronouncements. He showed me a number of memoranda he had composed at the time when he was still in a position to discuss foreign relations and economics with Hitler. It was here I found the extract from Hitler's speech of 7 March 1936: 'The nations of Europe are and will remain one family. It would be foolish to imagine that, in so limited an area as Europe, a community of nations can survive if each nation is to retain a different concept of law.' This indeed was a very different National Socialism – one aiming at a future Europe. This was a banner to which all European nations, great and small, could rally.

I took care to bring these ideas to the notice of Vlasov and his entourage. Daitz and certain friends of his produced a large number of memoranda which we had translated into Russian, and which were discussed at some length. Our Russians wasted no time over the frequent attacks on Anglo-American capitalism and diatribes against the Jews; they understood perfectly well that Germans had to make these concessions to Nazism if they were to get any hearing at all. But Vlasov and his circle welcomed and approved the idea of a reconstitution of Europe into a community of nations enjoying equal rights.

Their immediate reaction, however, was: 'The scheme in itself is a good one, but you Germans are just as far away from implementing it as is Stalin himself. So long as you are imbued with the spirit of "Greater Germany" and deny sovereign rights to Poles, Czechs, Balts and other nations, we can only counter with the idea of "Greater Russia". It is one thing or the other: either the community of European nations as proposed by Daitz, or else two big blocks – Greater Germany and Greater Russia. Germany would be entitled to assume the leading role in this community of nations, always provided that there be a fundamental change in German policy and that the rights of all other nations be recognized. At the same time, as Daitz points out, it is the productivity potential that is the decisive factor, and a day may well come when the centre of gravity is no longer Berlin but Moscow or Prague, or perhaps Paris or Rome.'

Such was the general line of the discussions in Dabendorf, in which Vlasov himself took a leading part. Our little group of Russians had shown a far clearer grasp of European national problems than had the government of the Reich. I was and am proud to have persuaded Vlasov to publish (in April 1943) his pamphlet on the nationalities question, based very largely on the theses worked out by Daitz.

Daitz never met Vlasov. He was conscious of his impotence. He told me once that any old-time court jester could say more to his monarch than he, Daitz, could now say to Hitler. His present status was not even that of a court jester. He still hoped that Hitler would come to his senses; but meanwhile he, as a German, was ashamed to meet the Russian Vlasov after all that the Russians had suffered at German hands. But he still hoped. After the war I learned that he had killed himself some time in 1945.

(iv)

In March 1943 Vlasov published his open letter 'Why I took up the struggle against Bolshevism'. Its origin was as follows.

The ban still held on the distribution of the Smolensk Proclamation in the occupied zone. Vlasov's German backers, who had hoped it would lead to a radical change of policy, saw their hopes evaporate. The Russians grouped round Vlasov were bitterly disillusioned. As already reported, the Russian population was asking, where is the Committee? What has happened to Vlasov? The atmosphere grew tenser. It was realized in OKW/Pr that something had to be done.

I do not know whether it was Martin or Grote to whom the thought occurred that the ban applied to the Liberation Committee, not to Vlasov personally. Martin had discovered a gap in the OKW fence. If, he suggested, General Vlasov were prepared to give some account of his experiences in the USSR and explain the reasons that had led him to take up arms against Stalin, there was nothing in the regulations to stop it.

But Vlasov was sick and tired of this sort of procedure. 'Unless,' he said, 'you people can decide on an open and clear-cut policy I shall go back to a prison camp. I am no longer prepared to take part in half measures.'

Malyshkin, Zhilenkov and Zykov thought otherwise. Now that it had come to be what they considered a war on two fronts – against Stalin and the Nazis – it was not the time to drop their weapons. 'It is for you, Andrei Andreyevich, to help our people –

in spite of everything. After all their set-backs the Germans still occupy an area with a population of 60–70 million Russians. These are our people. It is for us to free them from the German grip. Then there are the Russian prisoners and the *Ostarbeiter*; it is only we who can do something to help them. There is no one else, Andrei Andreyevich, to sow the seeds of freedom here in Germany or on Russian soil.'

I could not but agree to what they said. It was only from the little Vlasov group that a voice could be raised, a voice that Russians would listen to.

'Look, Andrei Andreyevich,' I said. 'Suppose I was not a German but an Englishman. You and your staff would be lodged in one of the best hotels and have everything you wanted. Whisky. Cigarettes. And no doubt the wily British would have produced a substantial cheque for your committee. You should be glad that we Germans have been too honest or too stupid to do anything of the kind – no one can accuse you of selling yourself to the Germans. Not a stitch of what you are wearing was given you by the Germans, and they still have not delivered your new spectacles.'

He listened carefully. 'What you are telling me,' he said, 'is hardly Great Power politics, but you are right. I can only smile at your thinking this is the way to conquer the world.'

Then he and Zykov set to and drafted that open letter so largely responsible for his popularity and renown. The nebulous committee was now replaced by a strong personality; and the aims and hopes once centred on that committee were transferred to that personality. Thanks to the publication of this letter the general's public image was such that before very long the terms Russian Liberation Movement and Vlasov Movement became synonymous.

'Why I took up the struggle against Bolshevism'[1] is a bitter attack on the Stalin regime. Vlasov addressed his compatriots as a son of a Russian peasant and as a former Red Army general. Stalin – not the Soviet system as such – was pilloried as the main enemy of the Russian people. (Here we see the influence of Zykov.) The war against Stalin was the concern, indeed the duty

[1] See Appendix II, page 253.

of all Russians; their true Fatherland was the Freedom Movement. Vlasov called upon his fellow-countrymen to fight for a
new and happy homeland, in alliance with the German people and
'in the framework of a European Community of free and equal
nations'. It should be noted that he speaks of 'alliance', not of
hirelings or quislings, and of the German people, not of the
German leadership. The letter contains no trace of subservience
to Hitler.

It is a proof of how the ideas of former Soviet citizens can
develop, once they are released from the grip of their Soviet
environment, and given the chance to think out their problems
for themselves.

The Ostministerium saw no objection to this 'unpolitical
operation', so that it was possible to have the letter issued and
distributed throughout the occupied zone and in the prisoner-
of-war camps. It was featured in our Russian language press.
Grote arranged for a German translation to be circulated to
officers at the front and to the German personnel in the camps.
The impact of the letter – clear, concise, factual – was enormous.
In due course I was to come across a considerable number of
Germans, many of them highly placed, whose first knowledge
of the existence of Vlasov (or indeed of the whole Russian
problem) had come from reading this letter.

(v)

So much was crowded into those early weeks of 1943. But before
going on to Vlasov's visit to the Northern Army Group, and to
the aftermath of that visit, I must mention certain developments
in Dabendorf.

One day in February an officer in an unfamiliar uniform, one
Sergei Fröhlich, called at my office in the OKW. His papers
showed him to be on the HQ staff of the SA, from which it
seemed likely that his superiors had appointed him liaison
officer with Vlasov's staff. I had known Fröhlich from my Riga
days; we had been members of rival ice-hockey teams. His
father was a prominent businessman. My first thought was that
Fröhlich had been sent by the SA to keep a watch on Vlasov and

my own organization. It seemed an unlikely role for the dedicated young ice-hockey player. But in the Germany of today one could never tell.

There was no point in beating about the bush.

'If,' I said, 'you have been sent by the party to keep a watch on me I expect you to tell me so. But if you are here as a friend, as I remember you from Riga, you are very welcome.'

He looked at me with wide open eyes, and I had no need of further explanation. But the reason he had called on me was of interest. His 'mission' was of his own devising, and arose from his conviction – shared by his friends – that it was only by means of the Vlasov movement that the chance was there to finish off Bolshevism and bring the war in the East to a satisfactory end. Fröhlich was at the same time a German, a Russian and a Latvian – that is, a real European. He had in mind, thanks to his contacts, all sorts of practical ways of helping Vlasov and his staff – arms, foodstuffs, quarters. Very soon we sealed our alliance. Fröhlich, within the limits of the possible and at the cost of personal sacrifice, was to maintain, right to the bitter end, his loyalty to the Liberation Movement and to his ideal of 'the other Germany'.

In view of Vlasov's special position it did not seem desirable that he should reside, permanently, in the Dabendorf camp. There was, of necessity, a set of camp rules, to which we could hardly expect the general to conform. Furthermore, Dabendorf was too far out of Berlin. We looked round for private quarters for him, and found a modest villa in Dahlem where he could settle along with his two principal aides – Malyshkin and Zhilenkov. It was Fröhlich who sought out well-disposed individuals who were willing to provide the necessary. It was he who took charge of the furnishing of the villa in the Kiebitzweg in Dahlem. It was he who, with the help of his contacts, produced the first arms our Russians ever had, machine-pistols, ammunition, W/T equipment. He had an air-raid shelter built in the garden. Then, over a period, the motor-cycles allotted to Dabendorf were one by one exchanged for cars. (There were car-owners who, in view of the shortage of petrol, were willing to take a

motor-bicycle instead.) Fröhlich's help was by no means limited
to the house in Dahlem, and very soon he had won the complete
confidence of Vlasov, Malyshkin and the others.

The regulation rations for the Kiebitzweg party were delivered
by Dabendorf, but Fröhlich personally arranged for extra foodstuffs to be sent by contacts in the Baltic; this was to enable
Vlasov to offer some hospitality to his numerous visitors. He
himself and Malyshkin would take no more than their very
modest regulation rations. My wife told me how touched she was
when she went to see them and Malyshkin insisted on sharing
with her his meagre bread ration and a little synthetic honey.

To start with Dabendorf provided a guard for the Kiebitzweg
house; but later a permanent guard under a Russian commandant
was established there.

(vi)

The appeal of the Russian Liberation Movement grew ever
stronger, due not to any efforts of German staff or front-line
officers but rather to the increasing demands of the Russian
population, and the increasing self-confidence of the Russian
volunteers. They looked to Vlasov as the man who could save
them from the harshness of the occupation authorities and also
from Stalin's reprisals should the Red Army reconquer the area.
And these of course were not their only motives.

Field-Marshal von Küchler and General Lindemann themselves asked that Vlasov should visit the Northern Army Group.
They were aware of the success of his visit to the Central Sector.
Vlasov's first reaction was to inquire whether any decision had
been reached on the demands he had passed to Grote on his
return from the Central Army Group; there was no sense in his
proceeding to Pskov and Gatchina unless the German leadership
was prepared seriously to consider the proposals he had formulated. Grote, as always, though tactful was perfectly frank. Such
stupidity, he remarked, was almost incredible. He was seldom as
outspoken as this but his words seemed to appease the general.
Dürksen, who by now had also won his confidence, talked in
similar strain.

'There are some,' said Vlasov, 'who make out that National Socialism and Bolshevism are much on a par. They are wrong. You people still criticize, you maintain your point of view, you stand up for what you think to be right. The two are as different as chalk from cheese.' He said this to Dürksen in my presence. We explained to Vlasov that he was now being offered the opportunity to meet personally the German field-marshals and army commanders, and win them over to the Liberation Movement. He realized that Grote and Dürksen had done their best, and declared his willingness to visit the Northern Army Group, if only, he added, to see General Lindemann who had behaved so well to him at the time of his capture. Vlasov's tour of the northern area lasted from the end of February to 11 March 1943, and on this occasion he was accompanied by my deputy, Captain von Dellingshausen. The visit was a great personal success for Vlasov – as far as the population was concerned it was a triumphal progress, as evidenced by Northern Army Group reports and the official photographs – but, as will be seen, was doomed to entail a serious set-back for the Liberation Movement.

On Vlasov's return from Gatchina he conferred in strict secrecy with his generals, and in due course I was informed of the following plan:

A strip of the coastal plain along the Gulf of Finland, between Oranienbaum and Peterhof and opposite the island fortress of Kronstadt, had never been occupied by the Germans. Vlasov proposed that he should be allowed to take over this sector with units of the Liberation Army. His objective would be to secure possession of both Oranienbaum and Kronstadt. He gave his reasons for believing this objective could be speedily attained by fraternization between his own troops and the Red Army garrisons. The plan had been worked out in thorough detail and was based on the latest appreciation of Red Army dispositions – including the names of the local Red commanders.

I confidentially discussed this proposal with Grote and Dürksen, and the latter insisted it should be submitted to the

OKH at once. It was 3 a.m. when Gehlen could see me at Mauerwald. He was tired and drawn but his eyes lit up and he smiled when he realized what the proposal was. 'Yes,' he said. 'That is something we can do not only at Kronstadt but on every single sector of the front.' He promised to discuss Vlasov's project with General Heusinger, Chief of the Operations Branch, and with the Chief of the General Staff, but explained he must first deal with urgent matters concerning the Central and Southern Army groups. Then, in spite of the lateness of the hour, he told me in some detail about his new plan – Operation *Silberstreif.*

Operation *Silberstreif* was to let the Red Army know that they had opposite them not only Germans but Russian national formations, fighting for a free Russia, and ready to welcome Red Army personnel. For Soviet line-crossers there would no more be the grim prospect of a prisoner-of-war camp; they could count on a warm reception by their own compatriots, given the chance to serve as free volunteers in their ranks, or at least be assured of employment and a decent livelihood. Gehlen put great hopes in this operation, provided it could be carried through with the cooperation of Vlasov and in connection with the Freedom Movement. Approval for this last had not been obtained. What had so far been agreed was that special Russian groups – each consisting of five officers and fifteen other ranks – be attached to every front-line division of the Wehrmacht. These Russians should have passed through special training courses at Dabendorf, and by the end of April there should be a total of some fifteen hundred available. They should be drawn from existing volunteer units and seconded by the GOC Osttruppen to attend the Dabendorf courses. It was hoped that the flow of line-crossers would enable each special group to grow into a battalion, or even, if all went well, into a regiment. 'Which means,' I ventured to say, 'that apart from the volunteer units already in being we should soon have a Russian Liberation Army.' Gehlen said nothing; but I gathered from his silence that he agreed with what I said.

Neither of us had any inkling of the blow that was to come.

10
A Set-back

THE authorities took no notice of the confidence in General Vlasov evinced by the Russian population during his northern tour, but they seized on a few words of his spoken openly at a luncheon party. He was in the habit of talking quite openly of past failures and errors alike, whether his hearers were Russians or Germans. He would go on to point out that one must learn from past mistakes and conclude by looking to a happier future. His speech of thanks to his German hosts in Gatchina, in which he expressed the hope that one day they would be his guests in Leningrad, was just as one would expect of him. Two months previously – in early January 1943 – when we were collecting clothes for him and his staff, I remember him telling my wife that his dearest wish was to see her as his guest in liberated Leningrad so as to make some return for all the kindness shown him. 'I would so like, dear Madam, to take you round the splendid city from which you were expelled as a small child on the outbreak of the First World War, because you were a German.' It was in just this spirit that he adressed his German officer hosts.

His enemies determined to exploit their opportunity. 'This impertinent Russian sees himself as lord and master of an independent Russia. Scandalous.' The matter was reported to the highest level, and on 14 April Field-Marshal Keitel issued a directive to the effect that in view of Vlasov's 'brazen pronouncements' he was forbidden to undertake any political activity in the army area. Apparently there was also a threat to return him to a prison camp or hand him over to the Gestapo. I personally never saw the order, but Martin informed me verbally of its contents. For Vlasov and Malyshkin this was one more disappointment, but we were agreed that it was just this sort of

\inst which we were fighting and that we had to
fight. Vlasov's own position was much as it had
explained that the Gestapo threat would not be
~y action unless Vlasov launched out on some new
~emarche. 'You have been warned,' said Martin. 'Be careful.
And carry on.'

But it made things very difficult for Gehlen. A visitor from
Fremde Heere Ost told me that Keitel's order had more or less
torpedoed the plans for Operation *Silberstreif*: the prohibition of
any mention of Vlasov or of the Russian Liberation Movement
would rob the proposed operation of its main appeal. My visitor
believed that somehow or other Gehlen would find a way round;
but meanwhile we in Dabendorf must be extremely cautious in
our training courses for the *Silberstreif* teams – nothing about the
Liberation Movement or about Vlasov. I discussed the matter
with Trukhin who grasped the situation at once. 'Don't worry,'
he said. 'This is our concern. We will find a way round without
telling any lies. The great thing is to avoid an open clash, even
though this means our working more or less underground.'

(ii)

What might not Germans and Russians together have achieved
even in that spring of 1943, had they only acted as loyal allies
to free Russia and the world from the Bolshevik yoke. Vlasov and
his colleagues knew very many of the Red Army generals. They
knew the victims of Stalin's purges. They knew whom they
could count on as comrades in their struggle not for German
interests but for freedom.

Vlasov would sometimes tell us of his past experiences. I
remember his account of the occasion, in November 1941, when
Stalin put him in command of the Twentieth Army to check the
German advance on Moscow. He described his wait in the ante-
room, his reception, the watchful reserve of the dictator, the
generals' situation reports, and then Stalin's clear-cut decision.

'I cannot give you many troops, Vlasov. Mostly gaol-birds at
that. But I give you, as I give my other generals, complete freedom
of action to destroy the invaders. The responsibility is yours.'

Vlasov gave a vivid picture of those present, the dictator with his little pipe, the generals, the indispensable and omniscient Malenkov. As he left the Kremlin he was proud to have been charged with so great a responsibility: the enemy were at the gates of Moscow. And then, suddenly, he realized that with the assumption of this responsibility he had delivered himself in pawn to Stalin's caprice. If his effort should be in vain! To be defeated is not merely to be the loser, it is to become a traitor. They were all traitors, he thought, these Red Army marshals and generals – Tukhachevski, Yegorov, Blücher, Yakir, Eidemann, Kork. . . . And their judges had been Stalin and this same Malenkov, and perhaps Molotov, Kaganovich, Shepilov, Bulganin – the men now sunning themselves in Stalin's favour. (Vlasov gave a thumbnail sketch of each of them, and his colleagues added their details. Bulganin seemed to possess some trace of human decency.)

'A declared enemy of the regime is any one who thinks otherwise than he is told. Or who is put up as a scapegoat to carry the blame. The Soviet citizen has learnt outwardly to conform to the requirements of the regime. What he really thinks he must keep strictly to himself. Hence an enforced schizophrenia, the greatest crime the men in the Kremlin have perpetrated.'

Vlasov went on to talk of Nikita Khrushchev, First Secretary of the Central Committee of the Ukrainian CP, whom he had got to know when in command of the Thirty-seventh Army at Kiev. 'I have myself seen this crawling lick-spittle of Stalin's fuming and raging at friend and foe alike. Always the same formula – Counter-revolutionaries! Mensheviks! SRs! Trotskyists! Followers of Bukharin or Zinoviev! When it is a matter of liquidating traitors anyone whose hand trembles or knees sag is an Enemy of the People. Do you imagine I and other officers can forget all this?'

A number of names came out, in a variety of lights, in these conversations – Voroshilov, Malinovski, Rokosovski and others. Malyshkin, Trukhin and Zhilenkov added new names and details. Everyone seemed to have his particular targets. Our Russians knew to whom in the Red Army they could (and wanted to) appeal. But to do so with effect they had to be sure of their own position – not as hirelings in German pay, but as independent Russian fighters for freedom, with a clear goal before them. Gehlen and Roenne were fully aware of the possibilities; but their efforts to create the essential preconditions had so far met with failure.

On one occasion Gehlen, who wished personally to meet Vlasov's principal collaborator, asked Malyshkin to come to Lötzen. In September 1943 the Russian generals had a further opportunity to submit proposals for a major operation. These proposals were passed by Gehlen to the Chief of the General Staff; but though the project envisaged action only in the enemy rear, thus conforming to Hitler's directive, it was completely ignored on the higher level.

(iii)

In the military chain of command Keitel and Jodl were General von Wedel's immediate superiors. One day in my OKW/ Pr office my phone rang. Field-Marshal Keitel was in urgent need of certain information, and as Wedel, Martin and Grote were none of them at the moment available the call was put through to me. A tense moment. Had I got to speak to the field-marshal? However it was his ADC who came on the line: a conference was in session, and the field-marshal must be told at once what 'the Russian Liberation Army' was. I considered rapidly. A false step would be a disaster, and yet I had to take a risk. I had learned something of inter-departmental diplomacy from Grote, though I was not anything like as expert as he was. 'The Russian Liberation Army,' I said, 'is the general term used to cover those Russian volunteer units serving with the Wehrmacht, who, like other locally raised formations, wear their national badges on their uniforms.' 'I understand,' said the ADC. 'Thank you.' He told me to confirm at once by teleprinter to Wehrmacht HQ.

This might have unpleasant consequences for the chief of the OKW/Pr, and I went to find General von Wedel. By this time he was back in his office. 'Things are coming to a head,' he

remarked. 'As it was you who did the talking the confirmation by
teleprinter must come from yourself. I agree with the line you
took, but would suggest you start your message with the prefix
"According to proposals not yet confirmed by the chief of OKW/
Pr, the Russian Liberation Army is the general term used to
cover etc., etc.". If they swallow it at Wehrmacht HQ and do
not start raising hell at me, that means there is tacit approval for
the term Liberation Army to be used for Russian units. And you
can then use it in your newspapers and in Dabendorf without
fear of consequences. Well, you go and sign the teleprinter
message and we will see what happens. I will stand by what I
have told you.'

This was a master stroke by Wedel and I was full of admiration.
There came no sign of dissent from Field-Marshal von Keitel.

(iv)

The work of Dabendorf went on. Our original Chief Training
Officer, General Blagoveshchenski, had announced he had no
wish to remain at his post since the Reich's government refused
to recognize the Liberation Movement. His successor, Trukhin,
maintained an outward show of calm, though inwardly he must
often have had moments of despair; but he welcomed Wedel's
manoeuvre, which helped him in his work, not least in the
training of officer teams for *Silberstreif*. We were now dispatching
teams to their divisions, though the actual operation was postponed.

Instead of the regulation caps and leather gloves as worn by
German officers our Russian officers had been issued with the
so-called *schiffchen* (forage caps) and grey cotton gloves. This they
regarded as an affront, and accordingly I told Pehla, our paymaster, to procure proper caps and gloves on the free market.
On the occasion of one of our passing-out parades General von
Wedel asked the paymaster why our officers were so turned out
in breach of the regulations. Pehla explained that the regulations
did in fact lay down that Russian officers should be equipped like
German officers, but that the supply services had refused to
issue caps or leather gloves; and that the Dabendorf commandant

had therefore arranged for them to be procured at his own expense. Wedel gave orders that the donor should at once be refunded from the OKW/Pr propaganda budget. I mention this little incident to show what could be achieved by private initiative even in the difficult year 1943.

(v)

To return to *Silberstreif*. Gehlen eventually had to launch the operation without Vlasov and his movement, and this no doubt affected the results achieved. Our special teams and propagandists continued to refer to the Liberation Army in their appeals to their compatriots; but the gap between propaganda promises and German realities robbed the appeals of the whole-heartedness they would have otherwise possessed. Some time later I was able to see the relevant reports sent in by divisional intelligence staffs. *Betreuer* teams had been sent to a hundred and thirty divisions in all. Of these ninety-seven had reported that their presence had been of definite value, nine of some value and the remaining twenty-four of little or no value. We agreed that success or failure depended largely on how far the various divisional staffs were prepared to give the operation their backing. As Gehlen himself had his hands tied, it could hardly be expected that divisional intelligence officers should show much enthusiasm for this half measure.

When, in July 1943, the Central and Southern Army Groups renewed their long-postponed offensive in the direction of Kursk, Operation *Silberstreif*, originally planned to support this offensive, had long been dismissed as of little importance.

The Red Army's counter-offensive north of Orel meant that the Soviet armies had regained the initiative.

11

Hitler's Decision

FOLLOWING Keitel's directive banning Vlasovite activity on our side of the front line, little attention was paid to us in the OKW. Wedel and Martin generously, and on their own responsibility, allowed me to carry on our normal routine, provided we did so without attracting notice. But Gehlen, Tresckow and Gersdorff tirelessly continued their efforts. Tresckow and Gersdorff found a favourable occasion to persuade Field-Marshal von Kluge to agree to a 'Russian Centre' being established in the Central Army Group, and Kluge (in mid-May) approached the chief of the General Staff. At Zeitzler's request, Gehlen provided him with a memorandum on how our political warfare had developed, and on the contribution of Vlasov's personality to its success; but Zeitzler carried little weight with Hitler, and in this instance he was not convinced himself.

Vlasov had endeavoured to ascertain Hitler's personal attitude towards the Russian Liberation Movement. In the course of his visits he had put this question direct to Kluge and Schenckendorff as well as to Küchler and Lindemann. The generals' replies had been evasive. None of them had discussed the matter with the Führer. Representations had been made to the Ostminister and the subject had been touched on in discussions (on the partisans and on the lack of security in the rear areas) with Field-Marshal Keitel and with General Schmundt of Hitler's personal staff. But none of these officers, except perhaps Schenckendorff, had a sufficiently clear conception of the problem to be able to put up a convincing case.

Vlasov had repeatedly tried to explain his views to the generals. Lindemann had promised to do his best to obtain a hearing for Vlasov's ideas on the highest level, but he could not approach

Hitler personally. All he could do was to take such opportunities as he could find to raise the matter in his discussions with Keitel and Schmundt. He emphasized that he, personally, was a firm supporter of Vlasov. Unfortunately this was not enough.

Martin told me that he, and other officers, had great hopes in Field-Marshal von Manstein. There was a rumour that Hitler intended to hand over the supreme command, very possibly to Manstein. Here we felt was a gleam of hope.

Captain Bolko von Richthofen who was seconded for some weeks to OKW/Pr was tireless in his efforts on Vlasov's behalf, and had already won over his cousin, Field-Marshal von Richthofen. Richthofen felt prospects of progress would be better served by working through the Air Force. Meanwhile it looked as if the Army General Staff and the field-marshals would be able to enforce a decision on the highest level, now that the situation on all fronts seemed ever more threatening.

So we continued, clutching at one hope and then at another.

A new factor which Gehlen had been able to include in his memorandum to Zeitzler was the Soviet reaction to Vlasov's Open Letter. Hitherto the Soviet authorities had ignored German leaflet propaganda. It was a fact that Red Army prisoners of war considered these German leaflets pointless and ridiculous. The Kremlin maintained silence. But now Russians were appealing to Russians, and the appeals were going home. Red Army personnel were strictly forbidden to pick up or read enemy leaflets. It was now no longer a question of German propaganda. What Vlasov wrote on present conditions and on future hopes was the concern of every Russian. The civilian population picked up the leaflets and the Red Army read them.

Vlasov and the Russian Freedom movement could no longer be silenced. The first Soviet reaction was to announce that Vlasov was dead – murdered by the Germans. Later, as it became obvious that Vlasov was still alive, he was branded as 'a traitor who had sold himself to the German bandits and imperialists'. The Soviet General Shcherbakov, in charge of the anti-Vlasov campaign, was ordered by Stalin to liquidate the

Vlasov myth, and if need be Vlasov himself. For this latter purpose agents were recruited. One of them was parachuted into occupied territory in the spring of 1943 and captured by a volunteer unit. He was interrogated by Malyshkin and Zykov, confessed the object of his mission and gave a number of details regarding Shcherbakov's operations. At Vlasov's insistence the man was pardoned, but Zhilenkov and Zykov insisted on his internment in a prisoner-of-war camp: they well knew the mentality of such agents. During the summer of 1943 two further agents were dispatched. Worth mention is the case of Vlasov's cook, Maria Ignatievna Voronova, who had been captured when he was and who later disappeared in Minsk. There she was worked on by Soviet agents and told to make her way back to Vlasov which she eventually succeeded in doing. Vlasov told us the task assigned to her was to poison him. However, she confessed, was forgiven and continued to serve as cook in the house in Dahlem.

All this was duly emphasized by Gehlen and Wedel in their reports. However, not even the importance attached by the Kremlin to Vlasov and his movement could modify the attitude of the German Supreme Command.

In fact what Stalin had been trying to do was done for him by Keitel and Rosenberg. On the German side of the line, as far as Vlasov was concerned, there was complete silence. When reports came in from the Northern and Central Army Groups of their grave concern at the growing unrest among the civil population and the Russian volunteers, Martin took a bold initiative. On 10 July 1943 he issued a circular statement 'to be passed verbally to German officers commanding Russian and other locally raised units', in which it was said that 'contrary to the assertions of Soviet Propaganda, General Vlasov is in excellent health and in full control of all his faculties'.[1]

Hitler's final decision against Vlasov was made on 8 June 1943.

[1] Martin's action was all the more courageous, because he must have been aware of the Berghof conversation. The minutes of the Berghof meeting on 8 June 1943 (Hitler, Keitel, Zeitzler, Schmundt and Scherff) were published by George Fischer in *The Journal of Modern History*, Vol. XXIII, No. 1 (March 1951), pp. 58–71.

Schmundt gave Gersdorff details of a meeting between Hitler, Keitel and Zeitzler. This was the occasion on which Zeitzler was to have brought up Kluge's and Gehlen's proposal for a Russian Centre. Apparently Zeitzler's performance was most unimpressive. It was at this meeting that Hitler declared straight out 'he had no need of Vlasov behind the front'. He could be of use on the enemy side, and propaganda about the Russian Liberation Army need cause no headaches. (Schmundt emphasized that one could still use the phrase Liberation Army.) But, Hitler added, it would be dangerous if Kluge and the other generals got it into their heads that he was ever going to help Vlasov – or any other Russian – into the saddle as Ludendorff had once done with Pilsudski and the Polish freedom leaders.

This is what we heard from Gersdorff. Wedel had his instructions direct from Keitel. I was told nothing about this meeting by the OKW. From the OKW standpoint the situation was unchanged. Any political activity by Vlasov in the army area had been forbidden following his visit to Gatchina; and the Führer had now formally agreed to the use of his name in propaganda directed at the enemy. There was no excitement in OKW/Pr.

Zeitzler seems to have given Gehlen a very muddled account of his intervention with the Führer, but Gehlen expressed no criticism of his chief when talking to me. For myself I became more than ever convinced that one can never successfully plead a cause unless one believes oneself that the cause is the right one.

(ii)

General Gehlen asked me how Vlasov would react. I could not answer him.

'I must,' I said, 'be completely frank with him. This is a basic and possibly final decision, which cuts away the ground from under my personal understanding with Vlasov.'

'The Führer,' Gehlen replied, 'does not need him. But we all do, and we shall. Tell him that.'

Vlasov and his followers had always hoped that one day reason would win out. It was the dire fate of the German nation that at that time there was no one who could prevail against the dictator.

I told Vlasov that all the officers' efforts to bring about a change of policy on the Liberation Movement had come to nothing. Hitler had rejected the proposals of Kluge, Schenckendorff, Lindemann and Gehlen. Our talk took place in the presence of Malyshkin and also Dellingshausen, on whose advice and help I could always rely. My news was the severest blow that Vlasov had suffered since he had staked his hopes for his nation on the German card.

Now he knew.

'I have always,' Vlasov said, 'respected the German officer – his chivalrous and comradely bearing, his competence, his courage. But these men are flinching when faced with brute force; they accept moral annihilation so as to avoid physical annihilation. I have done that myself. We have here what we have in my country – moral values trampled down by force. . . . I can foresee Germany's defeat and collapse when the *Untermenschen* from prison camps and workers' camps will rise up and take revenge for all that the Germans have done to them. . . . I had wished to spare you that . . . I know there will be varying verdicts on our struggle. We have been playing for big stakes. A man who has once heard the call of freedom must needs ever follow it, come what may. If your Führer imagines I could serve as a tool for his plans of conquest, he is wrong. I shall go back to a prison camp, back to my countrymen in their misery, whom I have not been able to help.'

I tried to tell him this was not necessarily the end of all things, and repeated Gehlen's parting words to me. There was nothing more that I could say.

Dellingshausen suggested we should think things over in the next few days and meet again. Malyshkin turned the conversation to the Decembrists,[1] and quoted the words of one of them under sentence of death: 'Our guilt lies only in our demand for freedom.' We talked for a little about the Decembrists. I cannot describe

[1] The young officers who staged an abortive insurrection against Tsar Nicholas I in 1825.

the aura of gloom hanging over our little circle. In the end we agreed to do as Dellingshausen suggested and think it all over in quiet.

(iii)

A few days later I had a phone call from a general known to me only by name. He asked if a discreet meeting could be arranged between him and Vlasov – myself to be the only other present. He suggested the room of a professor at the University of Berlin. Vlasov agreed. He and I arrived in civilian clothes. The general turned up in full uniform with decorations.

Having introduced himself he said: 'After what has happened I expect you are no longer eager to go on holding this Government's stirrup.' 'I have never held your Government's stirrup,' Vlasov replied. 'Nor your Führer's. It was in the interests of my country and for the sake of my country's freedom that I worked with the Germans since I believed that the German people, as ourselves, were concerned with the overthrow of Stalin. I was taking the same line as Churchill and Roosevelt with regard to Stalin, or, if you prefer, as Stalin in his alliance with Churchill and Roosevelt.'

'Quite,' said the general. 'I entirely understand. And therefore I am asking you not to throw away your rifle.'

Vlasov was going to answer, but the general continued: 'I do not want to hear any details. I am fully informed. All I can tell you today is that a modification or change of the government of the Reich is not impossible. The appointment of a new Supreme Commander is also not impossible. Then we would want to have you with us, General Vlasov. I can give you no dates. But I ask you to trust me as I am trusting you. I laid down no conditions when we began our talk, but now at its close I must request absolute secrecy on what has been said and on my identity. It must remain strictly between the three of us.'

He held out his hand to me as he said this, as if to seal my loyalty.

Vlasov was silent for some time.

'I had written the whole thing off,' he said at last. 'But I believe I understand you, General, and I will go on trying. I thank you for your trust in me.'

The interview had barely lasted twenty minutes.

We left the building separately. We found our little Volkswagen, and the general, without looking round, climbed into his Mercedes.

(iv)

Shortly before this meeting Vlasov had been talking to his most intimate colleagues, including Trukhin and Zykov. These two, particularly Zykov, did all they could to persuade the general to postpone the idea of going back to a prisoner-of-war camp.

'We are Russian conspirators, not Germans. What the Germans think of us is quite irrelevant. . . . If you let go the reins, shady opportunists will take over. And that would be the end of the Russian fight for freedom. Have no illusions, Andrei Andreyevich. There are fellow-countrymen of ours who are worse Nazis than the German Nazis. They are only waiting for you to go so as to take your place. One is already hearing the slogan of the Black Reaction – *bei zhidov, spassai Rossiyu* [Beat the Jews, save Russia]. A grim day for the people of Russia if these Black Reactionaries ever come into power.' Zykov proceeded to give examples. 'There are plenty of them with dubious motives of their own, who do not believe in freedom for Russia and who have sold themselves to the Germans. This last, Andrei Andreyevich, is something that you will never do, nor will anyone of our little conspiratorial group.'

Trukhin said: 'Hitler has shown his true face. The Russian Liberation Movement must now stand on its own, together with the few German friends who remain by our side. The movement lives, though it may not come to full fruition till after we all are gone.'

On that occasion it was Vlasov who asked for a few days to think things over. Then came the meeting with the German general, and he made his mind up. He would stay.

12

Tour of the Third Reich

A SHORT visit by Vlasov to Magdeburg proved to be the prelude to longer tours. As regards Magdeburg we informed the OKW that Vlasov wished to see something of the living conditions of German industrial workers. What we did not report was that following their informal conversations German officials and employers thanked Vlasov for his constructive criticism and advice, and pressed for better treatment and better rations for their *Ostarbeiter*.

Vlasov was now to get to know Germany, and this conformed to the Führer's directive that he should be kept well away from politics. We had already received a number of invitations, the most attractive being one from Erich Edwin Dwinger to Vienna and to the Allgäu. This would keep him well away from trouble. So we set off for Vienna.

Our programme was drawn up and organized by the admirable Gaubauernführer Mayrzedt,[1] who came with us and gave us the use of his car. We were shown round the old imperial city and the countryside in which it is set. We went to the Opera, attended a race meeting, visited a number of factories. In St Stephen's Cathedral a group of faithful stood in deep devotion before an image of the Virgin. As we left the cathedral Vlasov said: 'I wish that I could pray like that. I have lost the faith I had as a child, but I feel that there is some Power above us, and that to cut oneself away from this Power must mean the loss of one's spiritual self. The more I think the more I am convinced that to be cut away from this Power, from divine authority, is the root of all evil, alike for individuals and nations. With that gone there

---

[1] Himself one of the early Nazi Party members, he was executed by the Nazis towards the end of the war.

is nothing that can hold them to their course. But I myself can no longer find that simple faith and say that the Power over us is a personal God and is Our Father. And yet the two good Russian priests I talked to in Berlin are probably right. They say that, without this Father's love, belief in God or in any Power is unavailing. The Germans believe in Providence but that does not stop them being without love and therefore becoming dehumanized. In Russia the point of view is simpler. There is no God and no Providence. The lot of individuals and of nations alike depends upon the production relationships that are in force. And yet in his hour of greatest need Stalin appealed to patriotism and even to God, as mere brute force was seen to be not enough. Often in my village I have seen Russian women whose hearts shone through all the misery and godlessness around them. Was it God's love that was with them? I have read Dostoevsky, but then I was much too young. If I could only pray like these women.'

He was deeply moved as he left the cathedral.

The highlight of our stay in Vienna was a visit to the Spanish Riding School now evacuated to an estate outside the city. The Lippizaner dressage made an indelible impression. The commandant, Colonel Podhajski, arranged an intimate lunch. These Austrians had qualities the other Germans lacked; they were used to peoples of a different race. Their openness and friendliness to their Russian guests brought about a happy and relaxed atmosphere. The commandant made a short speech of welcome, and Vlasov's reply was greeted with warm applause.

'I must offer my thanks, Colonel Podhajski, to you, to your lady wife and to your officers. I am a foot-soldier; if you like, a simple Russian peasant. I know nothing about horses or about your skills and methods. If I were to praise your achievements I should be playing the hypocrite. In any case, what would my praise be worth to experts like yourselves? What I can do is to offer my thanks. I am profoundly moved. And what has moved me most is your love of your horses and your work with them. This, I maintain, is the secret of your success. And I know that we shall only succeed in our struggle for freedom and for peace if and when those working for the same cause come to love each other.

If the Germans would only treat Russians, their prisoners and their workers, in the way you look after your horses, there would then be no Russian problem, and this unhappy war would be long forgotten.'

The Volga peasant's son had found his way to the hearts of this sophisticated gathering.

But even this journey, 'right away from trouble', was not to mean no concern with politics. Either Günter Kaufmann or Mayrzedt arranged for Vlasov to be received by Baldur von Schirach, the Gauleiter of Vienna. The interview took place in what had been Metternich's private study in the Ballhausplatz, and one had the feeling that the ghosts of the Holy Alliance were looking down from the walls. Vlasov did most of the talking. Von Schirach listened attentively. I interpreted.

We had heard a good deal about Schirach, and my mood was one of caution. I was therefore agreeably surprised to find how clearly, and sympathetically, he grasped the points that Vlasov was making. He promised to raise the matter personally with the Führer. Was he really convinced? Had he really learned the lesson of history and of our position today? Or was it fear? (Further set-backs were being reported from the Eastern front.) Before we left he and Vlasov were photographed together: so that what had been said could not subsequently be denied. Then Schirach turned to Dwinger and myself and said: 'Lies and betrayal are no basis for a policy for Germany, let alone for Europe. I will do what I can to put things right before all is lost.'

I heard later that von Schirach kept his word and did in fact take it up clearly and firmly with Hitler; and was rebuffed as all the others had been. Rumour has it that the Führer broke into a violent tirade against Vlasov 'who was now trying to seduce his Schirach'. I cannot vouch for the truth of this last, but I gladly believe that von Schirach kept his promise.

(ii)

Dwinger escorted us to Munich, and from there to Hedwigshof, his country house in the Allgäu. As we entered the Munich hotel Vlasov, as his welcome to Munich, was confronted with a display of *Untermensch* on the bookstall. This nasty little periodical seemed mainly concerned to stigmatize Russians as criminals, cretins, in fact as *Untermenschen*. Frau Dwinger at once bought up all copies in stock, so that the bookstall was clear of it. There were angry comments at this piece of idiocy. But an hour later, as we left the hotel, we were astonished to see fifty fresh copies of *Untermensch* on show on the bookstall. Vlasov told Frau Dwinger not to buy any more. 'You see,' he said to her, 'a case of love's labour lost. Nothing that you can do can help – any more than anything that I have done.'

Apart from politics, Munich with its treasures was a wonderful experience. From Munich the Dwingers took us on to their house in the Allgäu. As already mentioned Dwinger, since the start of the campaign, had pressed for a sensible policy regarding Russia, and had, in consequence, been forbidden to publish. While we were with him he bitterly criticized the Reich's leadership and was able to give Vlasov some useful pointers. Vlasov asked him whether it was Hitler personally who was responsible for the line on Russia. Dwinger replied he could say nothing definite; but a good look at the hangers-on could give one ideas about the boss. At that time Dwinger had no knowledge of what had transpired at the Berghof meeting. A year later, after 20 July 1944, Dwinger spoke out regardless of the consequences. It was providential, he said, that Hitler had survived. Had the attempt on him been successful, the German nation would have ascribed defeat in the war (and the war was lost already) simply and solely to Hitler's death and not to the rottenness of the regime.

We had glorious summer weather at Hedwigshof. We toured the Allgäu, and Vlasov called on a number of peasants. Cleanliness, tidiness, prosperity. He saw the cattle in the pastures. He looked into cupboards and drawers – clothing, good footwear, woollen blankets, china – all treasures that a collective farm peasant could not even dream of. 'I understand,' Vlasov said, 'why the German soldier fights so well. He is fighting not only for his freedom and his country but for the peace and well being of his hearth and home.' He had never before realized that Western capitalist exploitation could offer its workers and peasants, and to each one of them, so high a standard of living. He was particularly impressed that here, in contradiction to the Soviet Union, there was no question of Potemkin villages.[1] Whenever he wished he could stop the car, knock at any peasant's door and ask permission to look round. It was as simple as that.

On a country road we met a group of Russian prisoners of war, returning to camp from their place of work. We stopped and Vlasov talked to them. They were in civilian clothes. They had nothing to complain of, working here with the Bavarian peasants. Food, and indeed treatment generally, had much improved in recent weeks. 'Now we have our own people in Berlin to look after us – Vlasov and the others – things are quite all right.' He asked if they would like to join the Russian volunteers and fight against the Reds, but they explained they had had enough of war, and for the rest of their spell as prisoners they would prefer to stay as they were. The young men could go and fight. Some day the war must come to an end, otherwise one would never get home again. Meanwhile one should leave the old ones in peace. Vlasov said he understood. He was in a blue civilian suit and no one so far had recognized him. But, suddenly, someone at the back pulled out a Dabendorf newspaper. Others crowded round him, looking at the paper and then at this strange Russian who was talking to them. 'It's him!' The paper had a photograph of Vlasov in uniform. Their faces lit up and there was no end to the questioning. But we had to break off. It was our last evening and we must return the borrowed car.

(iii)

Old Frankfurt at that time had suffered little damage from air-raids. We wandered through the ancient narrow streets, redolent of German and of Western history. In Mainz we embarked on a steamer and journeyed down the Rhine to Cologne. On board was a large party of German wounded, badly wounded for the most part. Many had lost an arm or leg; some were horribly dis-

[1] When Potemkin, Catherine II's favourite, took his royal mistress for a tour in south Russia, he had bogus façades of houses erected in the villages to give the impression of great prosperity.

figured by burns. Vlasov turned away and I could see him trying to conceal the depth of his feeling.

'We are all to blame that these gallant men must go through life as cripples. It is for us all to do our best to make amends – all of us, Russians, Germans, Englishmen, Americans, Japanese, Chinese.'

Vlasov stood out a head taller than most of the other passengers and the wounded soldiers must have noticed him. They were down on the hatch, sitting round a long table where a meal was being served them. Suddenly one of them, a sergeant-major, left the party and came up to our table on the upper deck. I was in uniform. Vlasov was standing by the rail, looking at the Rhine landscape. The sergeant-major saluted, and explained he had had a bet. Was that gentleman at the side the Russian General Vlasov? At one time he had served as instructor with a Russian unit in the Leningrad sector, and had now betted his friends this must be General Vlasov. I confirmed that he had won his bottle of Rhine wine.

We had no contacts in Cologne, but a Nazi Party office there had received a telegram from Frankfurt, and a delegation was waiting on the quay to greet us. Following a visit to the cathedral we were invited to an elaborate supper. A few days later, when we were back in Berlin, the party office sent me a bill for our share of the meal.

(iv)

One evening, back in Dahlem after our tour, Vlasov remarked: 'I think I told you that after having seen this splendid country of yours I well understand how the German soldier is inspired by his feelings for his home. But on thinking further there comes the question: this prosperity you have attained by your skill and your effort, does it make you Germans better men?'

I had to say no.

'There we are,' he said. 'This war can only be won by those who can create a better order of things. The Nazis ought to know this well enough. They came to power in Germany's hour of need because they promised a better order, and at first it was their sincere intention to fulfil their promise. I therefore cannot understand how it is that these same Nazis have abandoned their own principles. A higher mission has to be unselfish. But you are not unselfish, you try and rob us of our territory and our resources. That is why you will lose the war.'

The general, like a prophet of old, foretold the collapse of the Third Reich.

'Up to 1946–7 much blood will flow. German cities will be laid to dust and ashes. Terror will loom over Europe. And once the war is over it will be continued by other means and the nations will find no peace. Black will rise against white, the oppressed against their oppressors because these last have renounced their duty and their mission, have failed to be an example to the others . . .'

At this moment, as if to confirm these gloomy forebodings, the sirens sounded to announce yet another of the ever more frequent air-raids on Berlin. There were no public shelters near the Kiebitzweg. Vlasov had given orders that his immediate neighbours should make use of the little shelter in the villa's garden, and this in spite of the strict rule that strangers were not to be allowed on the premises. When we reached the steps down to the shelter the place was already packed. He would not agree that anyone should leave it, and he himself sat in the garden near the entrance till the all clear sounded.

13

Dabendorf under Fire

IN the latter part of 1943 the stream of callers at the Dahlem villa was such that Fröhlich and Vlasov's *chef de cabinet*, the émigré Colonel Kromiadi, had difficulty in keeping to their programme and timetable. Russian officers from the front, officials of the occupied zone, industrialists, clergy, émigré representatives, all seemed anxious for an interview with Vlasov.

The Russian Orthodox priests at that time in Berlin were men of high principle who could not and would not pass over in silence the sad lot of their fellow-countrymen, and who felt that the Vlasov movement opened up the way to an improvement of material conditions and also to the restoration of freedom and human values, so long denied and suppressed by the Marxists. More difficult was the establishment of satisfactory relations with the émigrés: each side regarded the other with deep mistrust. For the men from the USSR this mistrust was part of their background and upbringing. The émigrés, on their side, took the line, 'Can any good thing come out of Nazareth (i.e. the USSR)?' Old émigrés under General Biskupski and the Cossacks under General Krasnov could not and would not accept 'the Red General' as leader of a Russian Liberation movement. Some émigrés refused to understand that the struggle against Stalin could only be undertaken by Soviet citizens, and that the old emigration had a quite separate, and not less important, task in the sphere of culture, politics and economic matters. However, in course of time the difficulties were to some extent overcome. The die-hards on either side remained in opposition, but the realists declared their willingness to cooperate. These last among the émigrés included Professor Rudnev, Colonel Kromiadi, General Turkul, Y. S. Zherebkov and officers – Kravchenko, Count

Lamsdorff, Putilin, Tomashevski and Baron Lüdingshausen-Wolff. Mention must also be made of members of the Rigan student association Ruthenia – Rahr, Ryzhkov and others, who from the start volunteered to act as guards for the Kiebitzweg villa, and who later formed the core of Vlasov's first administrative staff.

Perhaps I have forgotten some of our most devoted helpers. They must forgive me. I have had to reconstruct this list from memory, as the notes I made at the time contain neither names nor dates: I had to reckon with the risk that my papers might come into the hands of the Gestapo.

The number of our German visitors continued to increase – it seemed as if many of our so far unknown well-wishers were choosing this juncture to express their sympathy with Vlasov's aims. Of our old friends we often heard from Dr Knüpffer of the Ostministerium, and the OKW/Pr officers and my former colleagues in 'the club' remained very much in the picture. But there were also newcomers – General Stapf, chief of the Eastern Economic Staff, Colonel I.G. Freytag-Loringhoven and other officers. I shall never forget Lieutenant-Colonel Krafft, commandant of a Russian prisoner-of-war camp in Saxony, who turned up with several copies of *Zarya* and a long list of questions. He was satisfied with his interview, and we soon heard he had introduced a number of measures which greatly improved conditions for his camp's inmates.

(ii)

Zhilenkov used to say, 'If we cannot make progress through military channels we must try the politicians and the party.' And Zykov would add, 'We have to fight on every possible front.'

Yes. But how were we to make the necessary contacts? It turned out that Zhilenkov knew some SS officers. They were not on the highest level, but it did seem that there was some understanding for our cause in the SS. Fröhlich said he could put out feelers through his friends in Riga. Where there is a will there is a way. And, in fact, there were opportunities that came to us.

Klaus Borries had served on various fronts and had been wounded; he was now assistant to the head of the Central Iron and Steel Office. On his own responsibility he multigraphed a number of 'revolutionary' memoranda by Professor Oberländer, Giselherr Wirsing and Günter Kaufmann. He next embarked on a similar campaign on behalf of Vlasov's scheme for Europe. It was Borries who set up the so-called Eastern Works Association (Arbeitsgemeinschaft Ost) in Unter den Linden, with Director Rasche of the Dresdner Bank as chairman. The first negotiations for raising funds for the Vlasov movement were conducted with Borries and Rasche. Vlasov's ideas on the subject, right from the start, were surprisingly clear-cut: no government subsidy, but a loan to the Russian Liberation Movement to be raised if possible from independent private financiers.

(I might mention here that about a year later, on the initiative of the two men named, and with the support of Finance Minister Schwerin-Krosigk, negotiations for a credit were sufficiently advanced for the sum of 1·5 million Reichsmarks to have been made ready. In this case it was a Reich government credit to 'The Russian Liberation Committee of General Vlasov', a condition being that this committee should have acquired the status of a sovereign power. The project was sabotaged, but a number of private banks declared themselves ready to make advances, which in fact they did. Once again Vlasov was astonished at the degree of private initiative still permissible in Nazi Germany. When, finally, the loan agreement was signed in January 1945 it was all too late. Though here again Vlasov's spirit of independence is worth noting. He was a true son of his peasant father, who had once accepted a loan, not a gift, from a German neighbour for the boy's education.)

A friend of ours succeeded in arousing the friendly interest of Dr Julius Lippert, Lord Mayor of Berlin. It is believed that Lippert once pressed Hitler to settle the Jewish question by means of a commission under the chairmanship of the distinguished banker Warburg, himself a member of a long-established Jewish family. To have made such a proposal speaks well for Lippert; but he now felt that nothing would come of any representations he might make on our behalf. Hitler, he explained, no longer listened to him.

Another possible line led to Sauckel, in charge of manpower, and to Dr Robert Ley, head of the Deutsche Arbeitsfront. We never contacted Sauckel. Our interview with Ley will be described later.

My meeting with Count Schwerin-Krosigk was arranged through Klaus Borries and a leading industrialist. It was the first opportunity I had had to explain our case to a minister of the Reich. He accorded me a long interview. He asked questions on the political and, especially, on the economic position in the occupied zone. He inquired about Vlasov himself and his immediate advisers. Finally he raised the matter of the *Ostarbeiter*, the special badge they had to wear and the slur thereby set on men and women working for the Reich. He disclaimed any sympathy with '*Untermensch*' theories, and expressed his disgust at slogans such as 'Russians, Jews, Poles and other rubbish'. These slogans were, alas, posted up in his own ministry; but he explained it was only under the protecting cover of such slogans that any reasonable progress could be made. Finally he thanked me for what I had told him. 'Policy,' he said, 'is of course for the Führer to decide.' But he now, for the first time, had a clear picture of the matters we had been discussing, and this he would bear in mind if and when an opportunity for action should come his way.

I was extremely impressed by his personality and grasp, and the interview filled me with new hope. I still believed that the views of a Reichsminister must carry weight.

On my way out I was called to see the Principal Under-Secretary Reinhardt. He was aware of the object of my visit and would himself like to be informed about the Vlasov movement. 'Today,' he said, 'it is the under-secretaries who count. They can often do more than a minister can.' He promised to put our case to well-disposed under-secretaries in other ministries. But I heard no more from him. No doubt he too ran up against a brick wall.

As weeks went by I became convinced that the Third Reich was ruled not by an élite and not by the party, but by one man, whose mind must be unhinged. . . .

'By one man?' Zhilenkov smiled. 'Not possible. The dictator cannot rule without his instruments, his chiefs of police, his firing squads.' We should win over Himmler and make use of him. Perhaps a way might be found.

Vlasov, Malyshkin and Trukhin did not agree. But before long it was fate that found a way.

Dürksen's energy and enthusiasm were indefatigable. He introduced us to Frau Melitta Wiedemann, who edited the anti-communist periodical *Die Aktion*, and she in her turn introduced us to senior SS officers. These last made a good impression. They did their duty as soldiers, but had for some time taken pains to stop malpractices within their sphere of competence. (This last we heard from Frau Wiedemann.) There were senior Waffen SS officers like Hildebrand and von Herff, and holders of important posts like Dr Wächter, Governor of Galicia. Some of them wished to meet Vlasov because their experiences in Russia had proved the falsity of *Untermensch* theories and had brought them to adopt views in harmony with ours. Every introduction she arranged brought Vlasov a new ally.

Frau Wiedemann was sincere, and at the same time a shrewd tactician. She could not, of course, make Himmler and his organization change their course. Her effort was directed to winning over individual highly placed SS officers to the cause of the Liberation Movement. What more could a woman do? If only there had been more men with her courage and persuasiveness.

No doubt these SS officers' change of heart was often due to purely practical considerations, as had been the case with the Wehrmacht. But even that was progress.

(iii)

Unsatisfactory as it was, our meeting with Dr Robert Ley of the Arbeitsfront is worth recording.

'An OKH officer as interpreter?' asked Ley before we had sat down. 'I have had enough of this OKH.' Then, to me: 'Don't be upset. I have my own interpreter.'

Vlasov was unhappy at the thought of a stranger as interpreter: he could never be sure he was being adequately interpreted. But Ley had with him Paul Walter, who had attended my old school in Petersburg and who whispered to me in Russian not to worry. This of course Vlasov overheard.

Ley asked Vlasov (who was wearing the Order of Lenin and other decorations) why it was that he was now fighting against the Bolsheviks. Vlasov began to explain in some detail. He described his early revolutionary enthusiasm, his civil war service against Denikin and Wrangel, the belief he had held in the rightness of his cause. 'But looking back,' he said, 'I now wonder whether these men were not as true patriots and freedom lovers as we were ourselves.'

He paused to think, and Ley, who had up to now been listening, broke in to say that was of no interest to him, it was all too long ago. He would like Vlasov to put his case more briefly.

Up to 1930, Vlasov continued, he had not been a party member. He then joined the party for the sake of his career as he wished to remain in the army. He went on to describe how his eyes were opened to Soviet realities. The higher he rose in rank the more he saw to condemn. He had seen the impoverishment of the common people as Five-Year Plan succeeded Five-Year Plan. He had seen the Purges and the Terror.

Ley interrupted. 'All that does not interest me either. I know your Open Letter – but that of course was just for idiots, for the common herd. What I want to know is the real reason for your change of mind.' Walter translated and Vlasov rose to his feet. 'Perhaps we should break off the conversation. If I cannot explain all this Dr Ley will never understand why I have taken up the struggle against Bolshevism.'

'I thought Stalin had offended him,' said Ley to Walter.

Vlasov by now had learned enough German to understand; and he recognized the note of contempt in Ley's voice. But he controlled himself.

'It is not a question of myself personally,' he said. 'My concern is with our cause, with our unhappy nation.' Ley asked him to continue. But the conversation became heated as Vlasov went on to describe his experiences in China in 1938-9. He was full of praise for Generalissimo Chiang Kai-shek, and foretold the defeat of the Japanese. Ley did not like such talk about his Japanese allies, and there was need of all Walter's tact.

The conversation turned to the *Ostarbeiter* and the stigma of *Untermensch*. Vlasov was unsparing in his criticism. Then he began to prophesy, as he loved to do. He painted Germany's future in the darkest colours if – which God forbid – the Red Army should approach the frontier. Then the enslaved and humiliated would arise and drive plundering through the German countryside. Woe to the German women and innocent children. But the blame for what was to come lay on those who today were treading human rights underfoot.

Ley interrupted him. 'Enough of crystal gazing.' But he kept his temper and went on to describe his own early work to found the Arbeitsfront. This was something much on his heart, and he lost himself in details. He went on to say that he too wished the Russian workers to be properly treated. But Eastern policy was for others to formulate – Rosenberg, Koch and Sauckel. The Führer had appointed them just for that. And the Führer was a genius – he knew what he wanted.

'But what does your Führer know about Russia?' said Vlasov. 'Perhaps you could tell him. You are a man of forceful personality. Tell Herr Hitler he will lose all Russian territory and will lose the war if he goes on as he is doing.'

'The Führer will manage. We have the Ukraine, and let Stalin try and take it back from us.'

Vlasov gave up his attempts at persuasion. Ley represented the cult of brute force, and seemed to have no idea that the whole edifice was undermined. This was the man whom Hitler once called his 'greatest idealist'. Vlasov rose to his feet and politely expressed his regret not to have succeeded in making clear why millions of Russians were fighting against Bolshevism. He, Vlasov, was only one of very many, a common man of the people.

Ley also expressed his regret. What the general had been saying had been all too highfalutin and complicated. He too was a common man, a man of the people. 'If, General, you had just told me you hated Jews and were fighting Stalin because of the Jews all round him I would have understood. Especially since you told me you had no personal grudge against Stalin. As it is I simply do not understand.'

'Just as I do not understand your attitude to Jews, who as a point of fact have today no influence on Stalin. You are fighting your war against little Jewish children instead of against Stalin. That is what I do not understand, and what you should say to your Führer.'

Walter had only started to translate when Ley sprang up, red in the face. Walter, who, I believe, had once been an enthusiastic Nazi and even a Reichskommissar, was obviously ashamed of his behaviour. '*Dubina*' (idiot), he whispered to me. We parted without a word.

Vlasov was in gloomy mood as we left the building in the Tiergartenstrasse. 'German officers are too polite and far too well-bred to get a hearing with Hitler. Only bulls like this can make any impression. I did my best to convince him but he is a bull with the smallest brain capacity I have ever come across. Josef Visarianovich can wish for no better allies than these men round your Führer.'

(iv)

Although Hitler and Keitel had no need of Vlasov it was now that we were approached both by the German Navy and the Luftwaffe. For the Navy the main concern was the treatment of the Russian auxiliaries they were employing in various capacities. We had a number of talks with Admiral Godt, during which Dellingshausen and I were able to set out the aims of the Vlasov movement. It was later suggested we should have an interview with the naval supreme commander Admiral Dönitz, believed to be sympathetic to schemes of a new European integration. But the interview never took place.

Our first contact with the Luftwaffe was with Lieutenant-

Colonel Holters. He was in charge of a department that undertook the repair of captured enemy material. Their prisoners of war were very well looked after. Holters's adjutant was an Estonian. (I must once again emphasize the importance of a good intermediary when men of different nations have to work together.) The adjutant and his wife were whole-hearted supporters of the Liberation Movement. There was a saying among the Russian pilots, 'Not from fear but from conscience' (*Ne sa strakh a sa savest*). Holters realized that with men like these mere briefing was not enough; there must be some firmer basis for real cooperation. Perhaps the Vlasov movement was the answer.

Vlasov, Fröhlich and I visited Holters's establishment, where his pilots were soon granted a similar status to that of our officers in Dabendorf. Holters arranged that they should attend our courses, where their grey-blue Luftwaffe uniforms excited the envy of our tattered volunteers from Orel or Zaporozhe. Holters thus laid the foundation for the future air squadrons of the Russian Liberation Army.

These pilots were not under the jurisdiction of the GOC Osttruppen – another administrative gap that we were able to exploit. For instance, such matters as leave and rations were not subjected to the Osttruppen norms. I took full advantage of the opportunities here offered. Göring would hardly have believed his eyes had he seen these well-turned-out *Untermenschen* whom one could hardly tell apart from his own Luftwaffe officers. Holters was both circumspect and resourceful. He hoped before long to win over his superiors to our cause. 'Things will move quicker with us than with you,' he used to say. (These hopes were very much like those that we in the OKH had once cherished, back in the Vinitsa days.) The Soviet air force colonel, Maltzev, made an excellent impression and was soon on the best terms with Vlasov. Among the plans discussed was the formation of Russian parachute units. To drop Russians from the air on Moscow might lead to incalculable results.

We soon secured the support of General Aschenbrenner, formerly Air Attaché in Moscow and now GOC *Ostflieger*. He came to Dabendorf and called on Vlasov in Dahlem; from the very beginning the two generals were in complete agreement. Aschenbrenner knew Moscow and the personalities in Stalin's entourage. There was, he held, no point in a blind campaign against Communism or against Judo-Bolshevism à la Goebbels. He knew the varying attitudes of the individual Soviet leaders; there were, he maintained, those among them with a thirst for freedom, and these would certainly be on our side. Indeed they might perhaps themselves have overthrown Stalin had we not played the part of brutal annexationists and labelled all in the Soviet camp as criminals and *Untermenschen*. Aschenbrenner named a number of Soviet leaders whom he counted as his friends – among them Mikoyan and Voroshilov. Vlasov for his part knew a number of senior generals who were, he maintained, anti-Stalin.

Later on, when Dabendorf came under sustained attack from every quarter and when the GOC Osttruppen refused to come to our aid, the suggestion was made that our training camp be transferred to some area under Luftwaffe command. Our ostensible motive for the move was the frequent interruption of our courses by the continuous air-raids on Berlin. We made several journeys, including one to Pillau in East Prussia where we found suitable accommodation available. General Gehlen agreed. As it was, the plan never materialized; but we had to be prepared for every eventuality.

(v)

A proposal of Zeitzler, approved by Hitler, ran: 'Locally raised formations are to be of not more than battalion strength. Remuneration should be of some kind or other, in money or promises.' But at the very moment when Hitler ruled out units of more than battalion strength there had come into being the Cossack Division under General von Pannwitz, the Russian Defence Corps in Serbia, under the émigré General Steifon, and other large formations as well. Professor Oberländer was commanding the so-called 'Mountaineers' Regiment, composed of Caucasians, which had served with distinction with the Southern Army Group. This I learned from a memorandum of Oberländer's, a copy of which reached me from the OKW.

Oberländer pressed for the setting up of Russian and Ukrainian Liberation Armies with the status of allies. Our Russians in Dabendorf knew of the contents of this memorandum, though of course they had not seen the actual document.

At about this time a number of Caucasian volunteers arrived in Dabendorf. As soon as the Ostministerium heard of this there was a sharp reaction. 'Vlasov is playing Great Russian politics. He is now getting his grip on the national minorities. The Georgians must be freed from the claws of these Great Russian chauvinists and returned to their Georgian units.' The Ostministerium always had time for this sort of thing, which of course made for bad feeling on the part of the Vlasovites.

At the same time in Dabendorf we were benefiting by the concessions secured for us by the GOC Osttruppen. In some respects, thanks to the tacit acquiescence of our superiors, we were faring rather better than the regulations allowed. The main difference between ourselves and the GOC Osttruppen was the political aspect. In Dabendorf we were laying the foundations of a new, free and national Russia as desired by Vlasov. The GOC Osttruppen, on the other hand, had merely to ensure that the volunteers' conditions of service were the same as those of the German troops alongside whom they were fighting. But no concessions to nationalism, and no nationalist war aims. This difference in attitude was later to lead to serious clashes between the GOC Osttruppen and Dabendorf. I have already explained that Grote, Dellingshausen and I regarded Dabendorf as the heart of the Russian Liberation Movement and as a purely Russian centre. So that from the beginning I had refrained from any sort of interference in Russian affairs: my role was that of liaison officer between Dabendorf and my official superiors, or of adviser or intermediary. Of course as officer commanding Dabendorf it was I who bore the responsibility, perhaps a wider one than could be found elsewhere. One of my former OKH colleagues tried to comfort me. 'Lawrence of Arabia had his difficulties, even though he had to do with Englishmen who are usually more flexible than we are.'

The role of intermediary was not always easy. Our new friends, thanks to their upbringing in the totalitarian USSR, had a way of thinking that was new even to us. Most of them approved not only of the February but also of the November Revolution with its slogans of liberty and social rights. This second revolution we ourselves saw only in its evil aspects. The attitudes of Vlasov and Trukhin, Malyshkin and Zhilenkov were not always in harmony. Zykov, on the left, took a line approximating to that of the Russian Menshevites. Zaitsev and his friends followed the NTS. No doubt there were internal arguments between the proponents of these different views: but they were united in their hostility to Stalin. We, the Dabendorf German officers, could not and would not become involved in questions of ideology and programme so long as all were working for our common aim. There were of course difficulties; but in spite of these, and thanks to the team spirit pervading all, the Dabendorf community remained intact.

(vi)

Our position grew more difficult from day to day. By the late autumn of 1943 the position was wellnigh intolerable. Dabendorf was shot at from all sides. The air-raids caused us least concern. We took cover in the trenches at the edge of the wood and suffered no casualties, though our huts were frequently hit with light incendiaries. Once a land-mine came down near the camp and blew off two of our roofs, but the damage was soon repaired. Daylight attacks interfered with our training, and some courses had to be prolonged.

Attacks from our German enemies were more dangerous. I have mentioned the Ostministerium's jealous watch over the national minorities, and their attacks on Vlasovite Great Russian chauvinism. The SD and other organizations under Himmler (we were never able to tell them apart) used ammunition of a different kind. 'Dabendorf is a hot-bed of Communists. Dabendorf is anti-German and anti-Nazi. There are no portraits of Hitler in Dabendorf. Dabendorf serves as refuge for Jews, Poles, spies and criminals. Dabendorf keeps up clandestine communication with the English, and with the French resistance.'

My officers were continually being called to Osttruppen HQ for interrogation by the Abwehr because, apparently, the SD had whole files of evidence against the Dabendorf commandant. He was even suspected of being an agent of the British Intelligence Service. Then there were complaints of lack of discipline, drunkenness, addiction to garlic and goodness knows what else – anything to discredit our cause. Even the high standard of catering in Dabendorf was held against its German administrators. The accusations were based on evidence from unidentified sources who, I guessed, might well include German communists as well as rabid Nazis, disgruntled émigrés, Red Army turncoats, NKVD agents and so on. Among the targets of course was our Abwehr security officer, von Kleist.

'Kleist is in the Russians' pocket. He spends his whole time with the senior Russian officers and is quite blind to anti-German infiltration on the lower level. He should be removed at once.' These charges, of course, were all supported by 'evidence'. As already mentioned it was the task of Russian leadership to guard against enemy infiltration, a task that was successfully and intelligently carried out.

There was also the difficulty that our defence against any one charge laid us open to another. If we showed that General Trukhin, as a Russian nationalist, could not possibly be a Bolshevik, the reply came back that as a Russian nationalist he must inevitably be anti-German.

Attacks from the GOC Osttruppen were often very dangerous. An officer of the general's staff there had been, in the early months, an active friend of our movement; but since our set-back following the Führer's ruling he had become a changed man. He knew little or nothing of Russian affairs, our cause had never been very near his heart, and so, like many others, he took the line of least resistance. Dabendorf, he suggested, must be 'assimilated' to the GOC Osttruppen's policy; Dabendorf must be supervised by responsible Abwehr organs; Russian generals and officers must be placed under control; they should, in fact, be Russians in German pay, a 'so-called Russian Liberation Army for purposes of Propaganda' – in the spirit and letter of Hitler's

June directive to Keitel. As already explained, Dabendorf as a Russian unit came under the GOC Osttruppen. When this officer told me that the general was setting up an inspection commission to look into the unsatisfactory state of affairs in my command I had no grounds on which I could protest.

Once again Gehlen took action. Instead of the inspection commission it was Captain Peterson of Gehlen's staff who appeared in Dabendorf.[1] When Peterson maintains that the Germans in charge of the camp 'had let go of the bridle', he merely confirms a fact of which we – those of us in charge – were proud. We had not 'let go of the bridle' (which, incidentally, would have been inevitable at some stage or other). We were merely following, as already explained, the policy of working through the Russian leadership which we had adopted from the very first. Peterson's dictum, 'Certainly anti-Bolshevik, but not pro-German', is further confirmation that the Vlasovites were not paid mercenaries but Russian patriots. His recommendations regarding 'stricter discipline', 'supervision of personnel when out of camp' and 'setting up of a security organization' are perfectly proper from the point of view of a German officer in charge of Russian auxiliaries; but our task was a different one and a higher one.

Peterson wrote me a private letter: 'When one is, officially, conforming to orders from above, action at the behest of one's own private conscience must be so devised that it does not come to notice and yet attains its aims.' Peterson achieved a reconciliation between the regulations and his private conscience with great skill. His conscience told him he must help us. So he concluded: 'The camp has fulfilled the task that was set it, as it provides trained (and for the most part competent) propagandists for the front and for the *Ostarbeiter*.' The GOC Osttruppen's attack was thus deflected by Peterson's report.

---

[1] Extracts from Peterson's report appear as Appendix III, see page 256.

(vii)

The contacts that our Dabendorf Russians had established outside Germany were also regarded with suspicion.

Yurey Z. Zherebkov was at the head of the Russian Émigré Centre in France. He came of a Cossack family, and his grandfather, at that time the senior Cossack general, had been ADC to the tsar. As already mentioned, young Zherebkov, unlike so many émigrés, had soon recognized the important role that the Vlasov movement could play in the liberation of Russia. He realized that the old émigrés were too out of touch with Russian realities effectively to lead a fight for freedom on Russian soil, though their knowledge and experience of the West could prove of great value to the recent émigrés. Zherebkov frequently visited Berlin and made the acquaintance of General Vlasov. The latter was invariably cautious and reserved when first meeting the old émigrés. All the same Zherebkov was most impressed by his personality, and decided to win over the support of the émigrés in France for the Liberation Movement. In this he met with remarkable success; and in due course Vlasov's relationship with the Paris émigrés was far more cordial than with those in the Reich – where some of them had become nazified and others unwilling to follow the lead of a former Soviet general.

Zherebkov invited Vlasov to come to Paris and address the émigrés there. For obvious reasons it was impossible for Vlasov to accept, and Malyshkin and Boyarski went instead of him. Malyshkin spoke at émigré meetings and to representatives of the press. His theme was the aims of the Russian Liberation Movement for a new, free and undivided Russia. His success was enormous. National feeling, so long suppressed, burst forth in spontaneous enthusiasm as this former Soviet general with the old imperial epaulettes on his uniform spoke to his émigré compatriots about their country. The anti-German element was impressed by the argument that, in the interests of the Russian people, the desirability of German cooperation in the struggle against Bolshevism should override former feelings of dislike. Any sensible German should have been delighted with the success of Malyshkin's appeal and grateful to him for having made it.

Not so the Nazi leadership. On the very next day Grote was bombarded with complaints by the SD, by the staff of the Wehrmacht and by other authorities. SD informers who had been present at the Paris meeting had reported that Malyshkin 'shamelessly challenged the policy laid down by the Führer'. The SD demanded immediate action, and punishment, but Zherebkov had good contacts with the staff of the Supreme Command in France and with other 'sensible authorities'. With their help he was able to produce what purported to be stenographic reports of the proceedings, which showed the accusations to be without foundation, so that what might have been a serious blow to the movement was averted.

14

The Volunteers in the West

I HAVE described the period from June 1941 up to the German check in front of Moscow as the era of the great anti-Stalin revolution, but this description no longer held good in the autumn of 1943. Vlasov and Malyshkin agreed with me but still maintained it was not too late for a turn of the tide. They must have been wiser than I was, for they were still prepared to lead the Russian anti-Stalin revolution. The so-called Russian Liberation Army was certainly no military factor: but Vlasov and his friends believed that a revolution of the Russian and other peoples of the Soviet Union was still possible. To anticipate, I might note here that a year later, in late 1944, line-crossers from the all-conquering Red Army were still coming over to the Vlasov units. The SS Standartenführer Gunther d'Alquen was reporting to Himmler that his 'Vlasov operation' (in June 1944) had increased the number of line-crossers tenfold. Later that year, following the Prague Manifesto, Fröhlich told that some 2,500–3,000 applications to join the Liberation Army were coming in daily from the occupied zone, from prisoner-of-war camps and from *Ostarbeiter*. Sacks full of applications were delivered by post every morning, so that back in 1943 Vlasov and Malyshkin seemed to have assessed the position more accurately than I did.

In autumn of 1943 blame for small-scale enemy penetrations along the Eastern front was laid by Hitler and Keitel at the door of the Osttruppen. It was even alleged that whole battalions had gone over to the partisans in the rear zone. On receipt of these reports Hitler, in a rage, declared that locally raised formations must be disarmed and disbanded, and the men – all 800,000 of them – sent to work in the mines and in factories. How all this could be carried out in face of ever-increasing enemy pressure was something no thinking officer could comprehend. Who would take responsibility for this drastic drop in effective strength? And, incidentally, how could the mines or industry usefully absorb this enormous intake of unskilled and unsuitable manpower?

The OKH raised valid objections. Hellmich and Herre prevailed upon the chief of the General Staff to delay implementation, and Hellmich put urgent inquiries to all divisional commanders throughout the front. Replies received enabled him to give Zeitzler convincing evidence that the reports reaching Führer HQ did not correspond to the facts. Incidence of desertion among the Osttruppen was by no means alarming: losses were more or less on a par with those of German units. We were told that even Field-Marshal Keitel was having grave misgivings about the proposed measure.

The final decision came in October 1943. No disarming. The Führer ordered that all Osttruppen be transferred to the west – to France, Italy and Denmark. 'We have at least saved the substance', said Colonel Herre. All that was left to us was to try and believe what he said.

But much harm was done while all the argument was going on on the higher levels. In Dabendorf we had orders to send officers and men from certain volunteer battalions for work in the mines. This order came in shortly before the end of the course, and the volunteers were still waiting for their new German uniforms. Dellingshausen and I, in agreement with Trukhin, decided to send the men back at once to their units in the east. This was possible because this particular course had been delayed, and according to the official timetable the men should already have left Dabendorf. The GOC Osttruppen laid down that all those on training courses with us should be sent to Sauckel's Labour Office, which led to sharp exchanges between Dabendorf and the Osttruppen staff. Before the argument was over the men were *en route* back to their units. It was only a very small number, those not yet assigned to any unit, who went to the mines. Following the decision to transfer the volunteers to the west the position became easier.

A far more difficult case was when Hellmich ordered a Russian unit in the rear army area to be disbanded. It happened that Zhilenkov, on Vlasov's orders, was then visiting the unit. The men threatened to mutiny. Zhilenkov put through a long-distance phone call to inform me that, to his regret, he must put himself at the head of the mutineers. Herre, Hellmich's chief of staff, was unable to help me and I hurried to Mauerwald. Once again Gehlen smoothed things over. Herre, of course, was in an impossible position. Who could dare act against the orders of the supreme commander even though these orders might be impossible to carry out?

Those were grim days. The ground had been cut away from our feet. The transfer to the west did indeed obviate the greater catastrophe – and for this I learned later we had Hellmich and Herre to thank; but the decision put an end to hopes of changing the course of the war in the east as envisaged by Gehlen and his friends in the OKH – Wagner, Stieff, Stauffenberg, Altenstadt and others. So much for German insight.

For the volunteers it meant the end of their hopes ever to see their homes again. They may not as yet have clearly realized this, but they had a sense of grim foreboding. Most of the volunteers had fallen into German hands in the early months of the campaign. Behind them was the Soviet terror. Of the West they as yet knew nothing. They recognized the Germans' superiority, and believed in a German victory. They were not revolutionaries. They had no political aims, no leader and no organization. Uppermost in the minds of most of them was to survive the war and not to starve. They were apprehensive of life in a prison camp in a strange country. They wanted to stay in their homeland, in familiar surroundings, where they had friends and relatives, where people spoke their language and where they could make their way home on foot. Stalin had declared all those taken prisoner to be traitors. The first Germans they had met had been friendly, spoke their language, understood their needs. Friendliness and understanding was something they had never met in their Soviet bosses. So they became auxiliaries or volunteers because fate had so decided, and because each of them had his own particular grudge against Stalin.

Once on the German side of the line they saw how different were the two worlds. But as months and years went by they came to realize that Germans thought of Russians as second-class citizens, though their own commanders and certain others with whom they had to deal might have been exceptions. Russians are quick to notice, and they saw how things were. At the front they had their ups and downs. There was still no victory and no return to their homes. Doubts came to them, and hopes grew dim. And then one day there was General Vlasov who spoke to them in their own language, who knew their needs, who opened up new vistas. Life and struggle once more seemed to have some meaning. And then, abruptly, nothing more was heard of Vlasov. Where was he? What was he doing for them? True they now had their pay and their rations. But what was the sense of it all? Was the war going to last for ever? The whole picture had changed. The Red Army was winning victories all along the front. Partisans in the forests were appealing to them to come over and join them, offering them Father Stalin's promise of a free pardon. And as the Germans retreated the partisans remained behind on their native soil. It was that that was so tempting.

But in spite of this tempting incentive the GOC Osttruppen's reports showed that the number of desertions was surprisingly small. That was evidence of the volunteers' morale; and showed how wrong had been the ideas of Hitler and Keitel.

(ii)

When I told Vlasov what they had decided he declared straight away that he would have nothing more to do with these hirelings. It would be a patent fraud to apply the name volunteer to men who were now mere German cannon fodder. The Russian Liberation Movement repudiated the whole idea of war against Americans, English and French. Hellmich's achievement in 'saving the substance' was branded by Vlasov as shame and as treachery. Russian volunteers had never undertaken to serve German interests. At Novgorod, in front of Moscow, at Kharkov and along the Don they declared themselves ready to fight for the liberation of their homeland. That was their sole objective. He himself would go back to a prison camp. 'We have heard no more from that general of yours with whom I had an interview in the university building.' I had no answer to this last remark.

Vlasov called a meeting of Malyshkin, Trukhin, Zhilenkov and Zykov. All of them took the opposite line. The decision, they maintained, was only what one had to expect from the 'Suiciders'; but the Russians at the front had been deceived by the Germans and were now in serious straits. In no circumstances could or should one leave them to their fate. 'The Russian Liberation Army does not exist. But these unfortunates are and remain our fellow-countrymen, and for us they are our Liberation Army.' This last was Trukhin's summing up. 'We have our cause,' Zykov added, 'and our own task. Not even Hitler can take this away from us.'

Vlasov fortunately had the quality of being able to listen to others. He postponed his decision.

(iii)

The transfer of the Osttruppen to the west was taken in hand at once. It was a Führer's order and thus took priority over all other matters, however urgent. The transfer was completed in January 1944. The operation was made easier by the fact that a number of German divisions whose auxiliaries' establishments were under strength switched their volunteers, with the latter's consent, to the category of auxiliaries and thus retained them under their command. This meant that there were considerably fewer volunteers to be moved to the west. Colonel Herre turned a blind eye to what was happening, and indeed he and his staff did what they could to help.

The volunteers still had no idea of why they were being transferred. The GOC Osttruppen staff issued explanatory notices, but the Russians by now were not prepared to accept everything the Germans told them. They had arrived in a new world, perhaps a better world, but even so they felt homeless and uprooted. Meanwhile, German officers and men in the west knew next to nothing about these Russian, Ukrainian, Caucasian and Turkic volunteers, apart from a recent rumour to the effect that they

were unreliable. A new post had been created, General of Osttruppen in the Western Command, but its holder, General
Niedermayer, was as helpless as anyone else.

Soon there was argument and misunderstanding. In addition
most of the battalions were inadequately equipped, and the men
untrained in matters of technique. So that quite apart from the
psychological aspect, tension and friction increased to an extent
that seriously alarmed the German command. Something had to
be done.

The volunteers insisted on being told why they had been removed from their own country and what they were doing in the
west. They demanded further that Vlasov himself should tell them.
The GOC Osttruppen was astonished at this evidence of Vlasov's
prestige: he had imagined that his influence was only in Dabendorf.

Meanwhile the call for a declaration from Vlasov was not confined to the volunteers. I do not know whether the initiative for a
second Open Letter came from the OKW/Pr or from General
Jodl. I was told that Jodl had remembered the existence of Vlasov
and gave orders that the Russian general should calm and
reassure his compatriots in France.

This new Vlasov letter was to inform the volunteers that the
object of their transfer to the west was to facilitate the amalgama-
tion of the small formations into regiments and divisions of the
Liberation Army – an operation that could not be undertaken
under enemy pressure on the Eastern front. Their transfer to the
west was merely temporary, and their ultimate task remained the
liberation of their homeland. Grote, Dürksen and certain Russians
worked out a draft on the lines laid down by Jodl, and the draft
was submitted to Vlasov. Vlasov asked me if Jodl really meant
what he said about the Liberation Army. This was a question I
could not answer. Grote explained the draft had been made on
orders from Jodl, and was to be submitted to him for confirmation. I believe Grote said this to save my conscience from twinges
over what I might have to say to Vlasov. But, I thought, supposing Jodl did confirm the draft, then he would have to keep his
word. He could not back out.

If, Vlasov declared, the military authorities had in fact decided to break with their previous policy, then he was ready to agree to the letter provided certain alterations were made – the most important being that all Russian units should be placed forthwith under his command. Grote said that that, unfortunately, could not be discussed at the moment.

The point, in fact, never was discussed. Jodl approved the draft and it was printed and distributed before any answer was given to Vlasov on his demands. He never signed the letter. When he heard what had happened he repeated that he would have nothing more to do with Russian troops in France so long as they were serving German interests under German command, and insisted that this declaration of his be brought to the notice of General Jodl and of the GOC Osttruppen.

To put some check on muddle and misunderstanding, Dabendorf was instructed to send propagandists to France to do their best to soothe the troubled spirits. But, as was natural, the briefing they received from Trukhin and Zhilenkov was inconsistent with the line laid down by the GOC Osttruppen. Some of these propagandists were arrested, others sent back to Dabendorf. And at the same time Dabendorf was ordered to dispatch more propagandists. It was complete chaos.

Malyshkin, Trukhin and Zhilenkov went to France, well aware that they would be exposed to all manner of attacks. Their task was ambiguous. These troops were not under their command, but might well before long be entrusted to them, and the one true fact that they had to put across was that 'General Jodl, and/or the German Supreme Command had approved the so-called Open Letter of General Vlasov.' The manner of presentation was left to the individual speakers. Malyshkin and Zhilenkov in their talks to the troops invariably emphasized that the transfer to the west was merely temporary. 'We are not here to fight the Americans or English. That is for the Germans. The Liberation Army, as soon as set up, will resume its struggle for the liberation of our homeland.' This was in direct contradiction to the directive of the GOC Osttruppen to the effect that the war against the Western Powers was part of the war against Bolshevism. The speeches of the two Russian generals were of course reported to the German command, and there ensued a new spate of attacks on Dabendorf. But for the time being these attacks were not dangerous. The OKW was quite satisfied if the unrest could only be calmed down. There was no need to worry if the Russian officers said more than what, strictly speaking, they should have said and thus gave the volunteers new hopes. It might be a deception, but it worked.

However, the volunteers soon realized that the promises were not being kept. Russian units were being incorporated as fourth battalions in German regiments, or split up in other ways. Malyshkin and Zhilenkov returned to Berlin in a state of extreme depression. They had to admit that Vlasov was right and that the volunteers were being tricked. But what could they do?

I went to France with Zykov to study the position on the spot. We had long discussions with our hard-pressed liaison officer, Rittmeister von Bremen. We called on the various military authorities including General Hellmich and his staff. The general, as ever, was straightforward and frank. He had done all he could, he said, and there was now nothing left for him but to obey orders. His conscience was uneasy at the recent develop-ments, and what he wished was to go back to the front and take command of a German division. But his underling, who had made trouble for us before, took a different line. He let it be seen that he regarded Dabendorf propaganda as contrary to the in-tentions and the will of the Führer: he was therefore bound to take action against the Dabendorf officers concerned. True, the Open Letter had been approved by General Jodl, but one should not therefore take the promises made too seriously. Dabendorf was becoming a nest of conspirators and anti-German elements. It was high time it was suppressed.

Hellmich said a few kind words designed to soothe me and we took our leave.

That evening Zykov, Zherebkov, von Bremen and I took a walk through the narrow streets of the Latin Quarter. Zykov suddenly stopped. 'Look, Wilfried Karlovich, these old houses with their beams and projecting gables. I feel any moment D'Artagnan might appear. And a horse and carriage. The Three

Musketeers! I have never been to Paris before. But all this – this is old-time Europe. And I feel that we belong here, and that I have seen it all before . . .'

Apart from France, volunteer units were also transferred to Italy, Denmark and Norway. So teams of Dabendorf propagandists had to be sent to these three countries, and German liaison officers appointed. But here we were spared the troubles with which we had been beset in France. In Italy Trukhin had a personal interview with Field-Marshal Kesselring which smoothed the path for our people, and in Denmark and Norway nobody seemed to bother about them.

A very large number of volunteers had, as I have mentioned, remained in the east. Communications had become an important matter for us, and here we were sometimes aided by other than military quarters. In Riga for instance, thanks to Fröhlich's personal contacts, we secured the cooperation of Dr Werner Kapp (who had helped us over the Dahlem villa and was now attached to the General Commissariat for Latvia) and the SS Gruppen-führer Schröder. Before very long Dabendorf had established a regular and reliable courier service, Berlin–Paris–Riga–Verona–Copenhagen–Oslo. My various chiefs knew little about what was going on. Von Dellingshausen, who organized the network, never said a word more than was strictly necessary.

Meanwhile Zykov and other close associates of Vlasov had established touch in Prague with former members of the Czech General Staff. This was not an anti-German manoeuvre. The task of these emissaries was to win over adherents to the idea of a European Community of Nations, first formulated by Werner Daitz and now firmly adopted by Vlasov. The seed fell on fruitful soil both in Prague and also in Yugoslavia where contact was made not only with the Russian Defence Corps but also with Yugoslav patriots of various shades of opinion.

(iv)

On 1 January 1944 General Köstring was nominated to succeed Hellmich as GOC Volunteer Formations. We believed that this

was a further attempt on the part of the OKH to revive the idea of
political warfare. Count Stauffenberg, severely wounded in North
Africa, had returned to become Chief of Staff in the Allgemeinen
Heeresamt and had been active in putting through this appointment.
Köstring had been, for many years, a highly successful German
Military Attaché in Moscow. Born in Russia, he knew the country
and the people and spoke perfect Russian. He had contacts
throughout the upper Soviet hierarchy, and had won the admiration, indeed the friendship, of a number of senior Red Army
generals. All this and more I had learned from a school friend soon
after the start of the war in the East. My friend added that
Köstring had warned Berlin that, notwithstanding the Tukhachevski purge, the Red Army must not be underestimated. He
had emphasized the growing potential of the Soviet armament
industry. He had disagreed with Hitler's view that it was the
Soviet intention to attack the Third Reich. Köstring knew his
Russia well enough to realize that Stalin aimed at world revolution; but he was also familiar with the classic Soviet precept that
the capitalist powers must first tear each other to pieces, and then
the ripe fruit would fall into the Kremlin's mouth.

What I found of particular interest, and was later told by
Köstring himself, was that long before 1939 he had reported on the
growth of patriotic propaganda in the USSR, and had foretold
that this might well become a decisive factor in the event of war.

This man with his knowledge of the enemy and with his
unique experience was not appointed as adviser to Führer HQ on
his return from Moscow; and no one at the time could understand
why this was so.

As already explained our volunteer detachment at Dabendorf
came under the command of the GOC Volunteer Formations.
Some weeks after his appointment I was summoned to report to
him at his HQ near Lötzen. I had heard so much about him that I
had a feeling of tension as I entered his room.

Our first interview lasted nearly three hours. He began in his
slow precise voice by asking me a whole series of questions: how
Dabendorf started, our relations with OKW/Pr, with the OKH,
Vlasov and his collaborators, our training policy and programme,

and so on and so on. My explanations were often interrupted by some sharp and humorous comment, which emboldened me to speak with complete frankness. I went so far as to speak of our recent differences with the staff of the GOC Volunteer Formations.

The old general seemed to know everything and to understand everything. He began to tell me, in another key, of his experiences over the last ten years. He remembered describing (on his return from Moscow in 1941) how correctly the Soviet authorities had treated the German Embassy staff on their journey south; and this had so disgusted Hitler that he did not address a word to his military attaché for the rest of the meal. And never since that day, Köstring added, had the Supreme Commander shown the slightest desire to hear his views on any current problem.

Stalin, he went on to say, had often abruptly changed his course. So had Churchill. But Hitler would never modify his policy regarding Russia. The Führer had declared once and for all that he had no intention of giving the peoples of Russia their independence. Accordingly the Russian Liberation Army must remain a fiction. He, Köstring, had had this clearly confirmed since taking up his new command. Therefore, to his regret, all he could do as a soldier was to conform to this directive. He would carry on the work of his predecessor Hellmich in assimilating the service conditions of the volunteers to those of the Wehrmacht. 'I can and I will do all that is possible to ensure humane and correct treatment for those men who are fighting on our side. I will endeavour to raise their status to that of our Germans. I will do what I can for the *Ostarbeiter*. But these are the limits of my activity.'

In spite of my disappointment I could not but respect the clarity and integrity of the man, carrying out his duty as a soldier and fully aware of the tragedy involved. Later I was to hear of striking instances where his devotion to the well-being of the volunteers went far beyond the strict letter of his instructions.

I found that his instinct and his experience had led him to think on 'Great Russian' lines, though he explained that in the nationalities question he would be bound to follow the policy laid down by Rosenberg. Like Vlasov he believed that after the overthrow of Bolshevism (now merely a theoretical concept) the peoples of Russia should have the opportunity to decide on their own future within the framework of a European community. We went on to discuss this project, as I was eager to find some common ground with him.

I asked if I should arrange a meeting with Vlasov. This he declined. 'Vlasov has become a sort of scarecrow for the Führer and for the men at the top of the OKW. Accordingly I prefer to carry on without personal contact with him. No one will be able to say, "Et tu Brute" – you too, Köstring, have been seduced by this Russian. It is better that I should not know him.'

I ventured to tell him of Vlasov's popularity, and of his remarkable impact on his compatriots, but this he would not accept.

'That I do not believe. In Russia military leaders do not have the popular appeal that they have in Germany. Russians think and feel differently. The fact is that Hitler will have nothing to do with Vlasov. If in the future we are forced to build up some Russian personality – as we should have done back in 1941 – then we must find some other Russian.'

On this we disagreed. In my eyes Vlasov was not just one of many military leaders. He had become a symbol. In the eyes of many millions he was the personification of their hopes and wishes for a better order and for a better life.

General Köstring assured me that as far as purely military matters were concerned I and my detachment could count on his help and support; but he must be left right out of anything to do with politics. Our interview then came to an end.

This was the first of a number of conversations I had with General Köstring during the first six months of 1944. In April his chief of staff, Colonel Herre, was given a command at the front and replaced by Major Voelkel.

It was not always possible to separate military matters from politics as General Köstring had wished. For instance, there was a memorandum by Vlasov and his staff on 'The attitude of the Russian Volunteers to the Jewish question' which Bormann, our

Dabendorf editor, had to submit to Köstring's staff for approval. The paper was approved, and this gave rise to a curious little incident at Köstring's HQ. A senior officer of out-and-out Nazi views took the opportunity to attack Captain von Herwarth, a diplomat in civilian life, who was acting as Köstring's ADC (and who strongly disapproved of the Nazi racial theories).

'It seems, Herr von Herwarth, that you approve of the pro-Jewish attitude of these former Russian Bolsheviks. Why?'

'Because,' Herwarth answered, 'I agree with what they say, and in any case I am not prepared to let this temporary nonsense ruin my whole future career.'

The young ex-Counsellor of Embassy knew the mentality of the man he was talking to.

'Yes. Your career. Yes, I understand.'

As Herwarth told me afterwards: 'You see, he would not have understood anything else.'

(v)

Vlasov and Köstring were not to meet till the Prague Congress towards the end of the year. I passed on to Vlasov what Köstring had said, and in doing so did not conceal my respect for the man himself. Vlasov, who had heard much good of Köstring, showed no understanding of the line he had taken.

'Uniforms, pay, leave warrants. Vastly important at a time when the front is cracking. What is the point of all this when the Red Army is on the point of overwhelming not only your hireling general but all Germany as well?'

Vlasov knew perfectly well that Köstring could do nothing to avert the impending doom. But in his eyes Köstring's efforts to improve conditions of service for the volunteers only emphasized their status as mercenaries. He refused to have anything to do with 'Köstring's hirelings'. It was in vain that I attempted to convince him of the German general's integrity and sense of responsibility.

(vi)

Thanks to Hellmich's and Herre's initiative plans were being worked out for a number of projects. Under Köstring the preparatory work was completed and the measures brought into force. Much of what we should have had in the autumn of 1941, and what Hellmich during his period of command had initiated, was now brought to fruition by Köstring.

Special sections to deal with matters concerning the volunteers were set up in each German division.

Köstring arranged for special field hospitals for volunteers, and also for convalescent homes and leave hostels.

Russian doctors and medical orderlies were given the opportunity to take qualifying courses.

Pension rights and care for widows and orphans were regularized.

A new disciplinary handbook for the personnel of locally raised formations was worked out.

Dabendorf had for some time been granting permission to marry on its own responsibility. Köstring arranged that this concession should be extended to all volunteers.

In the autumn of 1941 Russian volunteers had been awarded Iron Crosses by their German commanders. Such awards were subsequently annulled by a Führer's Order. Köstring arranged that volunteers should once more be eligible for the Iron Cross.

Russian officers were to be saluted by German military personnel.

This was one side of the medal, and due to the efforts of General Köstring; but as far as war aims were concerned, in the summer of 1944 we seemed farther away from our goal than ever.

15

The SS Show Interest

(i)

NATURALLY the threatening situation on all fronts caused great concern to Vlasov and his collaborators. In the small circle of those closest to him there were discussions (to which Dellingshausen, Fröhlich and I were invited) as to what should be done in the event of the final collapse of the Third Reich. The so-called Westerners were in favour of immediate contact with the Anglo-Saxons and the French Resistance. The NTS, as an émigré organization, had members everywhere, including enemy countries. Similar thoughts had occurred to me, and I hoped that after the fall of the Nazis there might be an alliance of all free nations, including the Germans, to oppose the second great threat to Europe, i.e. Bolshevism.

Vlasov saw the position more clearly than either I or his compatriots. Perhaps his experiences with Chiang Kai-shek had sharpened his judgement. 'In British and American eyes we are, presumably, neither *Untermenschen* nor "butcher boys" (to use Himmler's phrase). But we are traitors because we are fighting against our government. The fact that this government has no mandate from our people, has in fact enslaved our nation in defiance of the popular will, will today be regarded as irrelevant, although in 1918–20 these same British, Americans and French were supporting the White Armies with arms, stores and even troops against the Soviet regime. But today Stalin is an ally of the Anglo-Saxons against their common enemy Hitler. And therefore today we are traitors. What else can one expect of the Anglo-Saxons? They have forgotten the guarantees of freedom they gave to the Poles, the Baltic nations, the Czechs, the Yugoslavs and the Greeks. They will give our emissaries the cold shoulder so long as they come to them as suppliants with empty hands. Quite apart from this, it is a fact that an alliance of the Free Nations of Europe is only feasible in cooperation with a Germany willing and able to accept this concept – and here there is nothing whatever that we can do.

'So what can we do? I have no loyalty to Hitler. But I am and will be loyal to those Germans who have, all along, accepted us as fellow-beings and allies. Our only course is to rescue, or to create, a substance of Russian power, and to build it up, by every means in our power, *before* the Nazis collapse. Only if and when we become a power factor, along with Czechs, Poles, Yugoslavs, reasonable Germans and others, can we expect to get a hearing, sooner or later, from the Anglo-Saxons.'

Such was Vlasov's line of argument. There was no one in our little circle who could contradict him. The substance must be saved. The Russian fighters for freedom must now tread this path alone.

In January 1944 I had a long talk late at night with General Gehlen. I told him of my thoughts and fears regarding the coming end of the war. I told him what was in Vlasov's mind. And then I offered, should it be desirable, to go myself to Portugal in order to get into touch with an old school friend who had, up to 1929, been in a position to exercise considerable influence in London with regard to Russian affairs. I had heard nothing of my friend since the outbreak of war, so I would first have to re-establish contact. Gehlen thanked me for being so frank; and, with equal frankness, told me that another feeler, on similar lines, had recently been put out on the German side; one would have to wait and see what came of it. If need be, he, Gehlen, would revert to my offer at a later date.

Colonel Freytag-Loringhoven was a frequent visitor to the villa in Dahlem. He had successfully organized the employment of Cossack units on the Southern Army Group sector. Later he had been offered, and refused, the post of chief of staff to the GOC Osttruppen. He was a Balt, and could talk to Vlasov in Russian. He had seen the humiliation and hopelessness into which Germany had been plunged at the end of the First World War. He had seen how National Socialism had brought employment and prosperity, self-confidence and opportunity. He now had to see how the Third Reich, born of the reaction against the oppression of Versailles, was now engaged in the ruthless oppression of other nations.

In these talks with Vlasov the question was often mooted as to whether, in view of Nazi methods, one was justified in helping Hitler win his war against the Soviet Union.

'You say win his war,' said Vlasov. 'Your premise is false and so is your conclusion. A German victory in Russia is impossible, and has been so, ever since the failure back in 1941 to strike an alliance with the forces of freedom. Today it may still be possible for the Liberation Movement, with German or other help, to conquer Stalin. I say with German not because I love the Germans but because so far they are the only ones to fight against Stalin. In two years' time the picture may be different.'

Freytag-Loringhoven: 'But supposing German and Russian Nazis win the war?'

Vlasov: 'Well, I and my friends here are not Nazis, as you may have noticed. But if Hitler thinks he can use Russian stooges, that is his affair. A day will come when his puppet governments will not dance to his tune. That sort of thing cannot last. And this is important – Hitler is afraid of the nationalist Russia of tomorrow and he is losing his war against the Soviet Russia of today. My concern is that our Liberation Movement should not sink to the bottom with the German wreck.'

And then Vlasov developed his line of thought as I have reported above.

'Always with the proviso,' he added, 'that there will be German officers with whom we can take this last desperate step for the freedom of all the nations of Europe.'

(ii)

Meanwhile, in January 1944, the Red Army had broken through on the Northern sector. (It was here that Trotsky had routed the Whites under Yudenich in 1918, and the pattern of the operations was not dissimilar.) After heavy fighting the Northern Group of Armies retired to the line Narva–Lake Peipus–Pskov–Opotchka–Polotsk. Field-Marshal von Küchler was dismissed by Hitler, and replaced by General Model.

The gallant Finns under Field-Marshal Mannerheim were forced to plead for an armistice.

In the Central and Southern sectors the Red Armies, in the period December 1943 to April 1944, advanced up to the Bug and the Carpathians. The Reds were nearing the frontiers of the Baltic States, of Poland, Galicia, of Hungary and Roumania.

The Wehrmacht still occupied Russian territory of an area equivalent to that of Bavaria, Saxony, Württemberg-Baden and Hesse, and with a population of 12 million human beings – terrified, desperate, but still clinging to a ray of hope.

(iii)

While we were racking our brains to think of ways and means to save what could be saved, we were fully occupied, in early 1944, in defending Dabendorf from the ever-increasing spate of suspicions and accusations launched by the SD. A ever-recurring refrain was: too little space is allotted by the Vlasov papers *Zarya* and *Dobovolyets* to the requisite anti-Jewish campaign. Such items as ever do appear are unconvincing. The reason is that the editor-in-chief, M. A. Zykov, is, presumably, a Jew. The attitude of these papers amounts to sabotage. Zykov and his assistant Kovalchuk appealed to Grote and myself, as our German editor Bormann, who had hitherto shown intelligence and tact in his thankless post between the hammer of Nazi demands and the anvil of Russian aspirations, was now at his wits' end.

This time neither Grote nor I could think of a solution; and in the end it was Bormann himself who proposed that the authorities concerned should be asked to compose an agreed memorandum on 'The special position of locally raised volunteers with regard to the Jewish problem'. It was a brilliant idea: the ball was thus passed back to the Propaganda Ministry, the

Ostministerium and the SD, whose deliberations and arguments went on for months.

In this connection I should perhaps mention Vlasov's own attitude, the more so as since the end of the war certain allegations have been made to which he can no longer reply.

He seldom mentioned the influence of Jewish revolutionary intellectuals on developments in Russia since 1917. On the other hand, he frequently declared: 'Stalin is not a Jew. The Cheka and GPU butchers, Dzerzhinsky and Yezhov, were not Jews; Beria and Khrushchev, who made such a shambles in the Ukraine, are not Jews. Our struggle is directed exclusively against Stalin and his thugs, of whatever race they may be.' Vlasov made no bones about sharply attacking the 'racial lunacy' of the Nazis. 'You are waging a shabby war against the Jews, against unarmed men and women and innocent children.' Those were his words, which he inevitably repeated whenever the subject cropped up.

Vlasov was no hater. He was a keen critic of the Germans. Some traits he smiled at, others he condemned, but he was always ready to understand and to forgive. Dislike of Jews was not in his nature. A Jew for him was like anybody else. There were good Jews and bad Jews. As with Russians and Germans.

'But in general I have come to the conclusion that the Jews, whose cultural record goes back for so many centuries, have certain outstanding qualities. With their quickness, their shrewdness, their competence, their world-wide connections, they cannot fail to be a source of advantage to Russia. I would like us to have a great many Zykovs! Russia is healthy, and the percentage of Jews so small that the country could not come to any harm even if all Jews had the negative qualities that the Germans allege. But that is nonsense. If Germans maintain that the Jews were to blame for all their troubles in 1918, I would like to ask: is not the majority race, the Germans themselves, primarily responsible? Why did you let a minority take control? That is your fault. If you had been as clever and as united as the Jews all would have been well. And if Germans maintain that the German nation has suffered because of the Jews, I remember our old proverb, "A Russian can bear a lot that would kill a German."'

Malyshkin and Trukhin, who were often present at these talks, took the same line as Vlasov. But I must admit that not all his collaborators thought as he did.

A second SD attack was launched on the Dabendorf training courses, and the German chief training officer, Baron von der Ropp. He was accused of having told those attending the courses that the Jewish question formed part of the National Socialist programme but had nothing to do with Russians. Stalin was an absolute dictator on whom Jews exercised no influence. This, the SD maintained, was contrary to the attitude officially laid down and was contrary to the Führer's policy. They demanded an inquiry and appropriate punishment. Ropp's remarks had been in line with those of Vlasov. Vlasov had declared he knew of no Jews on the top Soviet level, except Kaganovich. Trotsky and Zinoviev had opposed the dictator, and in consequence had been liquidated along with countless Russians. The Liberation Movement was not anti-Jewish or anti any other race: they were solely against Stalin's oppression. Thus Vlasov. 'We cannot,' he said, 'blindly take over everything from the Germans. We naturally do not accept the theory that all Russians, Poles, Jews and gipsies should be branded as *Untermenschen*. Only skunks dirty their own nest.' This last was a reference to those who, even in Dabendorf, acted as informers for the SD. As already mentioned Trukhin and his officers were doing all they could against these creatures whom not only the Reds but also the SD were infiltrating into Dabendorf.

This particular bomb launched at us never exploded. A brave member of the SS, a contact of Fröhlich's, managed to ensure that nothing came of it.

A little incident in this connection showed the sort of thing that was keeping party officials busy while the German armies were being driven back on every front. Objection was raised to one of my leaflets on the treatment of Russians. 'The attention of the OKW department responsible for the publication of this leaflet is drawn to the fact that the word *Untermensch* is nowhere to be found in it.' Bormann took me to see a friend of his in the

Propaganda Ministry. 'No mention of *Untermensch*?' said Bormann. 'We can put that right. For instance, insert "every race has its *Untermenschen*, to whom we are resolutely opposed". So the word will be there and the censor should be satisfied.' Bormann's friend smiled. He was a cynical intellectual who did not believe in racial theories, and may perhaps have wished to score off the colleague who had so ineptly drafted the objection. Bormann's insertion was adopted and the brochure officially approved.

(iv)

What Count von Stauffenberg had feared in 1942 seemed to be coming true in 1944.

On 14 October 1943 Himmler had attacked Vlasov in an address at Bad Schachen to an audience of Waffen SS officers. It is very possible that Himmler's motive was to counter the ever-growing conviction among SS officers that the tide of war in the East could only be turned with Vlasov's help. The Reichsführer SS called Vlasov a 'butcher boy' and a pig. He denounced Vlasov's slogan, 'Russia can only be conquered by Russians', as 'impertinent arrogance'. He was apparently unaware that this phrase did not originate from Vlasov, but from Schiller more than a hundred years ago.

Colonel Martin told me of this speech in Bad Schachen. 'Carry on,' he said, 'but be particularly careful.'

In spite of Himmler's words, it was now that the SS was taking to the idea of using East European nationals. As well as Belgian, Dutch and Norwegian SS units, Estonian and Latvian formations were being set up. 'Galician' (i.e. Ukrainian) formations up to divisional strength were being organized. It was said that in spite of German military reverses the flow of recruits exceeded all expectation.

So why not Russian formations?

The SS had already taken over certain Russian units from the Wehrmacht. SS officers were engaged in setting up 'Eastern' formations. As had been the case with the army the SS had been unable to tell these men anything about war aims. If their

Russians asked 'Why are we fighting?' there was still no answer that the SS could give them. But the matter was now in the minds of certain SS leaders. I have mentioned the visits to Vlasov by senior SS officers. These men – like the tireless Dr R – were considering the revocation of the current anti-Slav policy and thus making possible a cooperation with Vlasov.

In the spring of 1944 Grote introduced me to the young Günther d'Alquen, who published the weekly *Das Schwarze Corps*. He had an open mind and was quick to see the point. If I could only make a Paul out of this Saul! Zhilenkov, Zykov and von Dellingshausen were present at this interview. D'Alquen was in charge of SS propaganda at the front, and had obtained Himmler's permission to employ Vlasovite officers in an operation designed to stimulate the flow of line-crossers from the Reds. At this interview our Russians explained the aims of the Liberation Movement and all that that implied. Dellingshausen and I kept to the practical points. But it was made clear that this would have to be a genuine Liberation Movement operation, not just one by the Waffen SS, whose role would be merely to provide technical facilities. D'Alquen saw the point. He assured us this was not a mere local operation, but one that he was determined should affect the course of the war on the whole of the Eastern front. What he said carried conviction, and the preliminaries were taken in hand at once. One of d'Alquen's aides had been at school at a German Church School in Petersburg, which made our co-operation easier.

(v)

Before ever Operation *Skorpion*, as it came to be called, was launched the Liberation Movement suffered a severe loss. I was in Hermannstadt when Sergei Fröhlich and Pastor Schabert brought me news of the abduction of M. A. Zykov. Zykov and his assistant Noshin were in Rüdersdorf (in East Berlin) and were taken off by unknown persons in civilian clothes. Accounts of witnesses were muddled and contradictory. Both Russians were armed: it seemed unthinkable that they could have surrendered to force without resistance. All possible inquiries by von Delling-

shausen and by Günther d'Alquen failed to lead to any trace of
their whereabouts. Was the abduction the work of the NKVD
underground or of the Gestapo? Were enemies of d'Alquen in
other Himmler organizations in any way involved? I often went
to Rüdersdorf with Zykov; was it only by chance that I had
escaped the same fate? The loss of Zykov was a heavy blow to
Vlasov. Later, when he was composing the Prague Manifesto he
sadly missed this independent but ever shrewd adviser. Zykov
was not universally loved. He could be a hard, sometimes ruthless
taskmaster. But he was a fighter by nature, and the most Western-
minded of the little group at the head of the movement. We had
been through difficult times together, and he had always been a
true and loyal comrade. His loss, and the consciousness of my
own impotence, left me shattered.

(vi)

Skorpion was started on a sector of the Southern front. I soon
had reports of its outstanding success from both Zhilenkov and
d'Alquen. Line-crossers in the sector where Vlasov's people
were operating showed a marked increase (according to d'Alquen,
tenfold). D'Alquen's main objective was to prove to Himmler
that all that now could weaken Red Army morale – in spite of
Red victories – was the announcement of the political aims
of a Russian Liberation Movement. It was to this hope of
course that Vlasov was clinging. Operation *Skorpion* provided
evidence.

Zhilenkov informed me that d'Alquen had proposed that he
should take over the leadership of this movement. This was not
an intrigue. D'Alquen knew that Vlasov, for Himmler, was like
a red rag to a bull and Himmler's attacks on Vlasov had been
too outspoken for him easily to change his tune. D'Alquen
was impatient for quick results, and the exchange of Vlasov
for Zhilenkov seemed the line of least resistance. However,
Zhilenkov had refused, and d'Alquen realized that it must be
Vlasov.

I have no details of how it was that the young Standartenführer secured the approval of the Reichsführer SS. To have

made the move at all entailed a real personal risk, and tribute must be paid to his courage and his willingness to assume responsibility. Perhaps Gehlen would have met with similar success over his Operation *Silberstreif* if only he had direct access to Hitler. As it was Zeitzler understood the position; being first and foremost a soldier, he would always bow to the will of his superiors. Keitel lacked understanding as well as moral courage.

As mentioned, I do not know what took place within the inner circles of the SS. What is certain is that at that time a number of SS leaders were beginning to realize that the very existence of the Third Reich was at stake; and I was bombarded by phone calls from business contacts and from Speer's Ministry asking me to call for unofficial talks. 'It is urgently required to have first-hand information on the Vlasov movement. It may be found possible to help Vlasov. And also ourselves.'

Sometimes I was not told beforehand whom it was that I was to talk to, and it was only afterwards that I could discover his position and sphere of competence. Among the names I now remember were Kehrl, Pleiger, Berger, Ohlendorf, Schellenberg, Wächter, Zimmermann and Arlt. What exactly was in their minds was not disclosed. There were merely polite generalities and the suggestion that some cooperation with Vlasov might be of mutual advantage. Naturally I took the opportunity to inform them in detail of Vlasov's attitude and aims.

The most forthcoming was Dr Arlt, head of the Freiwilligen-Leitstelle-Ost. I gathered from him that the SS intended to secure the cooperation of the various people of Russia under SS auspices. This would apply also to the Great Russians, not as dominant element, but on a par with the Ukrainians, Caucasians, Latvians and other races.

My talks with Pleiger and Kehrl were straightforward and confined to the treatment of the *Ostarbeiter*. They promised, as much as was in their power, to press for improvement in the treatment of these people on the lines recommended by Vlasov.

I well remember my call on the SS General Berger, head of the

SS Hauptamt. In the ante-room I found Thomas Girgensohn, now in some senior post with the SA, who complained to me that he had been kept waiting there an hour. He was a decent man, and I was somewhat embarrassed when, unexpectedly, I was called in to Berger before him.

Berger asked me to tell him about Vlasov, which I did on my accustomed lines. It seemed a good sign that he did not interrupt me, and showed no tendency either to be sarcastic or to read me lessons. When I had finished he told me he wished to meet Vlasov personally and asked me to arrange a luncheon. We had a few words about details and agreed, assuming Vlasov's consent, that an invitation should be sent through official channels. 'We mean to help your Vlasov,' said Berger genially. 'Bring him along.' That was all.

I have forgotten where the lunch took place. I sat between Berger and Vlasov. 'That makes it easier to talk,' said Berger. Vlasov realized at once that our host was sincere, and proceeded to explain his programme. Berger then declared that a great many mistakes had been made and not only over policy regarding Russia. It must now be put right. That was why he had asked Vlasov to meet him. He went on to speak of German political blunders with regard to the Balkans and Turkey. Had one only set about it properly Turkey would long have been in the war on the German side. Of the utmost importance was to treat people correctly and humanely. *All* people and *all* nations. . . . We should win over the Persians, the Indians, the Arabs . . .

His talk went on towards far horizons, but he was never overbearing and his tone was frank and friendly. His reference to the treatment of *all* people was something new. We were eager to watch out for the slightest nuance, especially from a high-placed SS officer.

Suddenly he turned to me.

'Supposing,' he said, 'we were to make Oberführer Kroeger liaison officer between the Reichsführer SS and Vlasov. You know Kroeger?'

(So it had got as far as that!)

It happened that I knew Kroeger. He had been head of the

'Home to the Reich' movement in the Baltic States in the autumn of 1939. I never adhered to that movement; but early in 1943 I had taken it on myself to call on him and explain the disastrous consequences of the *Untermensch* theory. He was the most highly placed SS officer I knew. He listened for a whole hour, took notes and promised his support. He too disapproved of the current policy regarding Russia. That was all I knew of the man, but when Berger unexpectedly mentioned his name I felt it would be to our advantage if I approved the suggestion. As a Balt he ought to be a more suitable intermediary than others I had met. At least that is what I thought.

Berger seemed to be pleased that I approved. 'You know Vlasov and his Russians,' he said, 'and you can best judge if Kroeger is suitable.' He took me by the arm. It was all very different from anything I had experienced before. As we parted Berger said to Vlasov: 'I hope we shall meet again very soon. The Reichsführer SS asked me if I knew you and now I do.'

It seemed that the SS now, in the early summer of 1944, were to take the opportunity that the Wehrmacht had missed back in 1941, but I was convinced that the change of course was due not to a change of heart but to dire necessity. Their aims were still not clear. We did not know the men we would now have to work with. Vlasov was reserved, though he had to admit this might be his last chance.

(vii)

It must have been shortly before our interview with Berger that d'Alquen had forced Himmler to agree to meet Vlasov. Our lunch showed that the Reichsführer SS had taken Berger into his confidence. According to d'Alquen Hitler had approved of what was happening. We were told that Himmler's meeting with the *Untermensch*, traitor and butcher-boy Vlasov would be fixed for 21 or 23 July. This absolute reversal of previous policy was so astounding that I could hardly believe it was true. Vlasov once more began to hope. He did not make plans in any detail. What he wanted was soldiers, arms and freedom of action. All else

would then follow. Zhilenkov took a cautious line. Malyshkin
and Trukhin were dubious.

Meanwhile the SD had resumed its offensive against us. The
NTS leaders were arrested. Trukhin belonged to this organization, but as an officer of the Russian Liberation Army he remained,
for the moment, at liberty. It was only by a miracle that A. N.
Zaitsev, our Russian training officer, was not arrested.

16

20 July

MEANWHILE the Western Allies had landed in Normandy. Malyshkin went off to France and what he had to report on his return to Berlin was alarming: 'With the Allied landing in Normandy, all Russian units in France can be written off. Russian volunteers cannot understand why they should fight in the West against the Americans, English and French. German propaganda, to the effect that the Russian soldier will gain his freedom by means of a German victory over the Western Powers, makes no sense whatever to Russians. The Germans have not kept their promise to assemble the small Russian formations into regiments and divisions under the supreme command of General Vlasov. Once again the volunteers have been cheated. Why have their Russian officers been removed? Where is General Vlasov? Why the incorporation of Russian battalions into German units? Nothing in this strange, unfriendly and mysterious West makes any sense at all.'

A number of the volunteers had been through thick and thin with the Germans since 1941–2, and always with the feeling, in spite of the retreats, that the German army was too good for their opponents. In Russia the volunteers were at home. There they could do something. There was a purpose. In France they were just cannon fodder: what was more, in the West it seemed that the Americans and English were the masters. Their air superiority and their superb technical equipment were alarming.

Malyshkin reported that certain volunteer units had fought bravely and had been wiped out. Others – Russian as well as Caucasian and Central Asian – had mutinied.

'Allied propaganda promises the volunteers either return to their Soviet homes or asylum in the USA or Canada. This shows the West has no inkling as to why these volunteers are on the German side. Return home means handing over to the Soviet authorities. The USA and Canada are far away.'

It appeared too that most of the German commanders were also bewildered. What should they do about these Russians, transferred from the East as being 'unreliable'? They demanded interpreters and Russian experts, but not from Dabendorf which was 'notorious as a nest of Great Russian traitors'.

The improvised German/Russian command of the volunteer formations was working badly, and often lost contact with the units concerned. Malyshkin and his officers were as helpless as their German opposite numbers. General Niedermayer, as deputy to the GOC Osttruppen, had done his best to bring together certain units under the command of the Russian Colonel Bunichenko, but the rapidity of the German army's withdrawal had made the venture hopeless. In France it was chaos.

Vlasov, ever since 'Jodl's betrayal', had written off the volunteers transferred to France; but inwardly he still hoped that one day they would come under his command. The Allied invasion seemed to have dashed these hopes. Malyshkin, from what he had seen on the spot, felt there was nothing that could be done. Nevertheless it was Vlasov's firm intention to plead for these men if his meeting with Himmler took place. One could only wait until 21 July.

(ii)

'What do you think of the state of things in France?' our Russians kept asking. What could we answer? Perhaps General Gehlen could help or advise. I took the train to Mauerwald. Gehlen was absent, on the sick list. I was unable to see General Köstring: his staff seemed to know even less about things in France than I did. Neither Altenstadt nor Freytag-Loringhoven were available. I took the night train back to Berlin and went straight on to Dabendorf.

Vlasov, Trukhin and Boyarski were waiting for me near the camp entrance. They told me of the attempt on Hitler on 20

July and its aftermath. For the moment only two were known to have been killed – General Olbricht and Count Stauffenberg.

I had grim forebodings. 'Our good friends,' I said.

'In these cases one does not speak of the dead as one's friends,' remarked Vlasov. 'One just did not know them. Bear that in mind, Wilfried Karlovich. I have been through Stalin's school. This is only the beginning. From now on it will be in Germany just as in the Soviet Union.'

I was soon to learn the names of the other friends we had lost. They were, most of them, those in the OKH who had since 1942 been working for a new policy with regard to Russia and, in this connection, for the inception of political warfare. These officers may well have held differing views on ultimate aims, and not all of them would have been prepared unconditionally to back Vlasov's plans. But it was this group who had done what they could on behalf of the Russian Liberation Movement. They were Colonel Freytag-Loringhoven, Lieutenant-Colonel Klammroth, General Olbricht, General Oster, Colonel von Roenne, Colonel Schmidt von Altenstadt, Lieutenant-Colonel Schrader, Colonel Count Stauffenberg, General Stieff, General von Tresckow, General Wagner and surely others whose names I do not remember. General Gehlen was not among the victims. A kindly fate had saved him for us.

(iii)

Of those who perished in the aftermath of 20 July I have special cause to think of Colonel Baron Freytag-Loringhoven.

I have mentioned the arrest by the SD of the leaders of the NTS. The SD were now after the blood of Trukhin, Boyarski and other Russians in Dabendorf. The OKW explained that they were powerless. The general of the Osttruppen refused to be involved. My third boss, the GOC of the Berlin Wehrkreis, informed me that he was not competent to deal with Russian political matters.

Charges brought by the SD included one against the Dabendorf commandant for having 'persistently given cover to the conspirators'. When Colonel Martin told me that he unfortunately could this time do nothing to help I reminded him that the accused Dabendorf commandant was under the orders of the OKH. My OKW regimental commander smiled. 'Then,' he said, 'in accordance with the proper procedure, I will refer the case, your case, to your competent authority, the OKH. And not for the first time.'

I went again to Mauerwald. I first saw the Fremde Heere Ost, then the Abwehr II section of the OKH. Colonel Freytag-Loringhoven looked into the matter himself and decided that all the accusations of the Gestapo were nonsense. 'The SD will be disappointed,' he remarked. 'No heads are going to roll.'

This was enough to avert the immediate threat: it was the Abwehr Section of the Wehrmacht, and not the SD, who were responsible for Dabendorf. Lieutenant-Colonel Schrader drafted the Abwehr's official decision. As he did so he remarked it was high time for Dabendorf to be removed from the OKW, and put entirely under the OKH. 'Sooner or later,' he said, 'the OKW will let you down, but here we are strong enough to cope with these machinations.' *Sancta simplicitas*,' said Freytag. 'Don't you realize Strik-Strikfeldt and his outfit are still in being only because he has four different masters, and accordingly no real master? He is with us today simply and solely because of the skilful way he has balanced, for years, on four chairs. No, let him carry on. For as long as he can.'

Next day I was told on the telephone that Freytag-Loringhoven had shot himself during the night. Deeply shattered I went to see Vlasov in Dahlem. With him were Malyshkin and Zhilenkov.

'Another very good friend is dead,' I said. 'Freytag-Loring-hoven.'

'I don't know him,' said Vlasov, with an air of complete indifference.

'But no, my good Andrei Andreyevich, that splendid staff colonel of ours who so often came to see you.'

'I don't remember.'

I left the room and went upstairs. A few minutes later Vlasov joined me.

'I have already told you one can*not* afford to know dead

friends like this one. I am as distressed as you are. He was a true
and gallant friend. But I am thinking of you. If you go on talking
like this you will be the next for the firing squad.'

I pointed out that the two generals now with him were our
best and closest friends.

'Two more witnesses,' he said calmly. 'I have no doubt whatever of their integrity. But why should they be involved? If they
should ever be asked, "Did Captain Strik ever speak of these
conspirators as his friends?" they would be in a dilemma. I
know how the Cheka and NKVD work. Your Gestapo will soon
be just the same.'

(iv)

The meeting with Himmler was indefinitely postponed. General
Berger proposed that in the meantime Vlasov should go to
Ruhpolding in Bavaria, where accommodation could be arranged
for him in the SS Convalescent Home. It was suggested that
Sergei Fröhlich should accompany him. The situation at
Dabendorf was so critical that I was reluctant to leave my
command. But Vlasov was so insistent that in the end I agreed
to go with him, though I knew that he could not have a more
suitable companion than Fröhlich.

In Ruhpolding we had a warm welcome from Frau Heidi
Bielenberg, the warden of the home. Her husband, a doctor with
the Waffen SS, had been killed in the war, and she now devoted
herself to her little daughter Frauke, and to her convalescents,
many of whom were permanently crippled. There was no trace
of internment about our stay. Berger seemed to trust us completely. There was no one watching to see what we were up to.
We went for long walks in the hills and no one bothered about
us. In the evening there was music. Frau Bielenberg sang to her
guitar, or accompanied on the piano. We laughed and joked,
but we also talked of those serious problems which we could not
get away from. Heidi Bielenberg spoke no Russian, but Andrei
Andreyevich had by now learned German. And one day they
found they were in love: and thus began a connection that was to
culminate in their marriage.

The peace and quiet of the little Bavarian mountain village was in sharp contrast to the grim realities of the world outside. But even here from time to time the bombers droned above our heads. And then one morning I was called to the telephone: the Reichsführer SS wished to see General Vlasov at his Field HQ in East Prussia on the morning of 16 September.

17

Himmler and After

ON 16 September 1944 Vlasov and I arrived at Himmler's HQ in Rastenburg. Himmler had meanwhile been placed in command of the Ersatz Army. He would thereby be able to supply all that was needed to set up our volunteer formations. So we thought. In complete ignorance of the deception awaiting us, we drew up our plans for the creation of a 'power factor' that would ensure that Vlasov acquired a real say in matters of high policy.

We were received by SS officers. Procedure was much as in the staff of the Wehrmacht. As we came to the door of the Reichsführer's private office the SS general escorting us remarked that before the conference began Himmler would like a ten-minute private talk with Vlasov alone. Vlasov hesitated, and declared he would not see Himmler without me; otherwise he would turn round and go back. I explained to him he must not turn back, if he had to go in alone he must go; he was quite capable of putting his case without my help, this was the decisive moment – and his German was perfectly adequate. 'Only for Ruhpolding,' he said.

The door was opened while he still hesitated. I pushed him in.

An SS colonel joined me and we waited in silence. Ten minutes went by, twenty, thirty. The colonel invited me to breakfast with him, as 'this intimate conversation is likely to go on for a long time'. He added that of course he did not know what was going on in the Reichsführer's office, but he was sure that now at last a satisfactory agreement would be reached with Vlasov. Oberführer Kroeger was there too. Kroeger was also 'a Russian' and could interpret. . . . It was unfortunate they seemed to have forgotten that I was there, but what mattered were the results.

'It was good,' Vlasov said when at last he rejoined me. 'But quite different from what I had thought. Himmler, Chief of the German Police. Reichsführer SS. I had imagined him a blood-thirsty Chekist à la Beria, a super Grand Inquisitor – for whom I was just a Russian *Untermensch*. But instead I felt I was meeting a decent well-brought-up bourgeois. Quiet, modest. Nothing of the gangster boss like Dr Ley. On the contrary, he was none too self-assured. Not a word about *Herrenmenschen*. No mention of Jews. He more or less apologized for having so long been taken in by *Untermensch* theories. I do not think he is intelligent; he seemed limited, narrow, pedantic. He has a farm – so he is a peasant like myself. He is fond of animals.

'He openly confessed all the mistakes that had been made, and I liked him for it. He said he had spoken to the Führer and obtained his approval for all measures to be taken to implement the new policy. If I understood rightly we are to have ten divisions. The Russian Liberation Committee is to start function-ing at once as a sovereign and independent authority. . . . The humiliating prefix 'Ost' will be abolished. Our workers and prisoners will have the same standing as those of other countries . . .'

His eyes were shining.

'I have attained much more than that,' he said. 'We are to have all the rights of an ally. Himmler proposed I should assume the rank of Head of a Government, but I explained that neither I nor the Liberation Committee now to be formed could assume the prerogatives of a government. That is for the Russian people or Russian peoples to decide later. I did not yield an inch. . . . I explained my political programme. First smash the enemy. Later all the minority races can decide their future in the frame of a New European Order. The minister agreed. Finally I asked, if not already too late, that all Russian units in France be with-drawn and placed under my command for the war against Stalin.'

Vlasov was proud and much moved. He had won his battle, after all the difficulties and humiliations of the past two years. For the good of his people he had struck just such a bargain with Himmler as Churchill once had with Stalin.

A group of SS officers waited tactfully and patiently some

distance away. After fifteen minutes or so one of them, a general, came up to me.

'It was due to a most unfortunate misunderstanding,' he said, 'that you were not present at the talk. We attach great importance to your having been there, both as long-standing adviser of General Vlasov and as representative of the Wehrmacht. I repeat you *were* present. The general has told you all about it, and I can fill in any gaps. So you were present, and please confirm this to the general's Russian associates. And of course to General von Wedel and to the officers of the OKW and OKH. I hope you understand me.'

'I do understand you,' I said. 'I can, if and when necessary, hold my tongue. But if my superiors ask me, then I can only tell them the truth. I was *not* present. I hope, General, you understand me. I am an officer.'

The SS general considered.

'I too am an officer,' he said. 'I respect your point of view and withdraw my request. But say nothing more than what you think is absolutely necessary for what is now our common cause.'

(ii)

Going back in the train to Berlin I shared a sleeper with Himmler's doctor, Felix Kersten, a somewhat unusual character who was an expert in nature cures. He told me he had long been doing his best for 'our good cause'. He talked about his influence over Himmler, how he had been a power for good and saved many innocent lives. 'Things happen,' he said, 'in wartime.' He would be pleased to offer his services to General Vlasov. I thanked him. So he too, I thought, is climbing on the bandwagon. I do not wish to be unfair to Dr Kersten. It is quite possible he may have been an influence for good. In fact I learned much later that this indeed had been the case. But at the time the conversation left a curious taste in my mouth.

'The Reichsführer SS Heinrich Himmler received at his field HQ General Vlasov, leader of the Russian Liberation Army. In the course of a long conversation complete agreement was reached on measures to ensure the deployment of all the forces of

the Russian nation for the liberation of their homeland.' Such
was the official communiqué. The German press gave considerable coverage to the Vlasov–Himmler meeting. It is true there
were certain passages we would have preferred otherwise; but
the development was so surprising that it caused considerable
stir. One heard suddenly of 'the new Wonder Weapon – Vlasov'
that was going to change the course of the war. We had an
enthusiastic reception in Dabendorf and Dahlem. Recognition of
equal status – the goal towards which we had been striving for
years – was now at last attained. We could now act as we had so
long desired.

When General Gehlen came back to duty I gave him an
unvarnished report. Himmler had appointed the SS General
Berger as his plenipotentiary in all Russian affairs. Kroeger was
liaison officer. SS Colonel Burg had the task of setting up the
Russian divisions. Gehlen asked me to stay with Vlasov for as
long as I could.

A telegram from Himmler to Vlasov spoke of only three Russian
divisions. Vlasov was deeply disappointed: ten divisions had been
promised. Kroeger explained Himmler had spoken only of three.
Had Vlasov misheard? Had Kroeger, in interpreting, given the
wrong figure? I was filled with mistrust.

Himmler's telegram referred to '*a* Russian Liberation Committee'. Grote told us that in the OKW, in Rosenberg's Ministry,
in the Foreign Ministry and in the Osttruppen HQ this was
taken to mean just a Russian Committee alongside the existing
minority races committees. Vlasov had understood Himmler to
promise that the committee that he (Vlasov) was to set up would
be the supreme central authority for all the peoples of Russia in
their anti-Stalin struggle.

General Köstring asked both Keitel and Jodl for their directives in view of the new course. He was told there was no intention 'to build up Vlasov'. General von Wedel (head of OKW/Pr)
was told by Jodl that this presumably was just one of Himmler's
manoeuvres, about which the OKW had no details. Jodl doubted
whether the Führer had in fact approved of the new course.

Rosenberg apparently was deeply hurt. There was feverish

activity in the Ostministerium, stirring up protests against the Himmler–Vlasov Pact from all the national minorities' committees – some of which existed only on paper. Rosenberg, we were told, was going to make a further personal appeal to Hitler. One must admit that Dr Kroeger took a strong line. He insisted, on Himmler's instructions, that the new Vlasov committee should enjoy an overall authority. Vlasov proposed that the committee should be named 'Committee for the Liberation of the Nations of Russia'. There followed long, wearisome and inconclusive negotiations between Vlasov and representatives of the minority races. These last were backed by Rosenberg and they naturally could not turn against their patron. Kroeger threatened drastic measures, but Vlasov refused to agree to any use of force. He was anxious that there should be no German interferences in something that solely concerned the peoples of Russia.

I was once more surprised to see how firmly rooted in Vlasov's mind was the idea of a genuine community of European nations.

In the end, for the sake of appearances, a certain number of members of the minority races were co-opted to the committee but their more prominent representatives refused to join. They refused to understand that in Vlasov and Malyshkin they would have had loyal and honourable partners, or that the way they were behaving could be of ultimate advantage only to the extreme Great Russian chauvinists.

The distinguished General P. N. Krasnov refused to serve under a former Red general. He demanded that Vlasov should guarantee that in a Russia of the future the Cossacks should enjoy their traditional rights and privileges. The old gentleman still lived in the clouds. He had no idea of the military situation, was still confident of a German victory and hoped that under Hitler he would be able to realize his schemes. His German sponsors naturally made use of him to queer Vlasov's pitch. Vlasov and Trukhin made every effort to come to some realistic agreement with Krasnov. I myself saw Krasnov and also his nephew and chief of staff S. N. Krasnov. There was a vast gulf between Vlasov's approach and the wild phantasies of the ageing Cossack general.

(iii)

The German officers of the Dabendorf staff retired to the background. They remained in touch with their Russian friends to advise and help, but this was mainly on a personal basis, in view of the confidence they had inspired as individuals. New Russian offices and organs had urgently to be created to deal with administration, press, propaganda, politics and, especially, military organization. Dabendorf was to be the HQ of the newly approved Liberation Movement. The event showed how well advised we had been in making our original plans. Trukhin seemed to have thought of everything. Of course our Dabendorf team included a few somewhat dubious types, who wanted to exploit the present situation to their own advantage. But by and large if it had not been for Dabendorf I feel the whole operation would have been doomed from the start. Though I doubt if this was ever realized by our SS contacts.

New living quarters and workrooms had to be built. There was a constant spate of uncoordinated meetings and conferences. SS officers and representatives kept appearing to take over liaison duties with Russian departments, whether already functioning or still in process of formation. There were arguments and incidents of all kinds between Russians and SS. For the time being the Dabendorf officers managed to smooth them over. Once Dr Kroeger threatened to have me arrested. 'You will not do that,' I said. 'Why not?' 'Because we are fellow-Balts.' He held out his hand.

(iv)

Colonel Martin was removed, and succeeded in his section of OKW/Pr by an SS officer, Kriegsbaum. He was a decent man, but it showed how the SS was infiltrating the OKW. There was no progress in the creation under SS auspices of the First Volunteer Division. In the end Himmler put Köstring, GOC Osttruppen, in charge of this. So in this respect we seemed to be back at square one.

The setting up of the various new Russian organs proceeded,

for various reasons, at a snail's pace. The uninterrupted air-raids on Berlin accentuated the delays.

Morale was low in the prisoner-of-war camps. The Prague Manifesto was not yet published. The mills of New Course ground slowly. The same held good for improvement of the conditions of the *Ostarbeiter*.

A promise was made to Vlasov that the arrested NTS leaders would be released. Nothing happened.

Volunteer formations in the West were disbanded and turned into labour battalions, just as Malyshkin had once foreseen.

Time went by and our hopes evaporated. No, Himmler's New Course meant no real change and no new beginning.

(v)

A number of committees were working on the draft of the manifesto to be issued at the ceremonial Constituent Assembly of the Committee for the Liberation of the Peoples of Russia. It was proposed by Zhilenkov that this should take place in some Slav town. Nearly all Russian territory had been reoccupied by the Red Army. It was agreed to hold it in Prague.

Point 7 of the manifesto provided for the recognition of private property acquired by work, and for the legalization of private enterprise in trade and industry. The majority of the Russian economists recommended a state monopoly for foreign trade. A Nazi economic expert, acting as adviser to the committee, agreed with this view. 'When we come to trade with Russia,' he remarked, 'it would be simpler to deal with one central authority than with a number of individual businessmen. This would certainly be the best solution from the German point of view.' I happened to be present at these talks. It was natural for the Russians to take this line: they saw in it the only means to save the weak and undeveloped Russian industry from exploitation by foreign capitalists. The attitude of the German expert confirmed their views.

I felt it my duty to inform Vlasov what was going on. He took up a line of his own. 'I know little about economics,' he said, 'and you experts must know what you are talking about. But if, later on, Americans, English and other free nations are likely to regard us as Bolsheviks because we have a foreign trade monopoly – to them anathema – then I would strongly advise against it.' Fröhlich took my place at the final meeting and came back smiling. Vlasov had carried his point. It may well have been the same in other committees.

The manifesto of the Committee for the Liberation of the Peoples of Russia was the work of Russians – mostly ex-Soviet citizens – and addressed to the people of Russia, to the Red Army, and to their 'brothers and sisters' in Western Europe.[1] This comes out in the manifesto's content and wording. Western experts were consulted so as to give some idea of the Free Europe to those living in the Soviet Union. It was natural that the SS should endeavour to impart a tinge of their own ideology; but in this they were unsuccessful.

The manifesto was issued in Prague on 14 November 1944. A full translation is given in the Appendix. It is worth reading as it has not entirely lost its validity today. Only in the third paragraph is an indictment of 'the imperialist powers under the leadership of English and American plutocrats'. This sentence is the sole concession to the Nazis. But the reproaches directed at the Anglo-Saxons should be taken as an echo of the sufferings of those oppressed by Hitler. The manifesto describes the sad lot of the peoples of Russia and attacks the crimes of Stalin and his clique against individuals and nations. Then comes the sentence, 'there can be no greater crime than the forced enslavement of another nation'. The manifesto attacks the annexation of foreign territory, the destruction of monuments and works of art, and lists all that Stalin had robbed from the peoples of Russia. For any reader who paused to consider, the name of Hitler might well be substituted for that of Stalin.

'The Committee for the Liberation of the Peoples of Russia acknowledges the help accorded by Germany on terms that respect the honour and independence of our Homeland. This help at the moment affords the only practical possibility of our carrying on our armed struggle against Stalin and his clique.'

[1] See Appendix IV, page 258.

No obeisance, or hint of such, to the Führer or to the Nazi Party. No mention of Jews: the legal rights of all citizens guaranteed. The manifesto concludes: 'Brothers and Sisters in the Homeland! Intensify your struggle against Stalin's tyranny, against the annexationist war! Take your stand for the rights of which you have been robbed, for justice and prosperity, for peace and for freedom.'

18

The Prague Congress

(i)

TIME went by, and all my hopes crumbled. Himmler's change of
course was no reversal and no new beginning. The story of the
vision on the road to Damascus had been a leading influence
in my life. It had brought me to Vlasov. This last hope which
had sustained me through the long weary struggle was now
dead.

I told Vlasov the ground had been cut from under my feet, and
I had no inner strength to continue.

We would talk far into the night in Vlasov's room in the Dahlem
villa when he came back, worn out, from his endless receptions
and conferences. We agreed that no Paul could be awaited
from the Saul of either Himmler or Hitler. We agreed it was too
late to hope for a change in the. course of the war. 'If,' Vlasov
said, 'Germany could resist for another twelve or fifteen months,
we would have time to set up an appreciable power factor.
This power factor, with the support of the Wehrmacht and the
small European countries, would presumably be something
that America and England as well as Moscow would have
to reckon with.' But it seemed that not one of the leading
Germans had either the insight or the power to work to such
an end.

Inevitably we always came back to what might possibly happen
after the collapse of the Third Reich.

'I can only see one course,' I said. 'You, Andrei Andreyevich,
must go to Prague and issue the manifesto. Then, when the whole
free world will have heard of you, when the Prague ceremony is
over, you must retire, explaining that the Nazi government has
failed to keep the promises made you. Only thus can you lay a
foundation for what comes after the Nazis. I know this is easier

said than done. No doubt it will mean your return to prison. But the Russian Liberation Movement will survive.'

It took him time to answer. He reminded me that I had always stood by him when he could see no way out. He thought of Zykov, no longer there to help him. 'Perhaps Zykov would have found a solution. He was so resourceful.' As it was there were millions of Russians for whom he, Vlasov, was now their only hope. He could not desert them now. He must continue on his way to the bitter end.

'And I must go my way,' I said. 'I have shared with you our difficulties, our troubles and our hopes and you have given me your confidence, given it too to all those Germans whose hopes and aims were the same as yours. Now there is nothing more that I can do for you. My role of intermediary is over. I cannot work with Himmler. I must ask you to release me from the promise I once gave you.'

It was four in the morning when we parted. Vlasov asked for twenty-four hours to think it over. When we met that evening he had made up his mind. 'You must go, good friend,' he said. There were tears in his eyes.

We talked on for another hour. What he said was something like this: I have thought it all over, again and again. I did not act because of ambition. I did not calculate. It was simply that circumstances forced me to act as I did. Your Stauffenberg, Roenne, Freytag and the others were not traitors. They wished no harm to their country. They tried to serve their nation. I and my friends have tried to serve our nation. In view of what we had experienced we had to act as we did, like those hundreds of thousands of Russians fighting on the German side against Stalin. Their circumstances forced them so to act, even if the immediate motive was to escape from starvation or from death. I have struggled with myself. I do not reproach anyone. A man's action can only be understood in the light of his circumstances. As for me I must continue on my path. For me there is no turning back, any more than for a soldier in the face of the enemy. You will understand. And if you understand, then I am satisfied. But you are free. Go, and God be with you.

I left Dahlem where I had been staying for the last few days, having been bombed out of my Berlin lodgings. I would shortly be going on leave, but for the moment I must await General Gehlen's orders.

(ii)

To see the war position one had to look at the map. Up till now I, and the Russian generals, had been able to form a reasonably accurate picture – at least geographically – of the situation on the fronts. But developments since the early summer had been so rapid that now one could hardly tell. When Vlasov read his manifesto in Prague on 14 November things were very different from what they had been during our early discussions with the SS in July. The position had so deteriorated that one could only suspect the very worst. Our ignorance of the relative strengths on the various fronts made any accurate assessment impossible.

Ever since the Allied landing in Normandy on 6 June the western theatre had been of prime importance. The Allies occupied Paris on 25 August. General von Choltitz, realizing that further resistance was senseless, had surrendered the town and thus prevented its destruction. His action made a deep impression on Vlasov's officers. 'You see,' said one of them, 'here again is the difference between Germans and Stalinists. There are still German officers who, in cases like this, are ready to take the responsibility of surrendering, and of disregarding, on grounds of humanity, the criminal orders of their superiors.'

Late June saw the start of the Red offensive against the Central Group of Armies. It was said that the heads of the Romanian and Hungarian governments were seeking contacts with the Western Allies or even considering separate peace negotiations with Moscow. Who can blame them? Like the little circle round Vlasov they were thinking of what would happen after the German collapse. Bucharest was occupied on 30 August and Budapest at the beginning of November.

The Baltic States were lost apart from the pocket held by the 'Courland Army'. The Reds were nearing Memel. They were approaching – perhaps even had crossed – the East Prussian frontier.

Churchill, in the very darkest hours, had spoken frankly and had realistically weighed up his chances against the facts. But in the Reich, leadership and population alike had shut their eyes to what, since the winter of 1941–2, had become inevitable.

The German people were conscious of their victorious advances from the Arctic to Africa and from the Atlantic to the Volga. They had still not lost their feeling of superiority. They maintained a blind, intoxicated, belief in the Führer – as if hypnotized. And as hard facts threatened to shatter their dreams they clung to their faith in the 'Wonder Weapons'. And not only the masses. I remember a general coming to the OKH in February 1945 and talking of the introduction of the 'Wonder Weapon' as imminent. 'Two months more, and the course of the war will be entirely changed.' Those that believed were fascinated. The others hid their disbelief – it would have been dangerous to show it. If officers held this faith, what could one expect of the masses, exposed as they were every day and every hour to the party's propaganda, press, broadcasts and finally the never-ending enemy air attacks? With the Allies' demand of unconditional surrender they were faced, all of them, with annihilation. The continued struggle day by day, in this chaos of tears, blood, destruction and hopelessness, had become an unreal reality, persistent, inevitable. And so they clung to the hope of a wonder weapon to bring about a change and, at last, an end.

(iii)

I was not invited to Prague. At the last minute, however, I was instructed by Gehlen to bring about a meeting between Vlasov and General Köstring who had not, so far, set eyes on each other. A condition was that Vlasov should agree. He was understood to have given out that Köstring was of no interest to him, and that he proposed to ignore the GOC Volunteer Formations. Quite apart from practical considerations it would be embarrassing if the commander of the Russian Liberation Army should cut dead the general in command of the volunteers. Vlasov was quite capable of doing so.

As instructed I duly approached Vlasov. He smiled and his immediate comment was unprintable, but in the end he showed himself once more willing to forget the past so as not to hurt the old gentleman's feelings. We agreed that it should be a strictly private meeting immediately on arrival in Prague and before the beginning of the official programme. When the time came Vlasov was relaxed and natural, and it was Köstring who was unforthcoming. In the last few weeks he had been too closely involved with anti-Vlasov circles. He may well have been oppressed by the thought that it was now all too late for what he himself had hoped back in 1941. There may too have been a sense of failure. I did my best to get the conversation going, as did Colonel Herre, the only other person present. It was an uncordial meeting, but at least an outer form was preserved and the two agreed they were no longer enemies.

In front of the railway station Vlasov was accorded all military honours by a company of German troops. He was welcomed by the Prague town commandant. There followed a luncheon given by the *Reichsprotektor*. The afternoon's proceedings and the formal announcement of the manifesto were arranged in the old citadel. Vlasov was much moved. The Reich government was represented only by Statthalter Frank and Obergruppenführer Lorenz, but the numerous generals and SS representatives made it an impressive assembly. The Russian officer corps proved to be superlative hosts. There were delegations from volunteer units and from *Ostarbeiter*. Obergruppenführer Lorenz in his speech made the first public reference to the 'new ally' and transmitted the greetings of the Reich government. Then the Committee for the Liberation of the Peoples of Russia was formally constituted, and General Andrei Andreyevich Vlasov, amid loud applause, was elected president.

(iv)

In the evening was a banquet. Dr Kroeger asked me to interpret the speech that Vlasov was expected to make. I refused. When the time came, Vlasov in the course of his speech proffered his thanks to the Wehrmacht for all the help they had given him: he went on to express his particular thanks to an unnamed German officer of the rank of captain who had stood by his side for all these years. Later in the evening a number of highly placed officers and officials came up to the captain and congratulated him: General Vlasov had mentioned no name, 'but there was no doubt as to whom he had in mind'. This tribute of Vlasov was to cause me much embarrassment. Later, I was invited to join Vlasov and Zhilenkov at a table where they were sitting with a senior SS officer. He turned out to be deputy head of the Personnel Department of the Waffen SS. They quickly came to the point: I should transfer to the SS and remain with Vlasov. Vlasov emphasized that this was not his proposal, though he would be glad if I were to come back to him. I replied that I would not cooperate voluntarily. The SS officer asked the reason for my refusal and I told him: 'Because I do not belong to you. My experience since 1941 has made it impossible for me to join any branch of the Nazi Party. As a soldier I had my duty.' I repeated this in Russian to the other two, to avoid any possible ambiguity. The German listened carefully. But he evidently had his orders. 'We must have you with us,' he said, 'alongside General Vlasov.'

'And Dr Kroeger?'

'And Dr Kroeger as well. In any case, if you do not wish to volunteer to join us, we can ask the army for you and they will transfer you. You can raise no objections to that.'

His tone was very determined. Then I remembered the case of Herwarth, and I had an idea.

'Twice during this war I have been recommended for promotion and each time it was refused – I imagine because of my feelings for Russians and my work with Vlasov. You, as a regular officer, should understand that after serving in two wars I naturally wish to be at least a major before leaving the Wehrmacht – especially as I already might have been a lieutenant-colonel.'

'I quite understand,' said the SS general. 'That is the right way to go about it. The army will promote you to major, and we will put you up to the rank of Standartenführer. I will fix things up at once with the army, and it should all be finished in two or three weeks. For an officer in the position you will be holding with General Vlasov the rank of Standartenführer is more appropriate. So the matter is settled.'

'To us,' said Zhilenkov, 'he will always be Captain Strik.'

After Prague I reported to General Gehlen.

'They are quite determined to force you to transfer to the SS,' he said. 'And once you are in the SS you will never get out again. The absolute confidence that Vlasov and the other Russians have in you is worth pure gold. Ever since those days in Vinitsa you have never lied to them. That is your capital. Once in the SS you will have to lie to them and your capital will be gone. And you will be a dead loss to us as well because some day or another we may want you again for Vlasov and the Liberation Movement.'

'Do you still think that?' I asked.

'One never knows.'

I had and have no idea what was in his mind. Since 20 July he had been less than ever inclined to talk. That affair had never been mentioned when we were together. But in our little club at Fremde Heere Ost it was firmly believed that, with all his cleverness and his caution, it was only good fortune that had saved Gehlen from the fate of the others.

'So we must now stop you getting picked up by the SS. At any rate for the moment. You will have to disappear from the scene. You will proceed to Pomerania where you will write the history of the Vlasov Movement. I will do the necessary.'

I do not remember whether it was Lieutenant-Colonel Nauck or von der Marwitz who gave me the address of a country house in Pomerania, to which I at once proceeded on orders from the OKH. Herr Kortüm's estate was deep in the Pomeranian countryside. Herr Kortüm had obviously been notified and welcomed me warmly. I was allotted a pleasant room and set about my work.

19

Last Meeting with Vlasov

(i)

VON DELLINGSHAUSEN came to see me on 12 December, and one of Gehlen's officers five days later. He brought me orders to leave my hiding-place and to investigate the possibility of finding quarters for units of the Russian Liberation Army in the Posen area. It was here that the First Division was to be given its baptism of fire. It was felt Russians would feel more at home on the Vistula than in East Prussia. There was also an idea of bringing armed or unarmed volunteer units from the west, or possibly *Ostarbeiter* 'volunteers', for the construction of defensive works in the area. In this way a centre could be formed for volunteers under Russian command, and the defences of the area strengthened. Dellingshausen told me that Colonel Herre was engaged, with considerable energy and drive, in organizing the First Division in Münsingen.

I called on General Petzel, commanding the Posen Wehrkreis, and his chief of staff. Petzel referred me to Gauleiter Greiser who had been given full powers over all matter connected with the defence of the Warthegau, and whose approval was required for any steps taken. I wondered if this meant I would be caught by the party and hauled off to the SS. But it seemed the right hand had no idea what the left hand was up to. A fellow-Balt provided an introduction to Greiser, who quickly grasped the position and promised his help: details should be arranged with General Petzel in the course of the next few days. There seemed no particular sense of urgency, though the Red Army had already reached the Vistula. I made my report over Christmas and returned to Pomerania.

(ii)

On 12 January 1945 the Red Army launched a general offensive from the Kurischer Haff to the Carpathians. I learned later that General Gehlen had not only provided accurate details of all enemy dispositions, but had also pinpointed the sectors of attack and foretold the probable objectives. He had produced a remarkable report, which Hitler proceeded to describe as 'bluff on the part of the Staff'. I was told Gehlen presented the report personally to Hitler in the presence of Guderian (who had now taken over from Zeitzler). Presumably Gehlen too would have been dismissed, if his predictions had not been so quickly and so completely confirmed.

When, a few months later, Malyshkin and I met Guderian in our prison camp he told us that he had reached the conclusion that all available forces must be deployed against the enemy in the east. The Red advance on Europe must be checked at all costs, even if it meant an enemy breakthrough in the west. This was the view that Vlasov for two and a half years had hoped would be accepted. There was, Guderian felt, a possibility of perhaps coming to terms with the Western Powers. These talks in the prison camp convinced me that Guderian still ignored the possibilities of political warfare against the Stalin regime. For him Moscow was not the heart of Russia but merely an important military, communications and industrial centre. In the prison camp he was still maintaining that, given certain conditions, Moscow could have been taken in 1941–2. He saw things only from the military standpoint. He never imagined that Russia would continue to resist even after the fall of Moscow, or that 'Russia can only be conquered by Russians'. When Malyshkin explained the idea of a Russian civil war and a national liberation government, and how it was just this that frightened Stalin, it came to Guderian as a revelation. He remembered that Field-Marshal von Bock had talked in similar strain.

(iii)

As the Red Army continued their relentless advance I remained
in the lonely house and lived in a haze of rumours. 'The Russians
are coming.' Bromberg, Deutsch-Krone, Posen. We even heard
they had reached Kreuz. My family were in Posen but I was no
longer in touch with them. I later learned they left the town on a
refugee train on 20 January. The day before, my wife had asked
for a permit to leave for my fourteen-year-old daughter. A party
fanatic shouted at her: 'The girl can pour boiling water into the
loopholes of Soviet tanks.' But there was a sensible Rhinelander
in the office. 'We can fix it,' he told my wife. 'They're all daft.'
Next morning there was an order for all women and children to
leave Posen.

On 23 January a phone call came through from Dabendorf. It
was Sergei Fröhlich. 'Get to Frankfurt at once,' he said. 'We are
arranging for a car to meet you. In Kunersdorf leave word at such
and such address.'

I shall not forget my parting with Herr Kortüm. The old
squire had sent his family off westwards in a farm cart. He brought
champagne from the cellar. He was a man who drank amply and
quickly.

'It had to be like this,' he said. 'Land and soil. Hitler never
possessed any land of his own. The old field-marshal (i.e.
Hindenburg) had only seen one of his faces when he made him
chancellor. The field-marshal had no idea there could ever be
so much nastiness in one man. I stay here, on my own soil, even
if the Russians do come. We have our rifles, my men and I.'

I tried to persuade the old gentleman to leave with me.

'I will let you have a horse and a good Polish driver; but I stay
here.'

'We don't shoot from behind hedges,' I ventured to say. 'That
is not our style of war.'

'Quite right. All the same I stay here.'

I do not know the old gentleman's fate. Perhaps he lies under
his soil.

I reached Frankfurt-an-der-Oder without incident. My friend

Hans Künkel and his wife gave me a hot bath and a warm bed. I was aroused at 4 a.m. There were Fröhlich and General Zhilenkov. No petrol was available except for a general, so both of them had come to fetch me. At Kunersdorf they had found my note with the Frankfurt address. By about 7 a.m. we were in Dabendorf. Dellingshausen warned me that I must not stay there. We drank tea and I took leave of my German officers and General Trukhin. Other Russians turned up in the mess to say goodbye to me, though no one was supposed to know that I was there. That dark January morning was my last in Dabendorf.

I went to Zossen to see General Gehlen, who told me to go and find my family. After many adventures I found them in the little village of Sallgast between Finsterwalde and Senftenberg. My mother wanted to stay there, she was tired of being on the move. All her life she had been a refugee.

I phoned one of my friends of our 'club' in the OKH to find out what was happening, and the answer was I should move my wife and family as far to the west as possible. I said goodbye to them and reported once more in Zossen. In the OKH, as well as the normal staff work, they were practising with anti-tank grenades. From Zossen I went with an advance party to Bad Reichenhall. As we arrived an English transmitter was announcing that the OKH was moving to Bad Reichenhall.

For the next few weeks Gehlen arranged for me to be posted as sick. There were various complications and I was continually on the move – Reichenhall, Mittenwald, Füssen and so on. I heard nothing about my promotion or my transfer to the SS, but twice I had notifications of some sort and once my marching orders. I happened then to be in Reichenhall. My immediate superior, Lieutenant-Colonel Nauck, phoned Gehlen and was told in reply that I must disappear.

In early April, in Füssen, I received a new fourteen-day sick-leave warrant, and went off to join my family, who had found refuge in a peasant's cottage near the Dwinger property in the Allgäu. They had been given a warm welcome by the peasant's wife – such as they had not always encountered in their wanderings.

(iv)

On my visits to Reichenhall I had been able to get some news of
Dabendorf, though Dabendorf itself no longer existed. A few
days after the air attack on Dresden, the inmates were transferred to Schloss Gieshübel in Sudetenland. Dellingshausen was
still assistant commandant, and the party owed much to his care
and foresight. Captain Balderschwang was temporarily appointed
commandant, but was soon succeeded by Captain Theodor
Oberländer. This was the same Oberländer whose criticism of
Himmler's *Untermensch* policy had once caused him to be arrested
and (as General Petzel told me) sentenced to death. The sentence
was not carried out. General Aschenbrenner was able to remove
him from the claws of the SD and instal him in his new
command.

I heard that Colonel Herre had done a magnificent job in
setting up and equipping the Liberation Army's First Division
in Münsingen, in spite of all the difficulties with which he was
faced. Vlasov had appointed Colonel (later General) Bunichenko
as commander. The division had its baptism of fire near
Frankfurt-an-der-Oder, and even at this period had a number
of line-crossers from the Reds.

A Second Division was formed at Heuberg, under General
Zveryev. Parachute, anti-aircraft and reconnaissance units were
being set up under the command of the Russian air force
General Maltsev and under the general supervision of General
Aschenbrenner, former Military Attaché in Moscow. Finally, a
military academy for officers had been started under the excep-
tionally able General Meandrov. What could not have been
achieved if we had had these splendid officers and soldiers on our
side from the start.

Chief of Staff of the Liberation Army was General Feodor
Ivanovich Trukhin, with Colonel I. G. Neryanin as head of the
Operations Branch.

Meanwhile an agreement had been reached between Vlasov
and General Shandruk, one of the leaders of the Ukrainian
National Committee, who had come to approve of Vlasov's views

and programme. The Cossacks had also come into line. And all this was happening four years too late.

General Trukhin sent me a message through Colonel Boyarski that Colonel Herre had accomplished an almost superhuman achievement in setting up the First Division. Trukhin and all the other Russian officers had expressed to him their warmest appreciation and their profound respect. 'At one time we called Herre the *Cunctator* and were always making complaints. Now he has restored the balance by his selfless dedication to his task. You too should know that, Wilfried Karlovich, and it is my duty to see that you know it.' Such was Trukhin's message. This was the last commission I ever received from Trukhin. When, after the war, I next met Herre I passed on the handshake of friendship as Trukhin had wished.

(v)

On 18 April 1945 my wife and I were in the living-room of the cottage when our daughter came running in. 'Out there on the hill, lots of officers, red stripes on their trousers, asking for you!'

There were Vlasov, Malyshkin, Zhilenkov, Boyarski, with their escort, General Aschenbrenner, and finally Dr Kroeger. No one knew of my hiding-place. The Russians had found me. We went together to Hedwigshof, Erich Edwin Dwinger's country house, and it was there that my last meeting with Vlasov took place.

'Germany,' said Vlasov, 'has collapsed sooner than I expected. So what now?'

He went on to explain the efforts he had made to keep intact 'the substance' of his following. He had agreed to his First Division going temporarily into action on the Eastern front, in order to show the Germans that his volunteers were still to be relied on when fighting for their nation's freedom under Russian leadership; but he had instructed his chief of staff, General Trukhin, and his intimates that 'the substance', come what may, must be preserved: the First Division and all available volunteer formations must be concentrated in the area Prague–Linz.

Aschenbrenner was privy to these plans, i.e. either in this area or on Yugoslav soil to form a kernel of 'Free European Resistance' out of the volunteers, the Cossacks, Czech and Yugoslav nationalists and freedom-loving Germans.

(The belief that the alliance of convenience between the Anglo-Saxons and the Kremlin could not endure was no empty dream. It was the conviction of all who knew what Bolshevism meant. What happened later proved us right. It was our timing that was wrong. We had, of course, no knowledge of what had been agreed at Yalta. So this belief shed a deceptive gleam over my last meeting with these men who had staked their all.)

However, Vlasov's scheme would be impracticable without the cooperation of the German officer commanding the area and his German garrison. Aschenbrenner had put out feelers which showed that nothing could be hoped from Field-Marshal Schörner now in command Prague–Linz. Further feelers, to Field-Marshal von Weichs in command in the Balkans, had led to no result.

So what now?

A proposal from Dwinger was to occupy a position in the Bavarian mountains and hold there a number of prominent prisoners in whom the Allies were believed to be interested. Dwinger suggested names. One could bargain with the Americans for these hostages in exchange for right of asylum for the volunteers. Vlasov would have none of it. 'Possibly effective,' he said, 'but I do not like the idea. So far we have fought with clean hands and clear hearts. We would be justified under the traditional rules of the game – loser has his head cut off. We have today no obligations to the Germans, but we do not want to abuse the confidence of those Germans who have helped us.'

Vlasov went on to say that some time before he had sent a member of the Liberation Committee, Zherebkov, to Geneva to contact the British and Americans through the International Red Cross. His brief was that the volunteers were political opponents of the Soviet regime and should be granted the right of political asylum. Nothing had been heard from Zherebkov.

Aschenbrenner urged an immediate approach to the Allied

Command. In the meantime the volunteer formations should be withdrawn towards the Prague–Linz area. He had already instructed Captain Oberländer to approach the British in the hope of saving the Russian air units under General Maltsev. Captain Strik-Strikfeldt should contact the Americans; but of course this must be a purely Russian, not a German, *démarche*.

Vlasov was definite. Malyshkin, not Strik-Strikfeldt, must undertake the mission, Then he turned to me. Would I go with Malyshkin? He added: 'The hardest service you could ever render us.' I had already decided I would accept. In any case Aschenbrenner, as representative of the GOC Volunteer Formations, was my superior officer and had the right to give me orders.

They made out for me a Vlasovite identity card as 'Verevkin, Colonel of the Volunteer Army of the Committee for the Liberation of the Peoples of Russia'. Dr Kroeger, who had taken no part in the discussion, wrote out a certificate assuring us freedom of movement in the front-line area without obligation to disclose the nature of our mission. This was to save us from arrest and execution by 'Werewolves' and other SS groups combing the advanced zone for deserters.

I stayed on for more than an hour alone with Vlasov. Inwardly he was a broken man. He pulled himself together when he had to exercise authority, but he knew that this was the end. Washington, he said, and Franklin were traitors in the eyes of the British crown. They won their fight for freedom and are now revered as heroes. 'I lost, so I remain a traitor until such time as in Russia freedom comes before bogus Soviet patriotism. As I told you, I do not believe in help from the Americans. We have nothing to offer. We are not a power factor; but to have trodden on our Russian hopes for freedom and for human worth, out of ignorance and opportunism, is something that Americans, Englishmen, Frenchmen, and perhaps Germans too, will one day bitterly regret.'

That night when he had gone to bed I went up to his room. 'Forgive me, Wilfried Karlovich,' he said. 'Of late I have been drinking heavily. Of course I used to drink before, but it never got hold of me. Now I want to forget. Kroeger keeps filling up my glass and perhaps he thinks that is the way to manage me. He is wrong. I can see and hear. I miss nothing. I just want to get right away from the nastiness of reality. I know my duty and my responsibilities. God give me the strength to hold out to the end. But you, Wilfried Karlovich, you will go with Malyshkin and help him. That I know. And one day you will tell the others that Vlasov and his friends loved their country and were not traitors. Promise me.'

He was nearly asleep and I left him.

20
The End

GERMAN columns were retreating towards Rosshaupten and
Lechbruck. My family and I and Malyshkin spent the night in
the woods; and it was my daughter Dela and her little friend
Karin who stopped drunken soldiers shooting at me. The next
day my mother died in Seeg. I had not been able to see her, and
could not go to the funeral. As I took leave of my wife and daughter
the little girl was impelled to give me this parting advice: 'Father,
if you ever get to the Americans you must tell them you are not a
Russian Colonel Verevkin but a German officer. You must
always speak the truth.'

A sergeant conducted us blindfold to an American divisional
staff. We produced our credentials from Vlasov.

'Russian officers? Allies. But how did Russian troops get here
to Nesselwang in Bavaria?'

I had to explain to Colonel Snyder who thought we were Red
Army officers. He phoned through to Army HQ and arranged
for us to be sent there next day. He suggested inviting a representative of the Soviet Military Mission.

'No, Colonel,' I broke in. 'Not that.'

'No,' he said on the phone. 'They don't want that. I will
explain . . .'

I had translated to Malyshkin, who suddenly grabbed the
receiver and broke off the call.

It was an irresistible impulse and Malyshkin kept apologizing.
Colonel Snyder smiled. Then he asked us to dine with him. 'You
first, General,' he said to Malyshkin as we reached the door.
Then, to me, 'Colonel, you next. I am only a lieutenant-colonel.'

I remembered what my daughter had said.

'I am only a captain,' I said. 'A German captain.' I explained that it was my task to interpret, and to do what I could to help the Russian Liberation Movement. I produced my pay-book. He told me to keep it as I might find it useful later on.

During the meal we took the opportunity to tell Colonel Snyder how the Russian Liberation Movement came into being, its aims and its purpose, and why it was that the movement was fighting on the side of one dictator against a dictator even more powerful and more brutal. We explained at length, and he listened attentively. He had, I gathered, held an important official post under President Hoover and had some knowledge of European affairs; but even so he found our complicated story not easy to understand.

'We do not always agree with Roosevelt's policy,' he said, 'but after all he is our president and we soldiers have got to obey orders.'

(As all soldiers in every country.)

'But supposing these orders were to commit crimes against humanity?'

'We have had no such orders from Roosevelt; but I admit there could be a difference between our obedience to our president and your obedience to Uncle Joe or Hitler. Hitler we know is a criminal. In my position I cannot talk about Uncle Joe for he is our ally. However, I think I understand you. I can envisage cases where one must refuse to obey.'

I shall not forget our meeting with this admirable American officer.

Colonel Snyder promised to make a full report to his superiors. He did not dangle any hopes before us. He was a soldier. He promised to try and trace my wife and pass her a letter from me, and also to let her know I had arrived at his quarters safe and sound. He kept his promise. His message was to be the only sign of life my wife had from me for eight months.

Next morning we were blindfolded once more and set off in a jeep. I admired the way Malyshkin could always tell the direction in which we were going – eastwards, now to the north again. In spite of the blindfold the Russian child of nature could always tell by the sun. *En route* we were parted and travelled in separate cars. I wondered what this might mean. When we halted I was led up a number of steps and only then was my bandage removed. I was in a large light room, with windows looking out on a garden. Then Malyshkin was brought in. We had no idea where we were.

Very soon we were taken into another large room where there was General Patch, Commander of the Seventh American Army. By his side was a youngish man in American officer's uniform, who told us, in Russian, he was son of the former tsarist, General Artamonov.

Their first questions were: 'Who is General Vlasov? What are Russian troops doing in Bavaria? What do you want?'

General Patch seemed to have been informed about us by Snyder or Snyder's superiors. All the same he listened carefully to Malyshkin. And this was Malyshkin's great moment. He told of the Russian people's fight for freedom against the tyranny of Stalin. He told how Russian volunteers had been already fighting – alongside the Germans but not for Germany – against Stalin before ever America had come into the war. He told how Vlasov had made it his task to prevent these volunteers becoming hirelings of the Third Reich, and how he had given sense and purpose to their struggle.

'You maintain your volunteers only fought against Stalin and were not German hirelings. Then how is it that we came across so many Russians in German uniform in our advance through France?'

This was the first time General Patch interrupted Malyshkin. It was a difficult point to explain. How could this American, how could any sensible being, understand that Hitler had rejected his natural allies against Stalin? That these anti-Stalinist volunteers had been forced against their will to be German hirelings and had been thrown willy nilly into the fighting in the west?

Malyshkin did his best, but it seemed that this was the one point that General Patch did not accept.

'But many Russians were fighting very hard on the German side against us.'

'General Vlasov had no truck with these auxiliaries as the Germans called them. They were never under his command. If they fought well it is simply because Russians are good soldiers.'

'You maintain they were forced to fight against the Americans. Good. But they volunteered to take the field against Stalin? After all, Stalin and the Russians are our allies.'

'We are your allies, General Patch. We are these same Russians. Vlasov was one of the Red Army heroes who defended Moscow against the German attack, who inflicted on the Germans their first serious defeat. We are all Russians and ex-Red Army men. But we had decided to choose the cause of freedom. What freedom means, you, General, as an American should know much better than I do.'

Malyshkin surpassed himself. What I can write here is but a feeble echo of his impassioned address. Colonel Artamonov was greatly moved and gave a spirited translation. General Patch seemed fascinated.

'Go on,' he said. (He must certainly have had more urgent matters to attend to.)

Malyshkin went back into the distant past. In 1917 Lenin and Trotsky had dissolved the freely elected Constituent Assembly, though the Bolsheviks were only a small minority. From 1918 to 1920 the British, French and Americans had supported the first Russian volunteers aginst the Bolshevik usurpers. 'And your compatriots were allies of anti-Bolshevik Russians. And therefore our allies. But now we are asking not for military support but for right of asylum. This right is laid down in the charter of the United Nations. And America is the citadel of freedom.'

Patch considered and then said: 'Unfortunately what you ask is right outside my competence as army commander; but I promise to pass your request to General Eisenhower. I will willingly do my best. Thank you.'

I had the chance of a few words with Artamonov, who, it seemed, held the same sort of post with General Patch that I had once held with Field-Marshal von Bock. I told him of my duties then and subsequently, and asked him to intervene on behalf of his fellow-countrymen with the Americans as I had once with the Germans. Presumably it was his official position that did not allow him to commit himself. He merely said he had once been enrolled in the Corps of Pages, and would try to do what he could. A cold fear came over me – supposing he was not an American colonel but a Soviet observer? I named one of the pages who might have been his contemporary. He had not heard of him. My suspicion grew. The way he spoke and his whole bearing made it seem he was speaking the truth, but my fears remained. In the spring of 1967 I learned by chance that by harbouring these suspicions I was wronging Artamonov.

Next day as I was conducted across the hall two American officers were shouting at an elderly Hungarian. He stood there, erect and dignified, and was declaring, once and for all, that he was not going to answer a certain question. The Americans bullied and threatened; the old Hungarian remained the image of a grand seigneur. My escort told me this was Admiral Horthy, the regent of Hungary.

General Patch's attitude, when we were brought in for our second interview, was very different from that of those two officers. He courteously informed us that as this was a matter of politics General Eisenhower would have to refer our case to Washington. That would, of course, take time; one could not say when a decision would be reached. He, Patch, accordingly proposed there should be no further loss of life. (This means, I thought, that here in the West human lives count for something.) The Russian divisions should lay down their arms at once. They would be treated exactly on a par with German prisoners of war.

I pricked up my ears.

'Does this mean, General, that the Russians will be treated according to the provisions of the Geneva Convention?'

'Why do you ask?'

'Because after the First World War I served on a Red Cross delegation in Geneva, because Hitler ignored the Convention on his Eastern front and because I know what that means.'

'I can only repeat,' said the general slowly, 'and I emphasize, that they will be treated in strict accordance with the regulations in force regarding German prisoners of war.'

Was this not clear? Did the Americans propose to ignore the provisions of the Convention that they themselves had recognized? So that meant no asylum for Russian volunteers. Did it also mean they would be handed back to the Reds? I shuddered.

This must be a reprisal for Hitler's infringement of the Geneva Convention.

I told Malyshkin and I then expressed my misgivings direct to General Patch. Artamonov remained silent.

General Patch abruptly held out his hand to Malyshkin. 'As general of the American Army I regret that this is all I can tell you. Speaking personally I must express my very great regret at having to do so. I understand your point of view and I want to assure you of my personal respect. You will understand I am a soldier.' This, or something very like it, was what he said to the sorely tried Russian general.

We were a delegation and, as such, the traditional rules of war provided that we should be sent back through the lines to General Vlasov.

'As soon as the position at the front allows.'

(ii)

Days went by, and for us time seemed to stand still. We had no news of the outside world. The Americans were friendly and polite. Then came 8 May and a major informed us Germany had capitulated. From that moment we were no longer delegates but prisoners of war. For some days we stayed on in the same quarters. Then we were moved to Augsburg. Our guards were rough but correct.

A workers' housing estate had been cleared of its residents and turned into a reception camp. This was what the Nazis had done in Poland and Russia, though the Americans apparently did not intend to keep us here permanently. General Malyshkin was lodged in a two-room flat along with other Russian officers. (One of them was unknown to us and we suspected he might be an informer.) The food was good. The guards were friendly Puerto Ricans. In a store cupboard we found some forty broomsticks. One of our officers was an expert at branding patterns and designs, and the broomsticks thus decorated were passed to the Puerto Ricans in exchange for cigarettes. Broomsticks with swastikas were much sought after.

In the mornings all prisoners came out for exercise in a large field, and one recognized a number of the leading Nazis, including Hermann Göring. One morning I unexpectedly saw General Gehlen. It turned out that he was lodged in the upper storey of the house where we were. It was arranged that I might take up tea to him. He maintained his self-possession and his confidence. He had plans stretching out far into a new future, whereas most of the camp's inmates could think only of the past.

At the Sunday divine service we noticed Zhilenkov. He too had seen us, and that same afternoon he made his way to us over a whole complex of roofs. That in itself was quite a feat; when blocked by a wall he removed the bricks. He was able to tell us that the First Division, at the appeal of the Czech nationalists, had marched into Prague and forcibly disposed of the SS garrison, but Czech jubilation came to an end when the Americans arrived and handed over Prague and its population to the Reds. General Bunichenko had to retire westwards; his division was disarmed, and most of the troops handed over to be prisoners of the Red Army. A great many committed suicide.

Zhilenkov had no news of what had happened to Vlasov. 'We, that is the Russians who were with me,' Zhilenkov continued, 'have so far been well treated by the Americans. But we noticed that when dealing with Germans the Americans behave as the Reds would behave. So I supplied the Germans in my party, all of them decent men, with identity cards and pay-books making them out to be Latvians, Estonians, Ukrainians and civilian officials, accountants and so on. One hopes this will give them the chance of getting better treatment. We know Soviet methods and German methods. American methods seem much the same. I thought I would try and improve on fortune, but now I am here in prison myself.'

A few days later Zhilenkov managed to arrange to be transferred to our quarters.

From Augsburg we were moved to Mannheim. It was evening when our train halted at a wayside station. Zhilenkov's Russian instincts came out.

'I drop off here,' he said. 'And into the bush.'

I asked him whatever he was thinking of. 'One day the Americans will come to realize that every good freedom-loving Russian is a welcome ally for the free world.'

My faith in Americans and in justice was then still unimpaired. I was afraid Zhilenkov might be discovered and shot in the course of his flight. Therefore I advised him to stay. The train was standing for perhaps half an hour at the little station. The guards were chatting among themselves and paying little attention to us. Zhilenkov stayed. Today I am haunted by the thought that his death is on my conscience. But he should never have asked me, he should have followed his instinct. He might quite possibly have got away and thus have been saved. Russians' guardian angels are quite different from ours.

In Mannheim we were lodged in an army barracks. I was kept with the Russian generals and officers to act as interpreter. We were allotted a large room. The Germans were not so well off. Prisoners included Field-Marshals von Blomberg, von List, von Weichs and von Leeb, and Generals Guderian, Köstring and Heusinger. I was glad to meet my old friend the Counsellor of Embassy, Gustav Hilger, and also several industrialists whom I knew. We were all prisoners together and there was no distinction between field-marshal and captain or between German and Russian. All were ashamed of the once vaunted *Untermensch* policy.

There were lively discussions between Malyshkin and Zhilenkov and the German marshals and generals regarding the operations in front of Moscow, round Leningrad, at Stalingrad, Kursk and in the Caucasus. Diagrams of dispositions and locations were drawn in the sand. Ritter von Leeb declared that his Northern Group of Armies could have captured Leningrad at the first onset, but Hitler's orders had held him back. He could never understand the motivation, among others put forward by Hitler, that it would be difficult to feed the town's population. With 50 million in the occupied zone who had to be fed already, the 2–3 million Leningraders would not make much difference. And in any case the blockade doomed them to starvation. The field-marshal knew nothing of Hitler's intention to decimate the population of Russia, or of his fear that Leningrad, most western of Russian cities, might again become a powerful centre of a free national Russia. He listened with great attention to Malyshkin and Zhilenkov and the scales seemed to drop from his eyes.

Field-Marshal von List told us of his arguments with Hitler over the simultaneous offensives against Stalingrad and the Caucasus. He had given warnings and offered his resignation which at first was not accepted. Then one day, when catastrophe was inevitable, Keitel had phoned him: 'You can do as you wanted.' That was List's dismissal.

Guderian, as already mentioned, still did not appreciate the political significance of Moscow. For him it was just an important centre of communications. What Malyshkin had to say on the subject seemed to bewilder him: he kept asking questions about Moscow. In general Guderian's bearing was dignified and soldierly, particularly when the American guards started to play tricks. I remember an American sergeant pointing a carbine at him and he stood there calmly facing him. I was close at hand and we managed to get the sergeant to drop his carbine.

It would, incidentally, be unfair to the 'unpolitical' General Guderian to reproach him for having, on Hitler's orders, accepted the post of Chief of the General Staff after 20 July 1944. He was close to those involved in this affair – a fact known to the very few. He had to reckon with the possibility that Hitler would appoint some SS personality as CGS. There was indeed a real danger of this, and the appointment of an unqualified amateur to this key post would have led to disastrous consequences.

Field-Marshal von Weichs had more understanding of the Liberation Movement than any of the others. He had been considering the problems involved ever since 1941. Another matter to which he had devoted thought was Hitler and his infallibility complex. He wrote Malyshkin a letter on the subject, which I translated into Russian and of which I have a copy.

Hilger had much of interest to tell us about his service in Moscow. With Malyshkin he spoke Russian. In him we had an experienced diplomat who had well and truly served his country and nation, who for decades had sown good seed and who had only harvested tares.

One day old von Thyssen was brought into the camp. In the early days he had supported Hitler, but later became estranged. The old man was quite senile, and only for short periods when playing chess did he seem able to forget his plight. Malyshkin was a good chess player, and he and I took it in turns to give the old man in his wide-brimmed straw hat this little relaxation.

Unfortunately there were also some rather dubious elements in the camp who engaged in shabby barter deals with their comrades in misfortune. There was Hitler's former 'court photographer', a certain Herr Hofmann. He now had no good word to say about 'Adolf', and maintained that he himself had never been a Nazi. Then there were certain German gentlemen who could not resist the temptation to pick up cigarette ends dropped by the guards. This is the sort of thing that happens in prison. Zhilenkov disapproved, and made a point of being first out in the yard in the mornings and collecting all the cigarette ends which he then destroyed. 'I do not propose to let the Americans have this satisfaction.'

Zhilenkov was the ideal comrade with whom to be in prison. Dignified and unbending towards the conquerors, he was always ready to do all he could for all who needed help. He gave away his cigarettes and often part of his rations. He mended shoes and clothes and once even made an artificial limb for one of the Germans. Some of the Russian officers helped him, and there were times when our room looked like a shoemaker's or tailor's workshop. Zhilenkov obtained his tools and material, legally or otherwise, from a store the Americans had in the cellar. One day Greiser, Gauleiter of the Warthegau, passed through the camp in transit. As we came to the canteen for the midday meal he was sitting at a table there, forlorn and avoided by the others. Zhilenkov in passing put down something to eat in front of him. He was sorry for this man whom he had never seen.

(iv)

One day the unimaginable happened. We were on our way to the canteen. In the yard was a small group of Russians with an American guard. Names were called out – Malyshkin, Zhilenkov and other Russian officers. I was put on one side. The Russians were told to fetch their luggage.

'This is the end,' said Malyshkin. 'Thank you for all you have done for us and for our people. One day the prisoners, the Red Army men and the *Ostarbeiter* will also want to thank you. But I and all of us here will not survive to see that day.'

The Russians took me in their arms and kissed me. Then I was parted from them. I ran to the field-marshals' quarters and shouted, 'They are handing them over.' List, Weichs and Guderian went across to a young American captain who had always been correct and even friendly.

'We must protest against the handing over of our Russian comrades to the Soviet authorities.'

The captain said he was merely carrying out his orders. The Russians were being transferred to another camp. He personally did not think they would be handed over. That would be against the American tradition.

I can still see them standing there, the two field-marshals and the general, once so powerful, now helpless and pleading; and the young American, obviously sincere, saying what his faith in his country bade him. 'With firmness in the right as God has given us to see the right.' We too had had faith in the right, and we did not yet know that in Yalta the right had foundered.

(v)

On the same evening Field-Marshal von Weichs and I were put in a lorry, driven off and unloaded in a prison yard. The old field-marshal was taken ill on the way; as he alighted he was bent double and could hardly walk. We were conducted along a long corridor. The last I ever saw of the field-marshal was when a guard kicked him into a cell and he collapsed on the ground.

My cell was No. 97. A tiny barred window. Two wooden bunks, one above the other. The cell was so narrow that I could not stretch out both arms. The door clanged behind me.

I should perhaps close here. An individual's experiences are of little interest, except perhaps to those very near to him; but having described my personal experiences against a background of big events, I perhaps may briefly look back on the solitude of my cell.

Meals were brought twice a day, at 8 a.m. and 4 p.m. Not ample, but what there was was good – pea soup, with one sardine or a piece of chocolate. Sometimes I had nothing – not I believe because of ill-will, but mine was the last door along the corridor and there may not always have been enough for all. Twice a week I was taken out to the yard for a few minutes, always with a guard. On one occasion I did my two rounds of the yard with the American guard pointing his machine-pistol at me all the way. He was not sober. A prisoner who wished to go to the latrine had to rattle a bar that went through into the corridor. It could happen that the guard's answer was, 'No – you have been enough today.'

Once I was inoculated. I was not told why or against what. Once I had such acute lumbago that I had to lie on the floor. A doctor helped me to my feet again after some days, and exempted me from being driven to the wash-room, which was the morning rule. There was nothing to read or to smoke. I had kept a copy of the New Testament which we had been given in Mannheim. The top left corner of my little window was broken and through the aperture one could see the end of the roof of the next block. I was happy and grateful when sparrows settled there so that I could look on something living. My personal details were checked, and on that occasion the sergeant threw a thick folder in my face. 'Have you seen this? Photographs from Dachau. Have a look.' Up to that moment I had had no inkling that in German concentration camps there had been bestialities such as in no other camps in the world. The sergeant did not believe me. The world still does not believe that these thugs managed to conceal their crimes from a great part of the German people. The Western world refused to believe it – just as we, at that time, refused to believe in the betrayal of freedom by free America.

When my personal details had been checked I was taken back to my cell. The guards were not allowed to speak to us beyond giving orders. The only contact with the outside world was the sounds coming through door and walls – sounds which were part of the prisoner's routine. The sense of hearing became keen. The click of an electric switch, the sound of plates on a tray, the opening and shutting of doors. The rumble of the ration trolley, when expectation became tense. Away on the right. Nearer. Nearer still. My door must be the next. No – they are wheeling it away. Will there be something to eat? Or not?

Once it happened to me as it had to old Field-Marshal von Weichs. I was being brought back from the surgery. I could not see properly in the semi-darkness and missed my open cell door. A kick in the back and I was sprawling on the floor. As I raised myself I said to myself I could not, should not accept this humiliation. I sat on my bunk. I had hidden a razor blade that would serve to open my veins. Then I looked at the New Testament and found these words in the Gospel of St John: 'Without me ye can do nothing.'

Yes. You can mangle this poor body – I looked down at the running sores on my legs – but myself, my honour, God's image that is in me, you cannot touch. This body is only a shell, not my real self. Without Him, without the Lord, my Lord, ye can do nothing.

New strength seemed to rise in me.

I was pondering over what seemed to me a miracle when the heavy lock turned in the cell door. A very young American soldier came in, put his finger to his lips to warn me not to speak.

'I saw it,' he said. 'Here are baked potatoes.' He pulled the potatoes out of his pocket and gave them to me, and then went out, locking the door behind him.

(vi)

In conclusion I must mention Captain David. Probably that was not his real name. We had met him in the camp at Mannheim where there was still some human relationship between victors and vanquished. He was a Jew, certainly of German background, presumably a victim of Nazi oppression. He had not returned evil for evil. It was he who had arranged for a room in Mannheim where church services could be held, and who had done much to lighten the prisoners' lot.

I had been for months in solitary confinement, with no idea of where I was or why. One day I was being brought back from the surgery, and there, in the dark passage, was Captain David. He recognized me and asked my cell number. A few minutes later he came in. 'How are you? A silly question, I can see you are not at all well. But you ought to be glad you are here in an American prison, for things are grim in the world outside. You are not a Soviet citizen, but you were always mixed up with the Russians, and you are better off here.'

It was long afterwards that I realized what this meant. I learned that the Americans and British had undertaken at Yalta to hand over all former Soviet citizens. In the event some German officers were also handed over. In the United Nations Declaration on Human Rights it is laid down that everyone has the right to seek political asylum in a foreign country. In 'liberated' Germany Russians, against their will – some even driven out of churches with machine-pistols – were handed over by American soldiers to their executioners. With the denial of human rights came the end of the Russian Liberation Movement.

Captain David asked a number of questions. He himself, he explained, was only here by chance as he was temporarily replacing a colleague. (Which meant, I concluded, that we could not be very far from Mannheim.) He remembered that back in Mannheim I used to recite my own poems about God and the world and high politics and the fate of prisoners.

'I will see you get paper and pencil. . . . And something to read. . . . And tobacco for your pipe. And matches.'

All these he brought personally to my cell. The book was Gullbrandson's *Und ewig singen die Wälder* . . .

This memoir is not a record of my innermost, intimate feeling. I do not wish to recall my desperation and my fears; but what I then experienced, and the grace that was accorded me, will be with me all my life.

It was Captain David that I had to thank for arranging that a cultured and congenial old émigré was brought to share my cell: I could not have borne solitary confinement much longer. My new colleague knew by heart long passages from Pushkin and Lermontov, and I made what I have been told are excellent translations. In the few weeks we were together we became fast friends.

And finally it was Captain David who arranged that after all these months I should be properly interrogated. He emphasized that in this, too, he was only standing in for a colleague.

It is to Captain David that I owe my release.

(vii)

General Vlasov was arrested by the Soviet authorities on Czechoslovak soil in May 1945. On 12 August 1946 Moscow Radio issued the following communiqué:

Within the last few days the Military Collegium of the Supreme Court of the USSR have been considering charges against Andrei Andreyevich Vlasov, Malyshkin, Zhilenkov, Trukhin, Zakutny, Blagoveshchenski, Maltsev, Bunichenko, Zveryev, Korbukov and Shatov. They were accused of treason and espionage and of terrorist activities against the USSR as agents of the German espionage service – that is to say, crimes under Section 58, paragraphs 1, 8, 9 and 10 of the Criminal Code of the USSR. All the accused admitted their guilt and were condemned to death under Point 1 of the Order of the Supreme Soviet of 19 April 1943. The sentences have been carried out.

Author's Epilogue

THIS account is as I wrote it during my 'exile' in Pomerania. It deals with my personal experience and is thus only a partial contribution to the history of that time. My notes gave no names and no dates and these I had to insert from memory. I have since revised certain passages. I made no notes after February 1944, and the last few pages were added, from memory, after my release from prison.

It is my duty to publish, because of my promise to General Vlasov to bear witness to the struggle for freedom, on the part of Russian men and women, against Stalin and Hitler. Ignorance and lies have blurred the image of these freedom fighters. But there comes a time when minds are free again, and there is search for the truth.

In the Soviet Union, following the official Moscow line, Vlasov and his supporters have been branded as traitors. And those in the Wehrmacht who helped them – on grounds of humanity and against the will of Hitler – are, for the Soviet public, set down as Gestapo agents or Hitlerian Fascists; but also in the West little is known of the Liberation Movement in spite of the literature that has appeared.[1]

German supporters of the movement are reproached for being so naïve as to embark on an undertaking that was doomed to failure from the start. 'One has only to read Hitler's *Mein Kampf* to realize that the Nazis would never modify their policy regarding Russia.'

A question that none of these critics has so far answered is: 'What should we then have done?'

The Spanish Jesuit Balthazar Gracian (1601–58) wrote: 'Mostly nothing happens because nothing comes of it.' We dared

[1] George Fischer, *Soviet Opposition to Stalin* (Harvard, 1952); Jürgen Thorwald, *Wen Sie Verderben Wollen* (Stuttgart, 1952); A. Kazantsev, *Tretya Sila* (Frankfurt a/M., 1952); Alexander Dallin, *German Rule in Russia* (New York, 1958); Sven Steenberg, *Wlassov—Verräter oder Patriot?* (Cologne, 1968).

to make an attempt and something did come of it. We acted as we did because we felt we must.

And who are 'we'?

There were Russian and other freedom fighters from Soviet territory, hoping for freedom and a better future. Of these there were many millions. Then there were not only members of the German Resistance, not only Balts, but countless Germans 'who wished to alter the evil that exists'. (I quote from my teacher, Dr Ernst Gelderblom – 'whoever wishes to be morally good must also wish to alter the evil that exists'.)

Our attempt is described in the foregoing pages. It covers the period 1941–5 – the period that calls to mind the fig tree that must be cut down should it bear no fruit.

1941 was the year in which history afforded Hitler one last opportunity to change his course. He had still the opportunity to refashion Europe on a basis of freedom, justice and equality. But, blinded by *hubris*, Hitler did not recognize this opportunity.

1942–3 were the years when German and Russian officers, out of inner conviction, endeavoured to open up the way to peace and freedom, in spite of Stalin and in spite of Hitler.

1944 saw Himmler's recognition of the Vlasov movement; but this change of heart was not sincere and came too late.

1945 saw the collapse and the end.

Vlasov and the little group around him made their own contribution to the idea of a community of nations. Their contribution was ignored, and not only by the Nazis. It is still ignored today.

Andrei Andreyevich Vlasov was not the founder of the Liberation Movement. This had come into being in the hearts of the oppressed and humiliated long before he ever appeared in the hearts of Russians, Ukrainians, Latvians, Estonians, Lithuanians, of the peoples of the Caucasus and of Central Asia. What Vlasov endeavoured to achieve was to endow their struggle with a policy and aim (in absolute negation of the spirit of Nazism); and to organize and build up the Power Factor required to bring the war to an end.

The various peoples of Russia doubtless harboured their own individual hopes and aims. Vlasov and his advisers saw the nationalities problem in a new light, envisaged its solution in a European context. Their point of view met with no recognition at the time and not only from the Nazis; it is still ignored today.

Vlasov was motivated neither by ambition nor by calculation. Fate, circumstances, his own personal experiences all combined to make it his duty to act as he did. He was not alone in assuming his responsibility. His principal associates were well aware that only the Second World War offered an opportunity – perhaps never to be offered again – to free the nations of Russia from the grip of their tyrants.

Can one then speak of treachery? If both Stalin and Himmler agree in saying this of Vlasov there must be something wrong.

When an American asked me whether Vlasov was a traitor, I put a counter question. Were Washington and Franklin also traitors?

If it be true that those are no traitors whose aim is to serve, not to harm their country, then the German Claus Graf von Stauffenberg and the Russian General A. A. Vlasov were not traitors. And this holds good for those who were with them.

If the late Social Democrat Julius Leber could declare that the whole world, *including the Communists*, must be rallied against Hitler, then the late General Vlasov was justified in demanding, also in the light of his experience, that the whole nation, yes, the whole world, *including the Nazis*, must be rallied against Stalin.

The Russian Liberation Movement was smashed and Vlasov and his friends were executed, just as Stauffenberg and the men of 20 July were executed; but because they gave their lives for freedom and justice, they have become a power that endures everywhere where freedom and justice are honoured.

Appendixes

The Russian as Human Being
[*Der Russische Mensch*]

CONCLUSIONS

The Russian, who knows nothing about our world and who looks to us for a lead, is now asking us a question, as important to ourselves as it is to him:

'What is going to happen now? Hitherto I have been a railway worker, an officer, a state employee; what am I going to be now? I have been a Soviet citizen; and all Soviet citizens were under the sway of a regime that did indeed keep us in bondage, but with the promise to lead us all into a better future. What will become of us now?'

This question has its psychological as well as its political aspect. This paper of mine is not a political treatise. The frontiers to be marked on any future map of Europe are not relevant to the issue with which I am here concerned. But whatever future frontier may be traced, we must face the fact that we shall be alongside some 100 million Russian men and women, and we shall be bound to devise some pattern of coexistence with them.

Two courses only will be open to us. Either we win them over and secure their cooperation; or else we do not win them over and must govern by force. In the latter event little regard need be paid to Russian psychology and Russian susceptibilities, or indeed to Russian political or economic aspirations.

But here there is a difficulty. As we have seen, Russian reactions to force, to the land and to suffering are not the same as ours. The force we would employ would be Western-style force, bound to appear to Russians to be far less formidable than the force they have hitherto known. We might well be constrained to change our approach and our methods, and set up a vast secret police apparatus, numbering a million and a half men or more. And if we fail to solve, or only half solve, the problem of the land we shall find ourselves forced, sooner or later, just as the hated Bolsheviks, to establish a totalitarian domination over body and soul.

That would be a return to the old Russian methods, carried out by

Westerners – always provided that Westerners are capable of carrying them out.

Unless we are prepared for this we must take the other alternative, and win the Russians over to our side; this indeed is psychologically possible, but first of all we must get to know the Russians with whom we have to deal.

General Vlasov's Open Letter: Why I Took Up Arms against Bolshevism

IF I now call on all Russians to rise in battle against Stalin and his clique and to strive for a New Russia without Bolsheviks and without capitalists, I feel it my duty to explain why I am doing so.

The Soviet regime has brought me no personal disadvantage.

I am the son of a peasant, born in the Nizhni-Novgorod province. I had no money, but in spite of that I received a higher education. I welcomed the People's Revolution, and I enrolled in the Red Army to fight for land for the peasants, for a better life for the workers, for a brighter future for the people of Russia.

From that day my whole life has been spent in the Red Army.

I have served in it, uninterruptedly, for twenty-four years. I rose from the rank of private soldier to that of Army Commander and of Acting Commander of an Army Group. I have been awarded the Order of Lenin, the Order of the Red Flag and the Twenty Years Red Army Service Medal. Since 1930 I have been a member of the Communist Party of the Soviet Union.

And now I have taken up the struggle against Bolshevism, and, myself a son of the people, call on the people to follow me. Why do I do so? This question is one that all who read my appeal are bound to ask, and one that I am bound to answer honestly.

During the Civil War I fought in the ranks of the Red Army because I believed that the Revolution would bring Land, Freedom and Happiness to the Russian People.

As Red Army officer I lived with the troops and their leaders – workers, peasants, intellectuals – all in our army uniform. I got to know their thoughts and their wishes, their cares and their difficulties. I never lost touch with my family and my village. I knew how the peasant lives and how he makes his living.

And so I realized that, after the Bolshevik victory, the Russian People had been given nothing of all those things for which it had been fighting during the years of the Civil War.

I saw how hard was the lot of the Russian worker, I saw the peasant driven by force into a collective farm, I saw how millions of Russian men and women disappeared, apprehended without due mandate or legal trial. I saw everything truly Russian trodden under foot. I saw the top civil and military appointments taken over by fawners and flatterers, to whom the interests of the Russian people meant nothing whatever. The Commissar system sapped the spirit of the Red Army. Irresponsibility, intrigue, espionage made of a commanding officer a mere pawn in the hands of the party manipulators.

From 1938 to 1939 I was in China, as military adviser to Chiang Kai-shek. On my return to the USSR I found that the higher ranks of the army had been arbitrarily decimated on Stalin's orders. Thousands and thousands of our best officers, up to and including the rank of marshal, had been arrested, executed or sent off to concentration camps where nothing more was ever heard of them. Terror raged over the whole nation – not just the army. There was not one single family that was spared. The army was weakened; the terrorized population looked to the future with foreboding, fearing the war that Stalin was preparing to unleash.

Then war broke out. I was at that time in command of the Fourth Mechanized Army Corps.

As soldier and patriot I felt that I must do my duty.

At Przemysl and at Lvov my Corps was attacked, held its ground and was ready to counter-attack; but my proposals were rejected. At Kiev I took over command of the Thirty-seventh Army and assumed the responsible post of Senior Military Officer in Kiev.

I realized there were two factors that must necessarily entail the loss of the war – firstly, the unwillingness of Russians to defend their Bolshevik masters and the rule of force these masters had imposed, and secondly, the inadequacy of a military leadership hamstrung by interference from the Commissars.

More than once I tried to suppress an ever-recurring doubt: Am I really defending our country? Is it for our country that I am sending men to their death? Or is it perhaps only for Bolshevism that our people shed their blood – Bolshevism that has usurped the sacred name of Homeland?

It became clear to me that Bolshevism had involved our people in a war on behalf of interests that are not our people's. Is it not then a crime to allow the blood bath to continue? Is not Bolshevism – and Stalin himself in particular – the main enemy of the Russian nation? Is it not the first, and sacred, duty of every honour-loving Russian to take up arms against Stalin and his gang?

I have become convinced that the tasks facing the Russian people can be successfully undertaken in alliance and in cooperation with the German people.

The Russian people must create a new and happy homeland, within a European community of free and equal nations. I call upon my people to join the struggle for a brighter future, for the realization of a national revolution, for the creation of a New Russia, Homeland of our great nation. I call for brotherhood and unity with the other European nations, and, first and foremost, for cooperation and lasting friendship with the great German nation.

My appeal has met with warm response not only from the prisoners of war but from the great mass of Russians still under Bolshevik sway.

In this struggle for our future I take my stand, firmly and whole-heartedly, for an alliance with Germany.

In the last few months it has become clear to Stalin that the Russian people will not fight for Bolshevik international aims. So he has made a show of changing his policy. He has abolished the Commissars. He is trying to win over the venal higher dignitaries of the Church that he once persecuted. He is trying to restore the old army traditions. To force Russians to shed their blood for foreign interests he invokes names like Alexander Nevski, Kutuzov Suvorov. He thus tries to convince the people that he is fighting for the Homeland, for Russia. He has need of this shabby deception, but only in order to keep himself in power.

Neither Stalin nor the Bolsheviks are fighting for Russia.

Our real Homeland is in the ranks of the Anti-Bolshevik movement. All Russians have a Cause, a Duty, to fight against Stalin for Peace and for a New Russia.

Russia is ours!

Russia's past is ours!

Russia's future is ours!

Throughout the course of history the Russian nation with its many millions has always found the strength to fight for national independence, to fight for the future. And so our Nation will not perish. Today, too, in these grim times in which we are living, our Russian People will find the strength to unite, to shake off the hated yoke and, united, to press forward to build a new State in which our nation will find happiness.[1]

[1] The above is a translation of the original leaflet as dropped from the air. Subsequently somewhat varying versions were in circulation.

Extracts from Report of Captain Peterson on His Inspection of the Dabendorf Camp, 13 and 14 September 1943

IN the camp on that date were a permanent staff of 164 (including Russians) and 286 men attending a course of training.

The course from 8 August to 25 September provided for 272 hours of instruction – 126 hours' theoretical, 36 practical, 68 physical training, 22 German language, 20 miscellaneous.

Guard: A German guard with Russian supernumeraries on the main entrance. There is also a side entrance with no guard. German and Russian Liberation Army flags at the main entrance.

Discipline: Slack. Bearing unsoldierly, though most of the inmates were former Red Army officers. Saluting slovenly. Men do not rise to their feet on the entrance of a German officer. Quarters untidy and dirty, due apparently to lack of supervision.

Food: Excellent, on Scale III. Scale IV would be adequate.

Clothing: Good.

Sanitation: Very satisfactory. The camp possesses its own delousing station, barber's shop, showers, latrine with water flushing.

Security: Inadequate. The Commandant is too busy to attend to such matters, and his deputy is mostly in Berlin from where he cannot exercise control. The camp authorities are therefore unaware of the state of morale within the camp and of influences exercised from without. Supervision is far too much left to the Russians themselves. Leave is feely granted and there is no check on the activities of personnel when outside the camp.

Feeling and Morale: Good in the case of soldiers from front-line units. Otherwise various rumours, e.g. early peace talks between Germany and the USSR, as both sides are exhausted. Peace to provide for the Liberation Army officers to be handed back to the Reds; officers should therefore be ready to escape to France, Norway or Italy.

General: The Germans in charge of the camp have let go of the reins, and confine themselves to organization.

Instruction: Russian history is on the whole well taught, but with too much emphasis on the nationalist aspect and on German–Russian differences. It is certainly anti-Bolshevik, but not pro-German.

Miscellaneous: No means of control over relationships with Russian and Polish women. Relationships with the latter are forbidden, but with the former seem to be inevitable.

Conclusions: The camp performs the task assigned to it, and is of great value in that it turns out adequate propagandists for the front and for the *Ostarbeiter*. But discipline must be appreciably tightened up, and the Germans in charge must assume firm control, albeit with due regard to Russian mentality. A proper security organization should be established to ensure effective supervision.

APPENDIX IV

The Prague Manifesto

FELLOW-COUNTRYMEN, brothers and sisters!

In this hour of trial it is for us to decide the fate of our Homeland, of our Peoples and of ourselves.

Humanity is living through a shattering epoch. This world war is proving to be a death struggle of conflicting political systems.

There are the forces of imperialism with, at their head, the pluto-crats of England and the USA, who derive their power from the oppression and exploitation of other nations. There are the forces of internationalism, at their head Stalin and his gang, who dream of world revolution and the destruction of the independence of other nations. And there are the freedom-loving nations, seeking to live their own life in accordance with their history and development.

There is no greater crime than that of Stalin, who lays waste whole countries and crushes those peoples whose aim it is to conserve the soil of their forbears and to build their happiness with their own hard work. There is no greater crime than to oppress another nation and force one's will upon it.

The powers of destruction and subjugation hide their criminal aims under slogans of defending freedom, democracy, culture, civilization. By defence of freedom they understand the annexation of foreign soil. By defence of democracy they understand the forceful imposition of their political system upon others. By defence of culture and civilization they mean the destruction of what others had taken a thousand years to build.

For what are the peoples of Russia fighting this war? For what are they exposed to such sacrifices and suffering?

Two years back it was still possible for Stalin to deceive the peoples by describing the war as patriotic and as one for liberation. Now the Red Army has advanced beyond the Soviet frontiers, into Romania, Bulgaria, Serbia, Croatia and Hungary, and is drenching with blood the soil of foreign lands. Now one can clearly see the real nature of the Bolsheviks in continuing the war. They wish to reinforce Stalin's tyranny over the peoples of Russia and to extend it to cover the whole world.

For more than twenty-five years the people of Russia have been suffering under Stalin's tyranny.

In the 1917 Revolution the peoples of Russia strove to establish Justice, the Common Good and National Independence. They rose against the antiquated regime of the tsars, which was neither willing nor able to put an end to social injustice, to the remnants of serfdom, to the economic and cultural backwardness for which it was responsible. But those then in power could not decide to bring in the bold necessary reforms once the tsar had been removed. Its leaders adopted an ambiguous policy, were opportunists, failed to assume responsibility for the future. They failed to justify themselves in the eyes of the people. And the people turned to those who promised them Peace, Land, Liberty and Bread, to those who put forward the most radical slogans.

It was not the fault of the People that the Bolsheviks who had promised a way of life in which the people could be happy and for which such sacrifices had been made, that these Bolsheviks seized for themselves the power that the people had won, ignored the demands of the people, strengthened their organs of repression, denied the people their rights and reduced them to misery and unscrupulous exploitation.

The Bolsheviks denied the Peoples of Russia the right of independence and the right to develop in freedom.

The Bolsheviks robbed the population of freedom of speech, freedom of opinion, freedom of domicile, freedom of choice of work, freedom of making a career. In place of these freedoms they brought in terror, privilege for party members and arbitrariness.

The Bolsheviks robbed the peasants of the land these peasants had won, robbed them of freedom to work their holdings and to enjoy their produce; drove them into collective farms, made them more exploited and oppressed than any class in the country.

The Bolsheviks robbed the workers of the right to choose their jobs and place of work, robbed them of the right to organize to improve their conditions or to exercise influence over production. They made workers the abject slaves of State Capitalism.

The Bolsheviks robbed intellectuals of the right to undertake creative work for the benefit of the community, and endeavoured by force, by fear and by bribery to make them the instruments of their lying propaganda.

The Bolsheviks have brought the peoples of our country to poverty, hunger, extinction, to physical and mental slavery, and, finally, have involved them in a criminal war for causes which are not theirs.

All this is cloaked with lies about the democratic nature of Stalin's Constitution, about the building up of a socialist society. No other country in the world has known so low a standard of living alongside such vast material resources, or seen such degradation of human values, as has been and is the case under Bolshevism.

The peoples of Russia have been, once and for all, disillusioned about Bolshevism, where the State becomes an insatiable machine, and men and women helpless unhappy slaves. They see the grim danger looming up: if Bolshevism should triumph – even for a time – over the blood and bones of the European nations, then the Russian peoples' struggle, carried on for years with great loss of life, will have proved in vain. Bolshevism would exploit the people's exhaustion to rob them of all their capacity to resist. Accordingly all must strive to destroy this inhuman Bolshevik machine, to ensure that all men and women be given the right to live freely according to their capabilities and to establish an order that will protect them and theirs from the arbitrary interference of any group or any state.

In view of these considerations, the representatives of the Peoples of Russia, fully conscious of their responsibility to their Peoples, to History and to Posterity have established The Committee for the Liberation of the Peoples of Russia in order to organize a united struggle against Bolshevism.

The aims of The Committee for the Liberation of the Peoples of Russia are as under:

(*a*) The overthrow of Stalin's tyranny, the liberation of the Peoples of Russia from Bolshevik rule and the restoration of those rights won by the People in the People's Revolution of 1917.

(*b*) Termination of the war and an honourable peace with Germany.

(*c*) The setting up of a new, free, democratic order without Bolsheviks and without exploiters.

The Committee lays down the following main basic principles for the establishment of a new political order:

(1) Equality for all the peoples of Russia, with absolute rights of self-determination, national development and independence.

(2) Establishment of a National-Solidarist form of government in which priority to be given to the raising of the standard of living and to national development.

(3) The maintenance of peace, the fostering of friendly relations with all nations and of international cooperation.

(4) Far-reaching state measures for the encouragement of family and marriage ties.

(5) Abolition of forced labour. Guarantees of free labour and

rights of workers. Regulations ensuring that wages provide for proper standards of living.

(6) Abolition of collective farms, free distribution of land to peasants. Freedom of choice of methods of farming. Freedom to dispose of the products of agricultural holdings. Abolition of forced deliveries, annulments of debts due to Soviet State organs.

(7) Inviolability of private property accruing from work. Re-establishment of trading, crafts, cottage industries; freedom of private initiative, opportunity to take part in the economic life of the country.

(8) Intellectuals to have opportunity for creative work for the good of the community.

(9) Guarantees of social justice. All workers, whatever their origin or former activity to be accorded protection against any form of exploitation.

(10) Free education, medical care, holidays and old-age pensions to be available to all without exception.

(11) Destruction of the regime of terror and force. Abolition of forced resettlement and mass deportation. Effective guarantees of freedom of religion, of conscience, of speech, of assembly, of press; inviolability of persons, property, dwellings; equality of all before the law; law courts to be independent and open to the public.

(12) Release and return home of all political prisoners of the Bolsheviks and of all detained because of their opposition to Bolshevism. No reprisals or revenge against those who have ceased fighting on behalf of Stalin – whether they were forced so to fight or did so from conviction.

(13) Restoration at government expense of all national property – towns, villages, factories and workshops – destroyed during the war.

(14) War disabled and their families to be cared for by the State.

The destruction of Bolshevism is the urgent task of all progressive forces. The Committee for the Liberation of the Peoples of Russia is convinced that the united efforts of the Peoples of Russia will be supported by all freedom-loving nations of the world.

The Liberation Movement of the Peoples of Russia is the continuation of many years of struggle against Bolshevism and on behalf of Freedom, Peace and Justice. The successful termination of this struggle is now assured by

(a) the greater experience now available – far greater than in 1917;

(b) the availability of ever-increasing organized armed forces – the Russian Liberation Army, Ukrainian Liberation forces, Cossack formations and national units;

(*c*) the existence of armed anti-Bolshevik forces behind the Soviet lines;

(*d*) the existence of growing opposition to Stalin among the population, among state employees and in the Soviet army.

The Committee for the Liberation of the Peoples of Russia considers it a precondition of victory that all national forces be unified and coordinated in their common task of overthrowing Bolshevik power. Accordingly the Committee supports all revolutionary and oppositional groups opposed to Stalin, while emphatically rejecting any projects tending to impinge on popular rights.

The Committee for the Liberation of the Peoples of Russia welcomes aid from Germany, always provided that such aid is consistent with the honour and independence of our Homeland. This aid, at the moment, provides the only practical possibility of armed struggle against the Stalinist clique.

In this struggle we have taken upon ourselves the responsibility for the fate of the peoples of Russia. With us are millions of our country's finest sons, who, with rifle in hand, have already shown their courage and readiness to offer their lives for the liberation of our Homeland from Bolshevism. With us are millions of men and women who have turned away from Bolshevism and are offering their labour to the common cause of our struggle. With us are tens of millions of brothers and sisters, still smarting under the yoke of Stalin's tyranny and now awaiting the hour of liberation.

Officers and soldiers of the Liberation Army! The blood that has been shed in our common struggle has reinforced the battle-tried friendship of our various nationalities. We have a common aim, and we must make a common effort. Only the unity of all armed anti-Bolshevik forces of the peoples of Russia can lead to victory. Do not let drop your weapons, strive for unity, march ruthlessly against the enemy of the peoples – Bolshevism and its abettors. Remember the tortured peoples of Russia now await you. Set them free!

Fellow-countrymen, brother and sisters now here in Europe! Your return to the Homeland as recognized citizens can only be made possible by victory over Bolshevism. You number millions. On you depends success in our struggle. Bear in mind that your labour is now on behalf of the common cause, on behalf of our Liberation Army heroes. Increase your effort, intensify your gallant work!

Officers and soldiers of the Red Army! Cease fighting in this criminal war, aimed at the suppression of the nations of Europe. Turn your arms against the Bolshevik usurpers who have enslaved the peoples of Russia and reduced them to hunger, suffering and loss of all rights.

Brothers and sisters in the Homeland! Intensify your struggle against Stalinist tyranny, against this brutal war. Organize your forces for the final assault against those who have robbed you of your rights of justice and of well-being!

The Committee for the Liberation of the Peoples of Russia calls upon you all to unite in the struggle for Peace and for Liberty!

PRAGUE, 14 November 1944

INDEX OF NAMES

Alexander I, Tsar, 91

d'Alquen, G., SS-Standartenführer, 173, 194-5, 198

Arlt, Dr F., SS-Obersturmbannführer, 196

Artamonov, Colonel, 233-6

Artamonov, General, 233

Aschenbrenner, General H., 165, 226-8

Balderschwang, Captain, 226

Berger, G., SS-Obergruppenführer, 196-8, 204, 209

Beria, L., 191, 207

Berndt, A. I., 51, 52, 60

Bielenberg, Heidi, 204

Biskupski, General V. V., 157

Blagoveshchenski, General R. F., 89, 115, 141, 245

Blomberg, Field-Marshal W. von, 238

Blossfeldt, Lieutenant, 67

Blücher, Marshal, 139

Bock, Field-Marshal Fedor von, 13, 19-21, 30, 31, 33, 38-42, 46, 49, 50, 52-6, 59, 93, 223, 234

Bormann, Werner, 102, 113, 114, 190, 192, 193

Borries, K., 159, 160

Boyarski, General, 75, 76, 91, 92, 171, 201, 202, 227

Brauchitsch, Field-Marshal W. von, 14, 49, 56, 59, 67, 91

Bräutigam, Dr O., 60, 103

Bremen, Captain E. von, 101, 180

Brieger, Lieutenant N., 101

Bukharin, N., 37, 85, 139

Bulganin, N., 139

Bunichenko, General S., 201, 226, 237, 245

Burg, SS-Standartenführer, 209

Canaris, Admiral Wilhelm, 57, 67

Chiang Kai-shek, 72, 163, 187, 254

Choltitz, General von, 217

Churchill, Winston, 15, 148, 183, 207, 218

Daitz, Werner, 128, 130, 181

Dallin, Alexander, 246

David, Captain, 243-5

Dellingshausen, Captain E. von, 101, 115, 135, 147, 148, 164, 167, 174, 181, 187, 194, 222, 225, 226

Denikin, General A., 162

Dietz, Lieutenant-Colonel, 60, 61

Dönitz, Admiral, 164

Dumpf, H., 40

Dürksen, Lieutenant, 78, 79, 83, 100, 134, 135, 178

Düsterlohe, Verena von, 101

Dwinger, Erich-Edwin, 123, 150, 152, 153, 225, 227, 228

Dzerzhinsky, J., 191

Dzhugashvili, Major Yacob, 32, 33

Eckert, Pastor F., 61, 63, 68

Eidemann, General, 139

Eisenhower, Dwight D., 234, 235

Elben, Major, 101

Fischer, George, 145, 246

Frank, Hans, 51

Frank, Karl-Hermann, 219

Franklin, Benjamin, 75, 229, 248

Frauenfeld, A., 52

Freytag-Loringhoven, Colonel Wessel von, 158, 188, 189, 201-3

Fröhlich, Sergei, 132-4, 157, 158, 165, 173, 181, 187, 192, 194, 201-4, 213

Gehlen, General Reinhard, 15, 25, 61, 65-9, 77, 78, 82, 92, 95, 97, 98, 115, 124, 136, 138, 140, 142-7, 166, 170, 175, 188, 196, 201, 202, 209, 221-3, 225, 237

Gelderblom, Dr Ernst, 247

Gersdorff, Colonel Rudolf von, 21, 22, 25, 30, 33, 40, 42, 48, 49, 65, 82, 91, 92, 142, 146

Girgensohn, Th., 197

Godt, Admiral, 164

Goebbels, Joseph, 42, 43, 60, 94, 109, 110, 166

Golovin, Professor General N. N., 48

Göring, Emmy, 51

Göring, Hermann, 57, 94, 164, 237

Gough, General, 13

Gracian, Balthazar, 246
Greiffenberg, General von, 23, 27, 42, 46, 47
Greiser, Arthur, 51, 222, 240
Grote, Captain N. von, 78, 83, 86, 87, 94, 96, 97, 100, 105, 107, 108, 113, 114, 116, 120, 121, 124, 127, 130, 134, 135, 140, 178, 179, 190, 209
Guderian, General Heinz, 223, 238, 239, 241

Halder, General Franz, 68, 69, 75, 77, 108
Hardenberg, Major Count von, 53, 54
Hellmich, General Heinz, 118–22, 174, 175, 176, 180, 183, 185
Herff, von, 161
Herre, Colonel Heinz, 174, 175, 177, 184, 185, 219, 222, 226, 227
Herwarth, Captain Hans von, 185, 220
Heusinger, General Adolf, 136, 238
Heygendorf, General Ralph von, 283
Hildebrand, 161
Hilger, Gustav, 78, 84, 238
Himmler, Heinrich, Reichsführer SS, 13, 20, 39, 43, 57, 82, 106, 107, 161, 168, 173, 187, 193–8, 201, 204–12, 215, 226, 247, 248
Hindenburg, Field-Marshal Paul von, 224
Hitler, Adolf, 13–15, 19, 21, 22, 26, 27, 38, 39, 41, 42, 49, 52, 53, 56, 58, 59, 62, 65–7, 69, 75, 77, 78, 80, 84, 93, 94, 101, 103, 106, 109, 110, 120, 121, 132, 140, 143–6, 152, 163, 164, 166, 168, 169, 173, 176, 183, 184, 187–9, 198, 201, 210, 213–16, 223, 224, 232, 235, 236, 239, 240, 246–8
Hoffmann, 240
Holters, Lieutenant-Colonel, 165
Hoover, Herbert, 19, 50, 232
Horthy, Admiral N., 235

Jodl, General Alfred, 140, 178–80, 201, 209

Kaehlbrandt, Captain Otto, 101
Kaganovich, Lazar, 139, 192
Kapp, Dr Werner, 181
Kaufmann, Günter, 123, 152, 159
Kazantsev, A. S., 94, 116, 246
Kehrl, Hans, 196

Keitel, Field-Marshal Wilhelm, 46, 62, 69, 103, 108, 137, 140, 141, 143–6, 164, 170, 173, 174, 176, 196, 209
Kerkovius, Captain, 61
Kersten, Dr Felix, 208
Kesselring, Field-Marshal A., 181
Khrushchev, Nikita, 139, 191
Klammroth, Lieutenant-Colonel, 66, 98, 115
Kleist, Field-Marshal Ewald von, 65, 104
Kleist, Lieutenant Hellmath von, 101, 169
Kleist, Dr Peter von, 125
Kluge, Field-Marshal Hans von, 55, 56, 91, 92, 124, 143, 146, 147
Knüpfer, Rudolf von, 60, 121, 125, 158
Korbukov, General, 245
Kork, General, 139
Kortüm, 221, 224
Köstring, General Ernst, 125, 181–6, 201, 209, 218, 219, 238
Kovalchuk, 113, 190
Kraft, Lieutenant-Colonel, 158
Krasnov, General P. N., 157, 210
Krasnov, S. N., 210
Krause, Th., 68, 102
Kravchenko, 157
Kriegbaum, SS-Sturmbannführer, 211
Kroeger, Dr E., SS-Oberführer, 197, 198, 206, 209–11, 219, 220, 227, 229
Kromiadi, Colonel K. G., 157
Küchler, Field-Marshal Georg, 134, 143, 190
Künkel, Dr Hans, 225
Kutuzov, Field-Marshal, 59, 255

Lamsdorff, Count, 158
Lawrence, T. E., 167
Leber, Julius, 248
Leeb, Field-Marshal Ritter von, 238, 239
Lehar, Franz, 21
Lehndorff, Count H. von, 30
Leibbrandt, G., 125
Lenin, V. I., 32
Ley, Dr Robert, 160, 161–4, 207
Lindemann, General G., 71, 74, 134, 135, 143
Lippert, Dr Julius, 159
List, Field-Marshal W., 62, 238, 239, 241
Lorenz, Werner, SS-Obergruppen-führer, 219

Ludendorf, General Erich, 146
Lüdinghausen-Wolff, Baron, 158
Lukin, General, M. F., 35, 36, 93, 94

Malenkov, G., 139
Malinovski, Marshal R., 139
Maltzev, Colonel V., 165, 226, 229, 245
Malyshkin, General V. F., 88–91, 121,
    130, 134, 137, 139, 140, 147, 168,
    171–3, 177, 179, 180, 198, 210, 212,
    223, 227, 229, 230–6, 240, 241, 245
Mannerheim, Marshal C., 190
Manstein, Field-Marshal E. von, 104,
    144
Martin, Colonel Hans, 83, 85, 90, 96,
    97, 108–10, 112, 130, 137, 138, 140,
    143, 144, 193, 202, 211
Marwitz, Major von der, 221
Mayrzedt, 150, 152
Meandrov, General M., 226
Mende, Professor G. von, 125
Mikoyan, A., 166
Milve, von der, 61
Model, Field-Marshal, 190
Molotov, V., 13, 139
Müller, SS-Gruppenführer, 44

Nansen, F., 19, 50
Napoleon, 23, 91
Nauck, Lieutenant-Colonel H., 221, 225
Neryanin, Colonel, 226
Nevski, Alexander, 255
Niedermeyer, General Ritter von, 178,
    201
Noshin, 194

Oberländer, Professor Th., 166, 167,
    226, 229
Ohlendorf, 196
Olbricht, General F., 202
Oster, General H., 202

Pannwitz, General von, 166
Patch, General, 16, 233–6
Paulus, Field-Marshal Friedrich, 153
Pehla, Paymaster, 101, 142
Peterson, Captain E., 71, 92, 125, 127,
    170, 256
Petzel, General, 222, 226
Pilsudski, President, 146
Pleiger, 196
Podhayski, Colonel, 151
Prokhorov, Colonel, 35

Putilin, 158
Pyatnitsky, Colonel N., 123

R., Dr, 106–8, 194
Rahr, 158
Rasche, 159
Reichenau, Field-Marshal W. von, 65
Reinhardt, 160
Ribbentrop, J. von, 13, 84
Richthofen, Bolko Freiherr von, 144
Richthofen, Field-Marshal, 144
Roenne, Colonel Alexis Freiherr von,
    61–3, 66, 67, 69, 71, 76–9, 82, 83, 92,
    96, 98, 104, 105, 115, 116, 118, 124,
    125, 140, 202, 217
Rogoshin, 101
Rokosovski, Marshal, 139
Ropp, Georg von der, 96, 101, 115, 116,
    192
Roosevelt, F. D., 15, 50, 148, 238
Rosenberg, Alfred, 39–42, 51, 57, 60,
    103, 106–8, 110, 115, 120, 121, 124,
    125, 127, 128, 145, 163, 209, 210
Rudnev, Professor, 157
Ryzhkov, 158

Sauckel, Fr., 160, 163, 174
Schabert, Arnold, 101
Schabert, Captain E., 61, 194
Schack, Major von, 30, 41, 49
Schellenberg, W., SS-Brigadeführer,
    196
Schenckendorff, General von, 65, 103,
    125, 143
Scherff, General, 145
Scherke, Professor F., 68
Schiller, Friedrich, 193
Schirach, Baldur von, 152
Schmidt, Captain Felix, 23, 24, 32, 33,
    42
Schmidt von Altenstadt, Colonel, 65, 98,
    103, 175, 201, 202
Schmundt, General R., 143–6
Schörner, Field-Marshal F., 228
Schrader, Lieutenant-Colonel W., 66,
    202, 203
Schroeder, SS-Gruppenführer, 181
Schubuth, Lieutenant-Colonel, 125
Schulz, Sonderführer, 101
Schulenberg, F. W. von der, 57
Schwerin-Krosigk, Count von, 159, 160
Semder, Lieutenant, 101
Shandruk, General P., 226

Shapovalov, Colonel M., 76
Shatov, General, 245
Shcherbakov, General, 144, 145
Shepilov, 139
Sivers, Andrik von, 58, 59
Sivers, General von, 58
Snyder, Lieutenant-Colonel, 231–3
Speer, Albert, 196
Stalin, J. V., 13, 15, 19, 27, 32, 33, 35, 37, 39, 45, 48, 58, 59, 62, 68, 72, 74–7, 80, 85–7, 89, 92–4, 97, 100, 101, 104, 113, 116, 119, 127, 129–31, 134, 138, 139, 144, 145, 148, 151, 162–4, 168, 175, 176, 182, 183, 187, 189, 191, 192, 207, 213, 214, 216, 223, 232–4, 246–8, 254, 255, 258, 262
Stapf, General Otto, 104, 158
Stauffenberg, Colonel Count Claus von, 15, 66, 79, 82, 95, 98, 112, 115, 175, 193, 202, 248
Steenberg, Sven, 246
Steifon, General, 166
Stieff, General Helmut, 65, 79, 98, 175, 202
Strauch, Captain Heinz, 102
Strik-Strikfeldt, Frau Adele, 21, 51, 134, 137, 224, 225, 227, 231, 232
Suvorov, General, 59, 255

Thorwald, Jürgen, 246
Thyssen, 240
Tomashevski, 158
Tresckow, General H. von, 42, 48, 49, 65, 67, 82, 91, 92, 103, 124, 143, 202
Trotsky, L., 189, 192
Trukhin, General F. Y., 115, 116, 139, 141, 161, 168, 169, 174, 177, 179, 181, 192, 198, 201, 202, 225, 227, 245
Tukhachevski, Marshal, 34, 37, 89, 139, 182
Turkul, General Andrei, 157

Vlasov, General A. A., 13, 15, 16, 69–90, 93, 95, 97, 100, 103–6, 108, 110, 111, 113, 115, 116, 119, 120, 123–40, 142–57, 158–68, 171, 173, 175–82, 184, 185, 187–98, 200–10, 212, 213,

215–21, 226–30, 233, 234, 236, 237, 245, 246–8, 253–5
Voelkel, Lieutenant-Colonel, 184
Voronova, M. Y., 145
Voroshilov, Marshal K. E., 139, 166

Wächter, Dr Otto, SS-Gruppenführer, 52, 161, 196
Wagner, General E., 65, 125, 175, 202
Walter, Paul, 162, 164
Warburg, 159
Washington, George, 75, 95, 229, 248
Wedel, General H. von, 69, 122, 127, 140–3, 145, 208, 209
Weichs, Field-Marshal F. von, 228, 238, 239, 241–3
Wiedemann, Melitta, 161
Wilhelm II, 51
Wirsing, G., 159
Wrangel, General P. N., 162

Yakir, General, 139
Yegorov, Marshal, 139
Yesenin, 89
Yezhov, 191
Yudenich, General N., 189

Zaitsev, Professor A. N., 116, 117, 168, 199
Zakutny, General, 245
Zeitzler, General K., 108, 143, 145–6, 196
Zherebkov, Y. Z., 48, 157, 171, 172, 180, 228
Zhilenkov, General G. N., 91, 92, 94, 109, 110, 130, 139, 158, 161, 168, 175, 177, 179, 180, 194, 195, 198, 200, 201, 203, 212, 220, 221, 227, 237, 238–41, 245
Zimmermann, 125, 196
Zinoviev, G., 139, 192
Zveryev, General, 226, 245
Zykov, M. A., 85, 86, 105, 106, 109, 111, 113, 114, 116, 123, 130, 131, 145, 149, 158, 168, 177, 180, 181, 190, 191, 194, 195, 216